Charles Dickens 1812-1870

A Centennial Volume   edited by E W F Tomlin

Simon and Schuster
New York

© 1969 by George Weidenfeld and Nicolson Limited

Designed by Alan Bartram

Published by Simon and Schuster
Rockefeller Center, 630 Fifth Avenue
New York, New York 10020

First printing
SBN 671-20424-6
Library of Congress Catalog Card Number: 70-87141
Manufactured in Great Britain by
C. Tinling and Co. Limited, London and Prescot
and Jarrold and Sons Limited, Norwich

Contents

Preface   E. W. F. Tomlin   7

The Great Inimitable   J. B. Priestley   13

The Life of Dickens   32

Dickens: The Dark Pilgrimage   Edgar Johnson   41

Dickens's London   64

Dickens's London   Christopher Hibbert   73

The Man of Letters   100

The Genesis of a Novel: Great Expectations   Harry Stone   109

Social Conditions   132

Dickens as Social Reformer   Ivor Brown   141

Dickens Characters   168

Dickens and the Theatre   Emlyn Williams   177

The Illustrators   196

Dickens and his Illustrators   Nicolas Bentley   205

Dickens in America   228

Dickens's Reputation: a Reassessment   E. W. F. Tomlin   237

Dickensiana   264

Notes   273

Acknowledgements   279

Index   280

Preface

E W F Tomlin

'Dickens is still ahead of us', wrote Jack Lindsay in his book on Dickens in 1950. He was referring to the remarkable way in which Dickens's art has survived, and indeed to some extent conquered, the age of mass-media. During the last decade or so Dickens has entered the world of television and that of the musical, while continuing to be read avidly by thousands. This enduring popularity may be due, as Lindsay suggests, to Dickens's 'fundamental method of fusing dream-process and realism in terms of essential human conflict'; for his gifts were basic and elemental to a degree unmatched by his contemporaries, and it is unlikely that a writer of comparable stature can appear again for a very long time, if ever.

The present book has been compiled with a view to showing the full scope of Dickens's genius. Although it represents a centenary tribute, the aim is not to engage in pious eulogy. No doubt the Centenary Year, 1970, will match the Shakespeare celebrations of 1964; and there will be a resumption of enthusiasm by lapsed Dickensians as well as the enlistment of new recruits. The contributors to this volume have been chosen for their expert knowledge of special aspects of Dickens's work, though some have a mastery of the whole. They are concerned with the promotion of Dickens studies, but also with the furtherance of true and discriminating appreciation. As Dickens was one of the world's great entertainers, the reading of the following pages should stimulate a new interest, while removing certain deep-rooted misconceptions, and thereby leave the reader with a keener appetite for the novels, the stories, and the miscellaneous prose.

The contributors have naturally been given complete liberty to say what they please about Dickens. A clash of judgments may sometimes be observed, and this is as inevitable as it is salutary and stimulating. At the same time, the essays, as they were assembled, revealed a remarkable consensus. This was the happy outcome of diverse studies, individual enthusiasms, and original approaches. The Editor sought no common factor, but he found one. The order in which the chapters are placed was determined with the reader's interest in mind. Similarly, my references to the authors in this Preface imply no degrees of precedence.

It is appropriate that the opening chapter should be the work of a novelist and essayist within the Dickens tradition. J. B. Priestley responded with enthusiasm to the invitation to assume the introductory role here assigned him; and the reader will welcome the views of this distinguished, lifelong admirer of Dickens. Priestley makes a number of important judgments concerning the secret of Dickens's success. In particular, he draws attention to the way in which Dickens triumphed over the conditions in which most of his work was published. This is not the moment to summarize remarks expounded in their place, but an observation from the same author's excellent *Charles Dickens: A Pictorial Biography* (1961) may be aptly cited. Whereas many critics have regarded the serial publication of the novels as having done damage to Dickens as an artist, Priestley believes that such a mode of publication compelled him 'to work at a speed and with an urgency that released the unconscious elements upon which genius depends'. We know that from *Sketches by Boz* onwards, Dickens was working against time; and as his life became more active and his public engagements multiplied, the pressure greatly increased. We know, too, that he several times tried a different tempo of working, and that at one moment he even toyed with the idea of abandoning the serial method altogether. (His idea was to bring out his novels in book form in Paris.) But he always returned to it; and he was battling strenuously along when, some way through *Edwin Drood*, the human engine broke down under the strain. Nevertheless, as *Edwin Drood* itself showed, the need to produce so much copy at regular intervals was a condition of the teeming life of the novels erupting on to the page; for there is considerable support for the view that, whatever the physical stress imposed on him, Dickens's invention grew richer and more complex as he entered middle age. Even contemporary novelists who, like Thackeray, decried his artistry, admitted and envied his unflagging creative impulse.

Nowhere has Dickens's vitality been better studied and revealed than in Edgar Johnson's masterly biography, *Charles Dickens: His Tragedy and Triumph* (1953). This book has superseded Forster, though by doing so it has lent Forster's devoted study a renewed interest. This is what one masterpiece should do to another. We were particularly gratified at Professor Johnson's acceptance of our invitation to write the biographical chapter, as any pronouncement on this subject from the acknowledged world authority was bound to be of interest and value. 'Dickens: The Dark Pilgrimage', while suggesting the more sombre view of Dickens which has crystallized out of recent studies, is a fresh and moving piece of writing. We are now beginning to see Dickens as a man whose personality, though in one sense irresistibly attractive, was complicated and darkened by the need to preserve two secrets: the first dating from his twelfth year, and the second persisting during his last twelve years. And yet, as Professor Johnson has said and as we have repeated in his own words elsewhere, the three or four months of agonized humiliation in the blacking factory produced both the man of aggressive determination and the writer whose imagination was thereafter haunted by victims of circumstance, 'a host of children suffering or dying young and other innocent victims of a stony-hearted and archaic social system': the writer whose resolve was 'to assimilate and understand the blacking warehouse and the Marshalsea, and the kind of world in which such things could be'.[1] The other secret, almost though not quite so well-kept, concerned the liaison with the young actress Ellen Ternan. In the final chapter of this book, it is pointed out how little the 'revelations' (such as they were) affected Dickens's popularity; and, to quote from Professor Johnson's biography again, 'the real importance of this autumnal love lies in the changes it wrought in the last twelve years of Dickens's life and development as a writer'.[2] These changes were profound. As a result, many critics, though by no means all, tend to the view that the last novels are by far superior to the earlier. This is because they reveal a deeper understanding of human nature, and because, to quote A. O. J. Cockshut on *Our Mutual Friend*, 'Dickens the fantastic, melodramatic symbolist and Dickens the hypnotic recorder of the dingy detail of life were at last reconciled'.[3]

Dickens was a world-famous writer at the age of twenty-five; and popularity is often 'founded . . . on the weakness and not on the strength of an author'.[4] Admittedly, Dickens realized early enough that he could hold his public by liberal indulgence in pathos as well as by humour; and he wrote at least one book, *The Old Curiosity Shop*, in which the balance between the two was so far weighted on the side of pathos as to alienate most modern readers. Both *The Old Curiosity Shop* and *Barnaby Rudge* stemmed, as we know, from the short-lived experiment of *Master Humphrey's Clock*. Here Dickens showed a slight hesitancy in his career as an author: for the *Clock* itself was a failure, and the only striking piece of writing it contained, apart from the two long tales, is a story, 'A Confession found in a Prison in the time of Charles II', which is perhaps the most horrific piece of writing he ever penned (it is rarely referred to, though far more macabre than the horror stories in *Pickwick*). This excursion into the extremes of melodrama gave place in due course to a more balanced approach; and by *Dombey and Son* Dickens's popularity rested securely on his strength rather than on his weakness. Nevertheless, the dramatic impulse was ever-present; and when Dickens's personal crisis was upon him, the need for some form of self-dramatization had become imperative, if only to sublimate the need for self-justification. Hence the Readings. Emlyn Williams, who has brought the novelist alive to thousands of people through his remarkable impersonation of Dickens as Reader, has here contributed an illuminating chapter on 'Dickens and the Theatre', concluding with some pertinent remarks on the adaptability of the novels to the cinema.

One of the masterpieces of Dickens's maturity, *Great Expectations*, is the subject of Professor Harry Stone's chapter, 'The Genesis of a Novel'. This contribution by one of America's leading Dickens scholars was invited in order to furnish the book with at least one essay in which minute attention to detail and original research were employed for the sake of shedding light upon the origin of a particular work. The result is to illuminate not merely *Great Expectations* itself, but Dickens's creative processes at perhaps their highest point of development. Scholars will find in Professor Stone's chapter new sources of interest and a fresh viewpoint from which to inspect Dickens's work in its entirety.

It is sufficient to read Dickens's instructions, advice, and sometimes protests, to realize that the artists who illustrated his books were in a very real sense collaborators; but few readers of Dickens appreciate the technical problems which confronted these often hard-pressed men, or the variety of talent which was enlisted by Dickens's publishers, from the ill-fated Seymour to the more conventional illustrators who succeeded Hablôt K. Browne. No one is better qualified to deal with this subject, and also with the modern illustrators of Dickens, than Nicolas Bentley, who contributes the chapter on 'Dickens and his Illustrators'. The practising artist and the specialist in Victoriana has given us in compact form the kind of information which sharpens our understanding of the way in which the novels were presented to an expectant, and not uncritical, public.

Of Dickens's political and social views, much has been written. Dickens has been claimed with equal vehemence by the radicals and by the conservatives. Ivor Brown, who needs no introduction, has interested himself in this aspect of Dickens all his life; and we were much gratified that the author of *Dickens in His Time* (1963) should have agreed to write on 'Dickens as Social Reformer'. This is a large and controversial subject, and there are aspects such as education upon which, given space, much more might be said. Not least there is Dickens's own experience of education, which was fitful and in one sense inadequate; but the inadequacy may have had its more positive side. 'He was an uneducated man of genius,' writes Angus Wilson, 'and as such was free and open to intuitive responses to the facts of his age which a better conventional education might have refused.'[5]

On the appearance of his study *The Making of Charles Dickens* in 1967, it was evident that Christopher Hibbert, the historian, was an unusually well-informed specialist on Dickens's London. Walter Dexter observes in his *London of Dickens* (1923) that Dickens's London 'is no imaginative London; it is the London of reality'. Indeed, Dickens knew London better than most of his contemporaries, and he experienced a particular pleasure, which in due course became a necessity, in traversing the streets on foot, both by day and in later years by night. Christopher Hibbert dwells particularly on the impact which the streets of London made on Dickens's boyish fancy: for it was his early wanderings that provided the raw material for so much that was later transmuted into art. Even though the face of London has greatly changed, especially since 1939, the districts most closely associated with Dickens are still recognizably his own.

The Editor's reassessment of Dickens's reputation, which concludes the book, makes no claim to be exhaustive. A thorough appraisal, taking into account the views of foreign critics of distinction, would occupy many more thousands of words. It would be necessary also to lay greater stress on the influence of Dickens on French, German, Scandinavian and not least Russian writers. A more thorough exploration of the 'Dickens Industry' would throw interesting light upon social psychology and the history of public taste. Above all, no reassessment should refuse to face the fact that much admiration for Dickens is grudging, but that much condemnation is so violent as to testify to his abiding power. No one can ignore Dickens, even through ignorance. As Lionel Trilling has observed, 'with a body of works as large and enduring as that of Dickens, taste and opinion will never be done'.[6]

I should like to thank the contributors to this volume on both sides of the Atlantic for the promptitude with which they delivered their chapters, and the way in which they lightened the editorial task. I should also like to express my thanks to the publishers of this book, who first proposed the form which it should take, and who gave me immense help at every stage. As a result, my work was rendered pleasurable: and I can only hope that something of our joint enthusiasm in compiling a volume not unworthy of the Dickens Centenary may communicate itself to our readers.

Morwenstow, April 1969   E. W. F. TOMLIN

The Great Inimitable

J B Priestley

The title of this essay demands some explanation. 'Inimitable' is no favourite word of mine; I cannot remember when I last used it. Adjectives come into fashion and then go out, as weekly reviewers are always demonstrating, and 'inimitable' ceased to be a vogue term, if it ever was one, many years ago. But one man when talking to his friends constantly referred to himself as 'the Inimitable', and that man of course was Charles Dickens. His tone must always have been jocular, for though he could be loud and perhaps over-hearty he was no braggart; but even so there was something more than comical swagger here. At heart he knew he *was* inimitable, and we have to remember that during his earlier years, from the time when everybody was talking about *Pickwick*, cheap imitations of him poured from the press. They never came within a million miles of him.

I have hoisted this title because it describes, in the smallest possible number of words, what I shall attempt to do in the essay that follows. First, I shall be concerned with *Great*, secondly, with *Inimitable*, observing the size of him and then trying to understand and appreciate his unique quality. It may be rough going, but then we shall not be driving round some neat little suburb but zigzagging our way through a huge roaring city.

In the earlier months of 1922, when I was spending a post-graduate year in Cambridge, Quiller-Couch, then Regius Professor of English, delivered some lectures on Victorian novelists that he published afterwards as *Charles Dickens and other Victorians*. Although Cambridge, even then, was no place for such enthusiasm, 'Q' came out, as Dickens himself would have said, 'hot and strong' for Dickens, whom he ranked next to Shakespeare as a master creator among us English. But he also said this:

I grant you that he [Dickens] has not yet passed – as he has not yet had time to pass – the *great* test of a classical writer; which is that, surviving the day's popularity and its conditions, his work goes on meaning more, under quite different conditions, to succeeding ages; the great test which Shakespeare has passed more than once or twice, remaining today, though quite differently, even more significant than he was to his contemporaries. . . .

No doubt 'Q' was thinking in terms of whole centuries; so we cannot say that Dickens has passed the test yet. Nevertheless – and this is why I began with the date of these lectures – nearly half a century has gone by, bringing with it immense changes in our national life and thought and literary values; and not only has Dickens survived these years but he has also started to pass this test in exactly the way 'Q' meant. This is proved by the fact that recent criticism, on both sides of the Atlantic, has been busy discovering and appreciating a new Dickens.

Sketch of Dickens, made by Spy (Leslie Ward) in February 1870, four months before his death.

For about forty years after his death, the usual critical estimate of Dickens ran as follows. His career began in glory and ended in comparative failure; his last novels, though more carefully contrived, were mere shadows of what had gone before. The glorious vitality that had blazed throughout his earlier work was no longer at his command; he was an increasingly sick man, old before his time. Too many of his later chapters suggest a writer painfully coping with the day's task, far removed from the headlong magnificent improviser he had once been. Alas! – alas! – the dazzling young enchanter, dashing all over the place, declined into the anxious and grizzle-bearded novelist toiling away at Gad's Hill Place. Asking some allowance for brevity, I think that is a fair account of general critical opinion on Dickens more or less up to the last thirty years. No doubt it is still being droned out in many an Eng. Lit. lecture room.

More recent criticism of the sharper sort has dismissed those judgements. It waves away *Nicholas Nickleby* or *Martin Chuzzlewit* or even *David Copperfield*, to concentrate upon *Bleak House, Little Dorrit, Great Expectations* and, perhaps above all, *Our Mutual Friend*. It discovers in these late novels, as well it might, a curious and quite original mixture of direct social criticism, often savagely satirical, and a broad symbolism – which gives us the fog in *Bleak House*, the prison in *Little Dorrit*, the wealth from the convict hulk in *Great Expectations*, the riches of the dust-heap in *Our Mutual Friend*. It came to be recognized that these novels largely represented their author's deepening despair. Critics now knew far more about Dickens's private life than earlier critics had done. At last that amazingly well-kept secret – his long and (I for one suspect) not very happy liaison with the young actress Ellen Ternan – was wrenched open, even though many significant details are missing and may now never be known. With Ellen to provide for, together with his large family, no doubt he felt a genuine and urgent need for the money his readings brought him; but deeper than that need was his desire for travel, excitement, applause, because he was now a restless and unhappy man, ready in the end to defy his doctors' orders because he no longer cared whether he lived or died. Most of us have known people who committed suicide by inches, and I have no doubt myself that Dickens was one of these people. Clearly this Dickens, at least below the surface, was very different indeed from the jolly Victorian idol, the life-and-soul-of-the-party Inimitable.

I must now return to the point I wished to make here. Dickens has begun to pass the test laid down by 'Q' in his lecture, obviously surviving 'the day's popularity and its conditions'. His name stands higher now among good critics and intelligent readers than it did, let us say, in the 1880s. A new generation of critics, with a different set of values, turn eagerly towards him. What were once thought to be the comparative failures among his novels are now regarded by critics as those most worthy of the closest attention. The older Dickens, writing at last about the life around him, is no longer seen as a rather desperate imitator of his younger self; he is another and in many respects a much stronger Dickens (except in his humour, but this decline hardly worries most contemporary critics). It is now agreed that Dickens, especially in his later work, has a very important part to play in the development of the novel. Instead of appearing merely quaint and old-fashioned, the author of *Little Dorrit* or *Our Mutual Friend* is suddenly discovered to belong to our time in a way that the other Victorian novelists cannot be said to do. We are almost ready to declare – quoting again one of 'Q's' conditions – that Dickens is 'even more significant than he was to his contemporaries'. So we are at least half-way towards calling him not only a great writer but a great classical writer.

There can never be another Dickens. But I am not now paying a further tribute to his astonishing genius; I am thinking about his equally astonishing career. If a novelist of similar genius appeared tomorrow, we could safely prophesy he would never arrive at the height of popularity Dickens held for thirty years. The Victorians wanted Dickens novels as nobody these days really wants anybody's novels. They were the great family entertainment, with something for everybody – an exciting story for Papa, fun for the boys, sentiment for Mama and the girls. Now the same kind of people have films, radio, and, above all, television. But it is not sufficient to say that Dickens had not to compete with these things.

Chesterton once pointed out that there is an important difference between a man who merely wants a book to read and a man who really wants to read a book. There is something largely passive now in our mass entertainment that was fiercely active when Dickens was writing. Setting aside a comparatively few excited youngsters, we can say that most people are not eagerly wanting something wonderful; they turn to films, radio, television, simply to pass the time. But Dickens's readers *pounced* on those fortnightly or monthly parts in which so many of his novels came out, then hurried away, gloating over them, ready to live intensely again with the characters found in them. It is true, as we chiefly learn from American sources, that television serials have only to go on long enough and then unsophisticated viewers will come to believe that their leading characters are real persons. But this comes from the sheer persistence of the highly realistic photographic image, the almost brutal illusion of the medium;

A family group reading the latest instalment of *Dombey*.

it is not, as with Dickens and his readers, one imagination setting fire to another. (Having worked with it and for it, and often enjoyed it, I do not despise television, but, whatever Professor McLuhan may tell us, I think it will be disastrous if and when television-viewing entirely displaces reading for pleasure. There are signs already that some committed viewers and non-readers, of all ages, are beginning to suffer from a blunting of imagination, a kind of curious new anaesthesia.) There is an old story that when *Dombey and Son* was coming out in parts, a horseman galloped through a village, late at night, shouting 'Carker's dead!' That suggests popularity and public excitement of a sort that no novelist has reached since Dickens.

Indeed, to understand what Dickens meant to his time, we have to forget writers altogether and to remember a man who achieved world fame in a different medium – Charles Chaplin. In the breadth and scope of his appeal, in his mixture of farce and pathos, even though he had not the depth of Dickens's genius, Chaplin of all twentieth-century figures comes nearest to Dickens. Nor can it be mere chance that the two men have much in common. If we look at the rather rare portraits of Dickens when he was out of his youth but had not yet grown a beard, portraits that show us an actor's face, we shall see a distinct resemblance. They both knew in their childhood and early youth the same poorer and darker quarters of London. Both of them deal comically and drastically with self-important official personages. Both of them are fascinated by the idea of innocent young girls in distress. Their careers, though so different in many other respects, are alike in being inspired by the same spirit of fiery independence, the same fiercely creative will, the same instinctive sympathy with the failures, the outcasts, the battered but still hopeful poor. Finally, they are alike in having been admired and applauded not simply by one nation, nor by certain sections of many nations, but by the whole wide world.

Most readers know that Dickens's reading tours in the provinces were a triumphal progress, not only inside the halls where he gave his extraordinary performances but also outside them, with crowds waiting just to catch a glimpse of him. But if we want to understand his unique status as a public figure – in a country that has always tended to undervalue rather than overvalue its authors – we must take a look at some events in the autumn and early winter of 1867 (at a time too when he was now bitterly satirizing Victorian society). Against the advice of many of his friends, who were concerned about his health, he had decided to pay a second visit to America, where he would repeat his readings. After several intimate 'farewell dinners', he was given an immense banquet at the Freemasons' Hall on 2 November. There were over four hundred (all male) guests; a hundred excited women filled the Ladies' Gallery; and in the other gallery was the band of the Grenadier Guards. The hall was decorated with British and American flags, together with large panels, in gold and crimson, each carrying the title of one of Dickens's novels. The chairman was his fellow novelist Lord Lytton, and he and Dickens entered together, tumultuously cheered, heading a procession that included the Lord Chief Justice, the Lord Mayor of London, and many other personages of the political or artistic Establishment. In his introductory speech, Lytton referred to the conquests of art and the royalty of genius, and concluded: 'Seldom, I say, has that kind of royalty been quietly conceded to any man of genius until his tomb becomes his throne, and yet there is not one of us now present who thinks it strange that it is granted without a murmur to the guest whom we receive tonight.' When Dickens rose to reply, the place went mad, the men jumping on to their chairs to shout and wave their napkins and glasses. The banquet went on and on, but at the end there was still a crowd waiting in the November night to say good-bye to their beloved Dickens.

He sailed to Boston, where he was to give his first reading. As soon as it was known he was coming, that hitherto staid city broke into a rash of Dickens portraits, the 'Dickens Collar', 'Little Nell Cigars', the 'Mantalini Plug', 'Pickwick Snuff'. His ship arrived like that of a conquering hero, with rockets bursting over it in the harbour. Tickets for the readings went in a rush both in Boston and New York, where people waited all through the bitter night to be there when the box office opened, and the ticket speculators – the 'scalpers' as they came to be called later – made profits of over two thousand per cent. No writer before had been given such a send-off as London gave Dickens; no writer before had created such a furore in the American cities; and it is safe to say that nothing like it has been known since and that, so far as novelists are concerned, nothing like it will ever be known again. We have had our own popular authors in this century, but their popularity has been a mere rushlight compared with the huge blaze of Dickens's popularity. He was fortunate in his time, when the novel came to be the great family entertainment, but he was even more fortunate in his unflagging industry, the force of his creative will, his unique genius.

Yet his career, like his personal life, bristled with sharp ironies. He did not escape them even in death. He had hoped for a small private funeral, a burial in a local graveyard. But this would not do for *The Times* and the Establishment it represented. So Dickens, who had cared nothing for tradition, who had laughed at solemn bigwigs, who had disliked official England, had to be buried in Westminster Abbey. However, this gave the people, who came in their thousands, a chance to file past his open grave; and we are told that for months afterwards his tomb was bright and fragrant with fresh flowers.

There is one important element in Dickens that many of our critics and their readers fail to understand. This failure is due to the fact that they have been brought up to believe that serious literature, as distinct from mere popular entertainment, is intensely private. The typical literary genius of our time is probably James Joyce, behaving like a one-man secret society, entirely withdrawn from any community in which he lived. (Indeed, writers of no great talent are often accepted as men of literary genius just because they have been neurotically introverted and social misfits.) Now Dickens lived and died before fashionable criticism took this sharp turn. As I hope to show, he was essentially an artist, and one with so rich a personality that in his depths he was often at war with himself. However, early in his career, as his work created more and more public excitement and his readers rapidly multiplied, he superimposed upon this artist in himself a figure who was both the master and the conscientious servant of his readers. His popularity made him feel deeply responsible. 'The Inimitable' must not take a wrong turning. He was now so striking and powerful a public figure that, increasingly, it was as if he were almost writing his novels in public. (The fact that they first appeared in fortnightly or monthly parts was important here: it was possible to make changes before the final publication in volume form.) He felt he *belonged* to his readers. If they wanted to know something about him, he felt he ought to tell them, which explains why he insisted, against all sensible advice, upon making a public statement about his separation from his wife. That he was not equally frank about his relations with Ellen Ternan does not prove him to be a hypocrite. He could not marry her, and all the evidence we possess does suggest that Ellen, unlike the mistresses of several other Victorian writers, was ashamed of their relationship, probably terrified of the publicity that would follow the discovery of the secret. Possibly Dickens, the novelist of cosy domesticity, was almost equally afraid of being found out: what is certain is that his increasing detestation of Victorian middle-class society and its humbug grew in the dark shadow of this secret. His sense of social responsibility, frustrated on one level, took refuge and then flourished on another deeper level, where a broad symbolism, found in all the later novels, was almost inevitable.

Dickens's idea of himself as a kind of responsible family magician, taking his place beside the family doctor or solicitor, does not have to be admired. I think myself that it weakened and never strengthened the artist in him. But we have to understand the attraction it had for him. It explains what might otherwise appear to be serious defects in his character, both as a man and as an artist. He wanted to retain his popularity, and he enjoyed making money just as he enjoyed spending it. (Writers who are loudly indifferent about making money are generally discovered to be living on other people's.) But when Dickens is found making hasty changes in his work, he is not being cynical about it, he is responding to this sense of responsibility, his idea of himself as a great public figure. For example, we know that he suddenly decided to send Martin Chuzzlewit and Mark Tapley to America because public interest in the novel, then coming out in parts, was declining. His readers were beginning to feel disappointed. *Martin Chuzzlewit* needed what we should call now 'a shot in the arm', and to the delight of most of us, even though we could do without Mark Tapley, it promptly received one. (And in spite of the grotesque absurdities in these American chapters, certain traits, noted and then wildly exaggerated there, still linger on.) Though Dickens wanted bigger sales and more money, behind and above this was the feeling that he ought to do better – that his readers were right and he was wrong – so, thank Heaven! he did better. This was not cynical potboiling; there was about it a kind of humility, which in turn had been created by his sense of responsibility towards his huge, eager, admiring public. Dickens was not a soft character; in many respects he was a hard man, fierily independent, strong-willed, driving himself ruthlessly; but there was never any arrogance in his attitude towards his public: he felt himself to be its faithful servant.

Martin Chuzzlewit was something of a hotchpotch anyhow, whereas *Great Expectations*, coming later, was carefully planned. We know how Dickens, staying with his friend Bulwer Lytton at Knebworth and taking the proofs of the final chapters of *Great Expectations* with him, was persuaded by Bulwer Lytton to change the end of the novel. The short final chapter that Dickens added – 'a very pretty piece of writing', he declared to John Forster – with its suggestion that Pip and Estella, now a widow and much improved by suffering, could be happy together, was really out of key with the whole tone of the novel. But Bulwer Lytton, himself a novelist who had always understood public taste in fiction, had pleaded hard, no doubt reminding Dickens of his responsibility towards his readers. (Moreover, though Ellen Ternan was no Estella, she was probably not free from touches of wilfulness and petulance, and a secret dream of being happy with her may have influenced this 'very pretty piece of writing'.) Certainly the artist in Dickens suffered a defeat here, but the point I wish to make is that it was not altogether an ignoble defeat. Mr Edmund Wilson, in his very fine essay on Dickens, seems to me to go wrong in attributing Dickens's habit of counter-balancing bad and good characters to his essential dualism. This dualism, the result of a deeply divided nature, certainly existed in Dickens, and we shall have to return to it. But on this superficial level of balancing characters – introducing a good Jew because he had formerly drawn a bad Jew, kindly and honest merchants and lawyers making up for cruel and dishonest merchants and lawyers – Dickens was not being the victim of his dualism but accepting his responsibility as a great public entertainer, a man always in the limelight. As I suggested earlier, this almost always weakened and never strengthened the artist in him. On the other hand, we should remember that the whole scheme, tone, symbolism, of his later novels defied the broader popular taste of his time.

Most of his nineteenth-century critics noticed the eager reformer in Dickens, the man quick to denounce abuses. Though I think more of Dickens than most of them did, I believe that in this matter they exaggerate his importance and misinterpret his motives. In his fiction, as distinct from his periodical-editing, much influenced by his concern for radical reform, Dickens was less personally concerned with denouncing and sweeping away public abuses than several other Victorian novelists. Once he had established himself with *Pickwick* and knew he had now a large and eager body of readers, it was his sense of social responsibility that made him turn, for example, to the horrible Yorkshire schools or Fagin's academy for young pickpockets. But these were familiar scandals: he had not suddenly discovered them himself. The true reformer dislikes something, wishes to abolish it, and knows what he wants to put in its place. Dickens as a man (and an editor and journalist) could adopt this attitude, but he was no reformer as a novelist, as a creator. To assume that he was, as many of his critics have done, only leads to confusion – if he didn't want that, then did he want this? – and then it appears that he didn't. Bernard Shaw declared that from *Dombey and Son* onwards, Dickens was a revolutionary, really a Shaw who had not read Marx. This is nearer the truth than the idea of him as a liberal reformer, but it will not do. He would have recoiled from and then outrageously mocked at Shaw and the Fabian Society. (Imagine what he would have done with the Webbs!) From *Dombey and Son* onwards, Dickens began to write out of a terrible despair, ruthlessly condemning one aspect of society after another. Yet, ironically enough, while dredging these black depths, he could not forget his responsibility as the 'great inimitable', remembered that he still had to be funny, sometimes with ineffective, almost painful, results. (*David Copperfield*, though it followed *Dombey and Son*, must be taken as an exception here: it was a novel on quite a different plane.) By the time we have followed him into the 1850s and then the '60s, though the humour may still crackle and sparkle here and there, the creator of the magnificent drolls, the characters most admired in his lifetime and for long afterwards, has been left behind.

'The characters of Dickens, then,' one of his critics tells us, 'are personified humours, his method is the method not of Shakespeare, but of Ben Jonson. Pecksniff is just another name for hypocrisy, Jonas Chuzzlewit for avarice, Quilp for cruelty.' There has been far too much of this solemn nonsense. If Dickens's characters are simply 'personified humours', so many mere caricatures, then what distinguishes him from the hundreds of mediocre novelists who also offer us such creatures? If Pecksniff is 'just another name for hypocrisy', then why do we remember him while forgetting almost all the other hypocrites in fiction? Cruelty is common enough in stories throughout the world, so why should we bother about Quilp? Parasitic dandies and impecunious middle-aged clerks were not unfamiliar figures in early Victorian London, but only Dickens could have transformed one of them into Mr Mantalini and one of the others into Mr Micawber. And if any contemporary young novelist thinks that comic creation on this level is easy, we can only advise him to try it and see, perhaps adding the final words of Mrs Sapsea's epitaph: 'Stranger pause. And ask thyself this question, Canst thou do likewise? If not, with a blush retire.'

In *Aspects of the Novel*, E. M. Forster, discussing what he calls 'flat and round characters', takes a potshot at explaining Dickens's comic characters:

The case of Dickens is significant. Dickens's people are nearly all flat (Pip and David Copperfield attempt roundness, but so diffidently that they seem more like bubbles than solids). Nearly every one can be summed up in a sentence, and yet there is this wonderful feeling of human depth. Probably the immense vitality of Dickens causes his characters to vibrate a little, so that they borrow his life and appear to lead one of their own. It is a conjuring trick. . . . Part of the genius of Dickens is that he does use types and caricatures, people whom we recognise the instant they re-enter, and yet achieves effects that are not mechanical and a vision of humanity that is not shallow. Those who dislike Dickens have an excellent case. He ought to be bad. He is actually one of our big writers, and his immense success with types suggests that there may be more in flatness than the severer critics admit.

And this is a handsome admission, because Forster makes no secret of his preference for 'round characters'. But his suggestion that Dickens's sheer vitality 'causes his characters to vibrate a little' does not take us very far. It does not explain why Sam Weller is not just another comic servant, Squeers not just another dreadful Yorkshire schoolmaster, Mantalini not just another affected rascal, Pecksniff not just another hypocrite, Toots not just another bashful stammering youth, and so on, throughout the great gallery of drolls. At least one element, found in profusion in Dickens but rather scarce, for example, in Ben Jonson, seems to be missing from this idea of flat characters merely being vibrated. It is an element that is also missing in the work of various minor early Victorian novelists – as for example Charles Lever, Samuel Warren, Albert Smith, and the Cockton who wrote *Valentine Vox* – who dealt heartily in types and caricatures and comic grotesques, all forgotten now. Vitality alone will not account for this profound difference. So we must try again.

For all his easier and rather slapdash manner, Chesterton comes nearer the truth:

The art of Dickens was the most exquisite of arts: it was the art of enjoying everybody. Dickens, being a very human writer, had to be a very human being; he had his faults and sensibilities in a strong degree; and I do not for a moment maintain that he enjoyed everybody in his daily life. But he enjoyed everybody in his books; and everybody has enjoyed everybody in those books even till today. His books are full of baffled villains stalking out or cowardly bullies kicked downstairs. But the villains and the cowards are such delightful people that the reader always hopes the villain will put his head through a side window and make a last remark; or that the bully will say one thing more, even from the bottom of the stairs. . . . Though Mr Pecksniff fell to be a borrower of money, and Mr Mantalini to turning a mangle, the human race has the comfort of thinking they are still alive: and one might have the rapture of receiving a begging letter from Mr Pecksniff, or even of catching Mr Mantalini collecting the washing, if one always lurked about on Monday mornings. . . .

I seem to remember Mr Edmund Wilson dismissing Chesterton-on-Dickens as 'boozy rhetoric' – his curious prejudice against us English for once clouding his perception. There is more in the above passage than met Mr Wilson's eye. It can begin to lead us through the undergrowth, all that dismal chatter about types and caricatures and personified humours, towards a clear height and a wider view.

When Chesterton, with some exaggeration, tells us that Dickens enjoyed everybody in his books, and that we find so many of his characters, however dubious as citizens, 'such delightful people', he is taking us closer to the secret of Dickens's peculiar magic. He is moving in the opposite direction from those critics, deficient in humour, who reduce Dickens's comic characters to some formula, which is about as sensible as trying to paraphrase a lyric by Shelley or Keats into a brief bald statement in prose. The point about Pecksniff is not that he is simply a hypocritical architect and a bogus moralist; it is that, as Dickens expands him, he flowers into such glorious absurdities of speech. Any competent Victorian novelist could have sketched a drunken irresponsible nurse like Mrs Gamp, but only Dickens could have given her such wonderfully daft dialogue. When Mr Crummles, expressing his admiration of Miss Petowker's talent and versatility, concludes by saying, 'She's the only sylph *I* ever saw, who could stand upon one leg, and play the tambourine on her other knee, *like* a sylph', he is rising to a height of absurdity far above any actual touring manager. Mr Mantalini is one more extravagant husband who sponges on his wife, but when he stares at her, apparently unable to believe she could be so hard on him, and cries, 'She is sitting there before me. There is the graceful outline of her form; it cannot be mistaken – there is nothing like it. The two countesses had no outlines at all, and the dowager's was a demn outline. Why is she so excruciatingly beautiful that I cannot be angry with her, even now?' Mr Mantalini, though still in character, is so exquisitely ludicrous that he is almost a poetic creation. Bashful suitors are common enough in fiction, but it is when Toots, after hanging about for hours to find courage to call and enquire after Florence Dombey, keeps muttering *It's of no consequence* before turning away at the front door, that he achieves memorable individuality: it is that inspired phrase which does the trick. While Toots is ringing the bell, so is Dickens.

I could happily supply scores of other examples but will content myself with one more – the Micawbers. It simply will not do to dismiss these two gigantic drolls by saying that Mr Micawber is waiting for something to turn up and that Mrs Micawber merely goes on declaring she will never desert Mr Micawber. Almost anybody, even a lecturer on the Victorian novel, might have got as far as *that*. It is Mr Micawber's actual manner and style, his grandiloquence that keeps collapsing ('The blossom is blighted, the leaf is withered, the God of Day goes down upon the dreary scene, and – in short, you are for ever floored. As I am'), the heights of absurdity he reaches, that keep him shining in our memory. Moreover, though Dickens out of sheer high spirits made him so wildly preposterous, so far as he is a type he is not altogether unreal. Most of us have known men not unlike him, men not engaged in one of the arts but in business of a sort, running dubious little agencies, and men too who defy misfortune, refuse to feel hopeless, just because they see their lives as so much romantic drama. Such men often have wives not unlike Mrs Micawber, though less rich and strange. Mrs Micawber, with her talk of corn and coal, brewing and banking, appears to be as severely practical as her husband is romantic and rhetorical; her logic cannot be challenged: 'Commission to the extent of two and ninepence in a fortnight cannot, however limited our ideas, be considered remunerative'. But she is not reasoning in the real world but in Mr Micawber's, feminine practicality having surrendered to masculine imagination. The huge daftness of this pair comes out of Dickens's comic fertility, but they cannot be dismissed as mere Punch-and-Judy figures. As characters they are larger and droller than life, yet cannot be entirely disconnected from it, which explains why the names of many of his comic characters soon became, like his own magazine, *Household Words*.

Even so, though few writers who ever lived have been more observant than Dickens, it was not observation but wonderfully comic invention, a huge expansion of the sense of absurdity, that really created these famous characters. This is the point in Chesterton's remark about Dickens enjoying everybody in his books, though of course his further remark, that we have all enjoyed everybody in those books ever since, is a wild overstatement. There are some characters, often playing an important part in the action, that simply do not come off: so I for one cannot accept Uriah Heep, who might almost be described as a Dickens character imagined by somebody who disliked Dickens. Naturally there had to be failures, even among the grotesques, but his comic triumphs, so numerous, varied and rich, make him unique among the world's novelists, at once 'great' and 'inimitable'. I may be thought to be too English here, making such a claim while forgetting that great novelists have existed elsewhere. Well, Tolstoy was a very great novelist and as Russian as Dickens was English and removed from him by a certain amount of time and a great deal of space. Yet Tolstoy, as 'Q' tells us, could say of Dickens: 'All his characters are my personal friends. I am constantly comparing them with living persons, and living persons with them. And what a *spirit* there was in all he wrote!'

Some further consideration of these comic characters will bring us nearer to an understanding of the *Inimitable*, even though I must not arrive too soon at the final points I want to make. There seem to me three good reasons why the humour of Dickens – at least on his own gigantic scale – appears to be unique. The first I have already indicated: the fertility and richness of his comic invention. The other two reasons are rather more subtle. One of them is concerned with the curious theatricality of Dickens's creative imagination, the other with his unusually close relation to his own childhood and ours.

To illustrate the theatricality, I will take one example out of scores, the first that comes to my mind, namely, the character of Wackford Squeers, the head of that nightmare academy, Dotheboys Hall. As a person encountered in the history of Nicholas Nickleby, a character moving in the plot, he is ignorant, brutal, and altogether a horrible fellow. But when, for instance, Squeers smacks his lips over his boys' wretched mixture of milk and water and then cries 'Here's richness!' we have to laugh at the sheer impudence of it. But then, if we are perceptive, we begin to wonder about Squeers. Perhaps he is trying to make us, the readers, laugh. Perhaps at such moments in the tale he is not really a horrible schoolmaster: *he is a superb comedian playing a horrible schoolmaster.* And as much might be said of many of the other characters, especially in the earlier novels. Perhaps other superb comedians are playing Sam Weller and his father, Dick Swiveller, Crummles, Mantalini, Pecksniff, and the rest. They deliberately overdo their characters, making them more and more preposterous but more and more laughable, to entertain us.

We know that Dickens himself was a magnificent actor, probably, as his highly dramatized readings suggest, the greatest English actor of his time. We know that he often acted his scenes as he created them. (Once he was discovered lurching and crawling in his study, and it appeared that he was about to write a scene for Quilp.) He wrote novels instead of plays because, after *Pickwick*, he realized that the novel was the more rewarding medium; moreover, he was naturally expansive and so needed the length, the breadth, the space, that fiction offered him. But he had been a frequent and enthusiastic playgoer, so now he turned his novels into what might be called super-theatre. This explains both what is bad and what is wonderfully good in his earlier work. His hard-hearted moneylenders and misers and his villainous aristocrats were borrowed from the theatre. His large-scale and overworked pathos, as distinct from his natural touches of real pathos, came from the theatre: we can almost see the lights fading and hear the muted strings in the orchestra pit in his lingering death-bed scenes. There was no gain here, only loss. But even the most tearful of the melo-dramas of the 1830s usually offered some comic relief, scenes dominated by the company's favourite comedians. Such scenes, however, were mostly written by hacks, certainly not by any humorist of genius. And now here, with comedy that had its roots in the theatre but was fruitfully and marvellously expanded by Dickens, there was no loss, all was sheer gain.

Moreover, there is nothing superficial, as some readers may imagine, about a character like Squeers apparently at certain moments being pre-sented to us by a comedian. On the contrary, there is here a fascinating double effect, which in fact is always discovered in rich high comedy. It wants to remind us that we all go through this life wearing a mask, hiding behind a *persona*. Our essential selves move and speak in a permanent masquerade. We are never quite what we seem to be. So the comedy that suggests this has far greater depth than the creation of character on a naturalistic level. I am not saying that Dickens consciously aimed at achieving this effect; but then a great artist is largely nourished by his unconscious, as Dickens certainly was throughout his career. It was be-cause the depths of his personality, revealed in his work, were not explored and understood by criticism, that he was belittled for so many years after his death. Now that we know more and discover so much more in his work, he is a giant again.

Finally, we come to the third good reason why the humour of Dickens – at least on his own gigantic scale – seems so original. As I have already suggested, it is concerned with his unusually close relation to his own childhood and ours. When is it that we seem to know so many comic Dickensian characters? It is in our childhood and early youth, when we keep meeting our parents' or grandparents' old friends, when fantastic distant relatives turn up at Christmas or at funerals. They may not re-semble any of Dickens's actual characters, but they seem to exist in the same atmosphere, to belong to the same odd world. They are always laugh-ably themselves, never appearing to change at all, and we can never imagine them as ever being anything different. Because we ourselves are living then in the long years of childhood and early youth, these comic family characters seem to us to live in a timeless world, cosily unchanging. When Dickens, still no more than a delicate child, was sent off to the black

ing factory, finding himself in a nightmare that went on and on, he did
not in fact have to stay there very long and was not too harshly treated;
but the deep wound it gave him never stopped bleeding for the rest of his
life. As a middle-aged man, famous throughout the world, he still dreamt
of being turned out, discarded, to go to the dark factory. It is this that
makes him turn again and again in the world of his imagination to the
bright hearth, the cosy domestic scene, the circle of familiar faces, among
them the comic figures, timeless and unchanging, that remind us of the
family friends, the peculiar relatives, the odd neighbours, we knew long
ago, in another half-fairy-tale world. It is not enough to say, as E. M.
Forster says, that this 'wonderful feeling of human depth' is due to
Dickens's immense vitality, enabling him to make his flat characters
'vibrate a little'. Certainly the vitality was there, but something else was
at work, a kind of imagination, fed by the unconscious, that we do not
expect to discover in a novelist.

So now I must keep the promise I made in the second introductory paragraph of this essay. I must move from *Great* to *Inimitable* and try to explain
his unique quality. Indeed, I must now contradict myself – I must declare
that this great novelist was not, strictly speaking, a novelist at all. He was
a great writer who wrote novels, but he was not a novelist in the sense that
contemporaries like Thackeray and Trollope were novelists. This of course
has never worried the vast number of ordinary readers who delight in him
and neither know nor care in what category he is placed. But it has foxed
many 'severe' critics from Leslie Stephen[1] years ago to some *Scrutiny* contributors. They cannot find in Dickens the qualities they admire in Thackeray or Trollope, George Eliot or Henry James, and at the same time they
are strangely blind, perhaps from lack of imagination, to all that is extraordinary and wonderful in Dickens. It is rather as if they read the romantic
poets, from Coleridge to Keats, and then accused them of a lack of common-
sense and soundly practical advice. This is not too wildly absurd an
analogy, if only because what they fail to perceive and then enjoy in
Dickens is the poetic quality of his creative imagination. There is a sense
in which Dickens's novels are merely pretending to be the usual prose
chronicles of man in society: they might be better described as huge
grotesque poems. They are not alone here, for there are other instances,
from Rabelais to Gogol (in the first part of *Dead Souls*) to James Joyce;
even though Dickens still has his own unique quality.

It is worth repeating here what E. M. Forster said: 'Those who dislike
Dickens have an excellent case. He ought to be bad. He is actually one of

our big writers, and his immense success with types suggests that there
may be more in flatness than the severer critics admit.' What this amounts
to is that Forster is aware of Dickens's weaknesses as a realistic novelist,
but, being an imaginative man himself, he is also aware that Dickens is
different and 'big', though he does not seem to understand why this
should be so. But there is no mystery if we begin to appreciate the character, size and force of Dickens's creative imagination. He is not primarily a
chronicler, commentator, social historian in fiction. He is a Maker, a
dramatic and epic poet working in prose, a haunted tragic-comedian of
mythopoeic genius. He creates his own world, his own atmosphere. It is a
world crammed with sharply observed realistic detail. (His power of
observation and his memory were phenomenal.) Yet in spite of all this
detail, it is a strange world, with lights and shadows in it not belonging to
our common day and night. While it shows us all manner of adult concerns,
legal, financial, criminal, and the rest, often we seem to wander through it
like dreaming children. Indeed, the atmosphere in which it exists might
come from some vast theatre in dreamland. The unconscious is always at
work here, first his and then ours, if we open ourselves to his spell.

Yeats, that great poet, said we make rhetoric out of our quarrel with
others, poetry out of the quarrel with ourselves.[2] Dickens used plenty of
rhetoric, not all of it welcome, but there was a kind of poetry, not verbal
and almost always grotesque, comic, dramatic, that inspired his furious
acts of creation. (But I must point out here that there is far more delicate
perception, together with more verbal felicities, in Dickens than he is
generally credited with: thus the childhood of David Copperfield is a
masterpiece of highly subjective narrative.) This poetry, though different
from what Yeats had in mind, also largely came out of the quarrel with
himself. He was a deeply divided man. I think Jung, the most profound
and rewarding of our depth psychologists, would have said that Dickens
was never able to come to terms with his Shadow, representing the dark
hidden side of ourselves, and his Anima, the magical symbol of the woman
in us. The influence of the Shadow was not responsible for his conscious
rebellion, for the warm-hearted protesting radical in him, but it was responsible for the unconscious deeply anti-social strain in him, as it was,
for example, in Dostoevsky, who admired Dickens and felt to some extent
his influence. This explains the fascination that murder had for Dickens
both in his work and his life, in spite of the fact that he was a conscientious
upright citizen. It explains too why his novels, setting in bright relief their
cosy domestic interiors, can be horrifyingly dark with violence, madness,
and death. So too, because he could not come to terms with his Anima,

projecting its magical image upon one young girl after another, he never found a satisfying mature relationship with a woman, which might have healed the wounds of his spirit. This largely accounts for that 'want of something' he confessed to his intimate friends, and perhaps for the fact that he seems to have had a curiously unsatisfactory relationship with his family for such an affectionate man. Certainly it accounts for his restlessness, his wearing himself out on reading tours, and the deeply hidden despair that welled up in the symbolism of his later novels, which reduces Victorian society – ours too, perhaps – to fog and dust and ashes.

'Yer pays yer money an' takes yer choice!' When I was very young, it was still the fashion to admire most the early novels, hastily improvised, with their zest and comic triumphs, and to deplore his later work. Now it is the fashion to dismiss all those earlier novels and to concentrate on the carefully plotted (often over-plotted) later work because of its social criticism and the surprising breadth and depth of its symbolism. In his own time it was probably his Christmas stories that his English readers loved best of all, and now, I suspect, only the very old turn to them. Dickens's nonfiction, pieces of *reportage* and comment that are easy to read and enjoy and are rich in social history, does not seem to attract much attention these days; but one good critical study of Dickens as a journalist, together with a sensible television series featuring him as a social historian and critic, might swing a large new body of readers in this direction. My own first choice among his books would be all novels, running from first to last as follows: *Pickwick, Nicholas Nickleby, Martin Chuzzlewit, David Copperfield, Bleak House, Our Mutual Friend*. There is, however, nothing fixed, nothing permanent, about this list: in a few years time, if I live that long, I might be ready to change it.

Finally, as I am to be followed here by writers who know as much about Dickens as I do, perhaps more than I do, I have deliberately omitted from this introductory essay many things that ought to be said about his personality and his work. I have left to my colleagues any appreciation of his warm humanity, the width and depth of his compassion, any consideration of the lack in him of religious, philosophical, political ideas, any account of the marked changes in his attitude towards the various Victorian social classes, comparing, for example, the villainous or imbecile aristocrats in *Nicholas Nickleby* with such a character, created twenty-five years later, as Eugene Wrayburn in *Our Mutual Friend*. Here, as Dickens himself might have said, I have only been banging the drum outside the show at the fair. But I hope I have suggested that this man was – and still is – great and truly inimitable.

The Life of Dickens

The life of Charles Dickens is as remarkable as any of his stories, and indeed
he drew upon his personal experience increasingly as he grew older. Without
doubt the humiliations of his boyhood acted in many ways as the spur which
made him the man and writer he became. As Edgar Johnson has written in
'Charles Dickens: His Tragedy and Triumph': 'In one sense, the grieving child
in the blacking warehouse might be said to have died, to be succeeded by the
man of deadly determination, of insuperable resolve, hard and aggressive
almost to fierceness. In another, that child never died, but was continually
reborn in a host of children suffering and dying young or other innocent
victims undergoing injustice and pain' [7 and 8]. Besides his own humiliation,
his father [17] was imprisoned for debt in the Marshalsea when the family
were living in Camden Town [9 and 10], and for some time they had a hard
battle for survival. These facts remained unknown to Dickens's children
[19 and 20] and also to his wife [11 and 25], until after his death they read
the biography of his great friend, John Forster [21]. Another profound
influence upon Dickens was the death in the flower of youth of his sister-in-
law, Mary Hogarth [12 and 13], who was probably the prototype of many of
his 'angelic' female characters. A poignant love-affair with Maria Beadnell [24],
together with the recollection of Mary, and the growing sympathy of his
other sister-in-law Georgina Hogarth [23], seem to have slowly alienated him
from his wife, with whom there were signs of incompatibility from the first.
But the final break was precipitated by his meeting in 1857 with the young
actress, Ellen Ternan [26], though his precise relationship with the latter still
remains something of a mystery. Apart from an early infatuation with a young
pianist, Mary Weller, and a strange relationship over a number of years with
a Mrs de la Rue, on whom he practised a form of mesmerism for a nervous
ailment, Dickens enjoyed the friendship and respect of several women of
distinction, notably Lady Blessington [27] and Baroness Burdett-Coutts [28].
Although his last years were clouded with unhappiness and burdened by
overwork, Dickens found in Gad's Hill Place [31] a home which he had
coveted from boyhood. It was a few hours after working on 'Edwin Drood'
in the Swiss chalet across the road [30] that he suffered a stroke on 8 June
1870, and died the next day. On 10 June, Millais made a drawing of Dickens's
bandaged head [32]. After his burial in Westminster Abbey, hundreds of
anonymous mourners came to strew flowers on his tomb.

1–6 Dickens: from the youth of eighteen
to the world-famous novelist of fifty.

1

2

3

4

5

6

7 Warren's Blacking Pots, on which the boy Dickens tied the covers and then pasted the labels.

8 'No words can express the secret agony of my soul.'

9 and 10 Bayham Street, Camden Town, where Dickens's family lived before his father was imprisoned for debt in the Marshalsea.

11

12

13

Monday, JANUARY 1, 1838.
1st day.   Circumcision.

A sad new year's day in one respect, for at the opening of last year poor Mary was with us. Very many things to be grateful for, since then, however. Increased reputation and means – Good health and prospects. We never know the full value of blessings 'till we lose them. I was not ignorant of this one when we had it, I hope, but if she were with us now, the same winning, happy, amiable companion – sympathizing with all my thoughts and feelings more than any one I knew ever did or will – I think I should have nothing to wish for, but a continuance of such happiness. But she is gone, and pray God I may one day through his mercy rejoin her.

14

deliberately upon it, except by means of this glossary

Faithfully Yours

[signature] Charles Dickens

Kate is better, I think, this morning. 1700 Grimaldis have been already sold, and the Demand increases daily !!!

11 Mrs Charles Dickens ('Kate'), 1842.
12 Her younger sister, Mary Hogarth, who died at 18, 'sympathizing with all my thoughts and feelings more than anyone I knew ever did or will'.
13 A page from Dickens's diary, the first day of the year after Mary's death.
14 A letter to John Forster in 1838 about the success of the *Memoirs of Joseph Grimaldi*.
☞ *overleaf*
15 Portrait of Dickens by W. P. Frith, 1859.
16 Some of Dickens's personal belongings.

FORSTER BEQUEST.

CHARLES DICKENS (1812-70) AT THE AGE OF 47. (SIGNED AND DATED). WILLIAM POWELL FRITH, R.A. (b 1819. d 1909)

15

16

17 John Dickens, the novelist's father.
18 Elizabeth, his mother.
19 and 20 Mamie and Katey Dickens in childhood, and with their father at Gad's Hill, c. 1865.

21 John Forster, lifelong friend and biographer.
22 William Charles Macready, famous actor and friend of Dickens.

23

24

25

26

27

28

23 Georgina Hogarth, the novelist's sister-in-law, in old age.
24 Mrs Henry Lewis Winter (Maria Beadnell), Dickens's first love.
25 Kate (Mrs Charles) Dickens in middle age.

26 One of the few surviving photographs of Ellen Ternan.
27 Lady Blessington, friend of Count D'Orsay, whose *salon* Dickens frequently attended.
28 Baroness Burdett-Coutts, his collaborator in many welfare schemes.

29

30

31

32

29 A cheque written by Dickens a month before his death
for payment of his servants' wages.
30 The chalet at Gad's Hill
presented to Dickens by his Swiss friend Fechter.
31 Gad's Hill Place, with Dickens in the foreground.
32 The last portrait: Millais' sketch of Dickens
on the day after his death at Gad's Hill.

Dickens: The Dark Pilgrimage

Edgar Johnson

'**O**ur Charles Dickens is dead' – 'Nostro Carlo Dickens è morto' – headlined some of the Italian newspapers when the telegraphed message of his death flashed around the globe. For one of his readers who saw the news in a Genoa paper it was as if the sun had been blotted from the heavens. Everywhere – in Europe, India, Australia, America – consternation mingled with sorrow; it seemed incredible that his enormous vitality could be gone, and people wept the tears of personal loss. The bond that united Dickens with his readers was deeper than an awed surrender to genius. It was a bond of love.

In the hundred years since Dickens died the love he kindled has not passed away, and the awareness of his mighty attainment has grown. He has come to loom among the writers of the nineteenth century like a rock-cut colossus towering into the sky. But his achievement is more than a matter of that tremendous stature, that magnetic force, which were almost universally felt even in his own day. Within and beneath his titanic creativeness the world has been discovering new depths – haunting undertones and overtones, thematic unity, variation, and development, profundities of awareness that wake buried vibrations in the mind and heart, and beneath the dazzling animation and the laughter shadows of tragic darkness. Far more than a great entertainer, a great comic writer, he looks into the abyss. He is one of the great poets of the novel, a genius of his art.

The overwhelming fact of genius still outsoars explanation. Who would have foreseen it in the grandchild of William Dickens the butler at Crewe Hall, and of Charles Barrow the embezzling civil servant? Who foretold it of the son of a minor naval clerk always tangled in financial difficulties? Who would have expected it to emerge from a sickly childhood and a meagre education, bursting forth, triumphant over every handicap, in one of the supreme writers of all time? Often the forces that shape the nature of great attainment lie buried deep beyond recovery – in the unrecorded, the forgotten, the deliberately hidden; in childhood days of suffering and of shining joy, miseries, delights, terrors, exaltations; wounds obliterated by the will but ineradicably scarred upon the heart. How recapture the strange and perilous influences that hammered out the powers of imagination and forged them in the furnace of the soul?

Of these ultimate mysteries there is, of course, no solution, but in the childhood of Charles Dickens some, at least, of the shaping forces are almost transparently clear. The short sunlit happiness of his early days, the despairing misery into which he was plunged when he was only twelve, the fierce struggles of his youth, all moulded the dominant qualities of his sensibility and gave his powers a direction that determined the entire course of his career and flowered in the glorious achievements of his art. The Greek Fates could hardly have spun and woven more inevitably than those experiences of Dickens's early life that made him what he became.

He was born at Portsea on 7 February 1812. His father, John Dickens, was a clerk in the Navy Pay Office; in 1817 he was transferred to the government dockyard at Chatham. John Dickens was hard-working, able, voluble, and magniloquent; he was also one of those glowingly improvident men who never manage to live within even a rising income. He loved the splendid gesture, unbounded hospitality, grandiose display. Ultimately his fecklessness was to lead to disaster.

But for little Charles the six years the family spent at Chatham was a happy time. Though he had been a sickly child, he grew stronger in its hilltop air, playing glorious games in the daisied meadow before the house and on rainy days having magic-lantern shows indoors. When there were guests John Dickens proudly perched him on a table to sing comic songs in a piping voice. Trotting beside his father, he visited the shipyard, with its clamorous anchor-smiths and hammering carpenters, the rising walls of the vessels, the smell of oakum and tarred rope, the gangs of convict labourers, and the black convict hulk moored out in the River Medway 'like a wicked Noah's ark'. Sometimes they sailed in the Navy Pay Yacht as far as Sheerness, gliding by tall ships that enraptured the child with far visions of the sea.

Chatham melted into the cathedral city of Rochester, with its hoary Norman Cathedral and rook-haunted tower, and, over the hill, the ruined Castle, its bare holes of windows staring out like the empty sockets of a skull. Over the bridge, across the Medway, on longer rambles with his father, the child passed the Elizabethan mansion of Cobham Hall, with its mellow brickwork towers, and came out of Cobham Wood at Gad's Hill. Here the little boy stared in admiration at a rose-madder Georgian dwelling and listened with incredulous longing while his father told him that if he worked very hard and saved his money he himself might one day live there. But the fabulous dream came true; forty years later he bought that very house and it was his home for the last twelve years of his life.

In a little attic nook near his own bedroom the child found a small collection of forgotten books. While the other boys were shouting outdoors, he precociously began devouring the pages of the *Arabian Nights*, *Robinson Crusoe*, *Gil Blas*, *Tales of the Genii*, *Don Quixote*, and the novels of Smollett, Fielding, and Goldsmith. 'I have been Tom Jones . . . for a week together. I have sustained my own idea of Roderick Random for a month at a stretch,

I verily believe.' From the age of seven the child was taken to Christmas pantomimes, where he shouted with laughter at Pantaloon and Harlequin and fell in love with Columbine. In the tiny Theatre Royal he clapped joyfully at the clown Grimaldi; before he was ten he shivered in terror at *Richard III* and *Macbeth*.

All these excitements are core elements in Dickens's imagination. The breezy world of Fielding and the brutal world of Smollett he suffuses inextricably with the fairy-tale world of fantasy and the highly coloured world of the theatre. The sharpest and most everyday realism, seen in the most concrete detail, mingles with romance, farce, and melodrama, the magic of Ali Baba's cave and Sinbad's valley of diamonds with Fagin's greasy cellar in Saffron Hill, the broken-hearted toil of David Copperfield in the rat-infested warehouse, the glowing good cheer of Bob Cratchit's Camden Town fireside. It is but a leap for Dickens from hilarity to bitter anger, from wild absurdity to deep pathos. His vision blends the comic, the tender, the grotesque, the pathetic, and the horrible.

The Chatham days ended in the winter of 1822–3, when John Dickens was transferred to London. His debts had become a hopeless weight; before the family moved they had to sell all their household goods. Their new home was a shabby tenement in Camden Town. No attempt was made to continue the schooling Charles had begun at Chatham. Instead, he ran errands, blacked his father's boots, and helped keep the wolf from the door by pledging small articles of silver at the pawnshop. Two days after his twelfth birthday he began wrapping bottles in a blacking warehouse, at a wage of six shillings a week. Eleven days later still, his father was arrested for debt and gaoled in the Marshalsea. At the prison gates the weeping child heard his father's parting words: the sun had set upon him forever.

The blacking warehouse was a dirty, tumbledown old building at Hungerford Stairs. For the boy it was as if, like his father, he was being sent to prison, but for some mysterious crime he did not understand. This descent into menial labour was an appalling shock that plunged him into bewildered misery. His father had led him to think of himself as a young gentleman; now his fellow workers were Cockney boys with ragged clothes and uncouth accents. 'No words,' he wrote later, 'can express the secret agony of my soul as I sunk into this companionship . . . and felt my early hopes of growing up to be a learned and distinguished man crushed in my breast.'

To save money, his mother, with his younger brothers and sisters, moved into the prison with John Dickens, and Charles was lodged in a garret in Camden Town. His loneliness deepened his despair. 'No advice, no counsel, no encouragement, no consolation, no support, from any one that I can call to mind, so help me God.' 'I know that I lounged about in the streets, insufficiently and unsatisfactorily fed. I know that, but for the mercy of God, I might easily have been, for any care that was taken of me, a little robber or a little vagabond.'

Presently a small legacy enabled John Dickens to pay his debts and emerge from the Marshalsea, and a little later, after a quarrel with the manager of the warehouse, he announced that the boy should cease working and be sent back to school. The time Charles had spent in the warehouse amounted to no more than five months, but the lonely anguish he endured had made it seem an eternity of suffering. The wound was so deep that its emotional scar remained with Dickens forever. All the remainder of his life he lay under the double shadow of the Marshalsea and the workroom dungeon where he had toiled in despair.

The experience was crucial for Dickens's entire future course. It is hardly fanciful to say that in the blacking warehouse that unhappy child died, and into his frail body entered the spirit of a man of relentless determination. Deep within him, he resolved that he should never again be so victimized. He would toil, he would fall prey to none of his father's financial imprudence, he would let nothing stand between him and ambition. He would batter his way out of all the gaols that confine the human spirit.

But the child that died was reborn in all the unhappy children of Dickens's books, from Oliver Twist to crippled little Miss Jenny Wren. Instead of remaining gaol-locked in mere self-pity, Dickens opened the floodgates of his sympathy for all the neglected, unloved, and misused, all the innocent and suffering victims of society, all the prisoners of injustice and pain. Their cause became his cause, for in his deepest heart he and they and the sorrowing child he had been were one.

At the school Charles attended for the next two and a half years, Wellington House Academy, he never spoke of the blacking warehouse to the other boys. All they saw was a jolly, laughing youngster who dressed with extreme neatness and held his head spiritedly high. 'How could it affect them, who were so innocent of London life and London streets,' David Copperfield echoes his creator, 'to discover how knowing I was (and ashamed to be) in the meanest phases of both?'

Leaving school in 1827 – the family was again in financial straits – Charles started work in a law office. But to him the law seemed merely a dull and involved labyrinth for entangling troubled clients, and advancement was far too slow for his impatient demands. He decided to become a reporter; with characteristic energy he taught himself shorthand – a task,

A note sent by the twelve-year-old Dickens to a fellow schoolboy.

he was told, equivalent to mastering six languages. But he accomplished it. At the age of seventeen he was a shorthand reporter efficiently taking down cases in the law courts while he waited restlessly to be old enough to get a post as a newspaper reporter.

Impatience and the longing for more exciting work still tormented him. In his impetuosity he thought of the stage. Since he had left school he had been haunting the galleries of the theatres; could he not, he asked himself, attain a more speedy success as an actor? Industriously he began memorizing roles and teaching himself gestures and movement; when he thought himself adept he applied to the stage-manager of the Lyceum Theatre for a trial hearing. The day came, but he was ill with a frightful cold. Before he could renew his application the offer of a post on the *Mirror of Parliament* gave him his long awaited opportunity to become a reporter. Through so narrow a margin were his dramatic talents deflected from the stage.

Dickens was still only nineteen, but to him it seemed to have taken long enough to reach his goal. And almost at once he 'made a great splash' among the eighty or ninety newspaper veterans who took down the debates in Parliament. One of them exclaimed decades later, 'There never *was* such a shorthand writer!' Within less than two years, he found a still better position, on the *Morning Chronicle*, and was soon one of the star reporters, covering all the most spectacular news events of the day, from the notorious Melbourne-Norton trial to the fire at Hatfield House in which the Marchioness of Salisbury was burned to death.

The iron resolve with which he had driven himself had grown all the more desperate because when he was seventeen he had fallen violently in love with the dark ringlets, bright eyes, and vivacious chatter of a tiny siren named Maria Beadnell, a banker's daughter, who filled his nights and days with ecstasy and agonized longing. He must be a success, and that speedily. For almost four years she teased and smiled, tortured and relented; he laboured in a fog of heartache and fruitless devotion. Only when he had battered down all the obstacles to his professional career did he at last realize that his suit was hopeless, and find the courage to say farewell and try to blot her memory from his heart.

Meanwhile he had begun writing short fictional sketches. One of them he dropped, 'with fear and trembling', into the letterbox of the *Monthly Magazine* on a winter night in 1833. It was accepted; when he saw it in print he had to hurry from the Strand into Westminster Hall to hide from passers-by his tears of joy and pride. His sketches began appearing in other periodicals; the editor of the *Evening Chronicle*, George Hogarth, invited him to do an entire series for that paper. Presently all these pieces were collected under the title *Sketches by Boz*, with illustrations by the great caricaturist George Cruikshank. They were published on the young author's twenty-fourth birthday.

The book was successful enough to bring from the new publishing house of Chapman and Hall a proposal that Dickens write a novel to be published in monthly instalments. It was really only a hack-job: he was to provide the narrative for a series of comic pictures by a well-known cartoonist. But

48 Doughty Street, Mecklenburgh Square, where Dickens moved in 1837, soon after his marriage.

Dickens agreed almost at once, though in a superb feat of self-assured salesmanship he made himself the dominant partner in the enterprise, with the artist illustrating his story instead of the text following the artist's lead. Thus was *Pickwick Papers* born. Exuberantly Dickens announced, 'Pickwick is begun in all his might and glory!'

Part of his reason for accepting the offer was that the £14 a month he was to be paid for the novel would enable him to marry. In the three years since he had said farewell to Maria Beadnell he had fallen in love with George Hogarth's daughter Catherine, a dark-haired, blue-eyed young woman whose quietness was in languid contrast to Maria's prattling vivacity. Catherine was pensive, sometimes a little melancholy, but Dickens was swept away by her sleepy voluptuousness. They were married on 2 April 1836, just two days after the first number of *Pickwick Papers* appeared.

The novel made so disappointing a start that for a time there was danger of the enterprise being abandoned. But then it caught on; by July it had swelled into such popularity that one of Dickens's letters announced in excited capitals, 'PICKWICK TRIUMPHANT'. Before the end of its monthly course it was selling forty thousand copies a number. It became a mania; there were Pickwick cigars, Weller corduroys, Pickwick chintzes, Boz caps, Pickwick hats. At the age of twenty-five, within little more than two years of his first appearance in print, Dickens was famous.

Pickwick is a great happy book, full of a young man's fierce delight in the idiocy of humanity, but no less overflowing with a high-spirited vision of human goodness, of the heroic and at the same time comic struggle between good and evil. It even manages gloriously to transcend Dickens's darker memories of his unhappy boyhood and the parental neglect that had left him to struggle upward with a scanty education. 'I took a good deal o' pains with his eddication, sir,' Sam Weller's father tells Mr Pickwick; 'let him run in the streets when he was wery young, and shift for hisself. It's the only way to make a boy sharp, sir.'

With the spectacular triumph of his very first novel, Dickens promptly gave up reporting and assumed the editorship of the newly established magazine *Bentley's Miscellany*. For this periodical he began writing *Oliver Twist*, while he was still hardly more than midway through *Pickwick*. This second novel too soared into popularity; readers hated Bumble and loathed Fagin as vigorously as they loved Mr Pickwick and Sam Weller. But Richard Bentley, the owner of the *Miscellany*, was close about money and tenacious of authority. Dickens felt resentfully that he was being exploited financially and his dignity as an editor impugned. The two men clashed repeatedly; and after two years of conflict Dickens stormily resigned and concentrated all his literary activities with Chapman and Hall.

He had begun his married life in three rooms in Furnival's Inn, where Catherine's younger sister Mary came to live with them. There, on 6 January 1837, Catherine Dickens gave birth to a boy, who was named after his father – the first of their ten children. Shortly after this Dickens signalized his prosperity by renting a comfortable house in Doughty Street, and it was here that Mary died 'with awful suddenness' on 7 May 1837. Two years later, grown larger by the successive births of two daughters, Mary ('Mamie') and Katey, the family moved to the luxury of Devonshire Terrace, which was almost a small mansion, with a walled garden.

The young author was in the highest of spirits. He was forever sending his friend John Forster little notes proposing rural jaunts: 'What a brilliant morning for a country walk!' 'Is it possible that you can't, oughtn't, shouldn't, mustn't, *won't* be tempted this gorgeous day!' Within this period Dickens rapidly and ebulliently wrote two further novels, *Nicholas Nickleby* and *The Old Curiosity Shop*. The first fuses a melodramatic exposure of the cruelties of the Yorkshire schools with the hilarious farce of the Mantalinis, the Kenwigses, and the Vincent Crummles theatrical troupe; the second mingles the comedy of Dick Swiveller and the grotesquerie of Daniel Quilp with the tearful pathos of little Nell's death. No sooner had Dickens killed Nell than he plunged at once into writing *Barnaby Rudge*. When that novel had run its course, in November, 1841, Dickens had placed beyond all doubt that he was the foremost novelist of the day.

But in six years he had written well over a million words, and for all his enormous energy felt a little tired. He decided to take a six months' vacation and visit the United States of America. He was sure that he would understand that democratic country with a sympathy impossible to the Tory prejudices of previous European visitors; he would write a travel book celebrating its glorious achievements. He and Catherine embarked, in January, 1842, on a ship sailing for Boston. His first sight of the New World there was indeed all a love feast; the Bostonians welcomed him with delirious enthusiasm. The Americans, Dickens wrote glowingly, were 'friendly, earnest, hospitable, kind, frank, . . . warm-hearted, fervent, and enthusiastic'.

But at Hartford when he ventured to remark on American piracies of books by foreign authors, there were howls of fury in the press. He was 'no gentleman', he was a 'mercenary scoundrel'. Thereafter, his ill impressions multiplied. Intrusive celebrity hunters left him no moment of privacy; newspapers and politicians were even more corrupt than in England; in the

tin chuzzlew'g

tin Sweezledew

utin chuzzletoe

utin Sweezlebach

martin Sweezlewag

South intolerance on the slavery question was rampant; the country despised art and literature; the pursuit of the dollar swallowed up everything else. 'I tremble,' Dickens wrote, 'for a radical coming here, unless he is a radical on principle, by reason and reflection.' 'I do fear that the heaviest blow ever dealt at liberty will be dealt by this country, in the failure of its example to the earth.'

Home again, in the summer of 1842, he wrote *American Notes*, generously praising what he could, but unable to hide his disappointment. That autumn he began *Martin Chuzzlewit*, which despite its satiric brilliance sold disappointingly in England and because of its pyrotechnical American caricatures enraged the citizens of that country still more violently. But its relative unpopularity is no measure of its achievement; Dickens's energies had never been more electric or his powers of comic criticism more glittering, pouring out a profusion of sharply realized characters above whom tower the garrulous and fusty Sairey Gamp and the blandly unctuous Pecksniff.

Even as Dickens was writing the monthly instalments for *Martin Chuzzlewit*, his inspiration reached new heights in *A Christmas Carol*, the most widely known and best beloved of all his fictions. It is indeed the very core of Dickens's vision of what the relations between men should be, a warm and glowing celebration of sympathy and love. It is also a serio-comic parable of social redemption: the miserly Scrooge is an embodiment of the pursuit of material gain and indifference to human welfare represented by both the businessmen and the nineteenth-century economists, and his conversion is a symbol of that change of heart in society on which Dickens had set his own heart.

Villa Bagnarello, the house near Genoa where Dickens stayed during summer of 1844.

But in spite of the *Carol's* enormous success, its earnings were not as great as Dickens had hoped. Already irritated with his publishers about the unsatisfactory sales of *Martin Chuzzlewit*, he blamed Chapman and Hall for poor management and skimpy advertising, and severed his connection with them. The dark days of his childhood had made him sensitive about money and being victimized, both of which he furiously saw as issues in the present disappointments. The publication of his books he now transferred to Bradbury and Evans, who had been their printers.

Meanwhile, to cut down on his expenditures, Dickens sublet his luxurious Devonshire Terrace home and in July, 1844, took his entire family – there were now six children – abroad for a year in Italy. Most of it was spent in the neighbourhood of Genoa, but he went sightseeing as far south as Rome and Naples and as far north as Venice, distilling his experiences in the vividly coloured *Pictures from Italy*. His only other literary work of the year was the Christmas story, *The Chimes*, which had an even greater popular success than the *Carol*. The attack on social heartlessness Dickens had launched with the portrayal of Scrooge, this story sharpened to fiery satire; there are acid caricatures of the brutal Alderman Cute, the condescendingly benevolent Sir Joseph Bowley, and the coldheartedly utilitarian Filer.

Returning to England in June 1845, Dickens threw himself simultaneously into an amateur production of *Every Man in His Humour* and the founding of a great liberal newspaper, the *Daily News*. For a brief time he was its editor, but the proprietors irritated his always touchy sense of his own dignity by disputing, as Bentley had done, his editorial control, and he threw up the editorship. He went abroad for another year, this time to Lausanne, and later to Paris, where he began writing *Dombey and Son*.

The story is the first masterpiece of Dickens's maturity. In it he no longer sees evil and suffering as the consequences of individual villainy, but as social phenomena, the inevitable products of that *laissez-faire* philosophy that tried to reduce all relations to barter and sale. Mr Dombey is the living symbol of his century's theory of pecuniary enterprise, its belief in ruthless competition, its harsh indifference to the welfare of the poor, its coldhearted determination that nothing must impede its pursuit of monetary power. It is really society's financial rulers, he is now insisting, who are its great malefactors, who are responsible for its urban slums, its starved labourers, its maimed factory children, the vice and crime of its cities.

As the world approached the middle of the nineteenth century Dickens was at the pinnacle of his fame. Never had his position been more unassailable, his renown more glittering. He wrote *David Copperfield*, into the

(Personal History and adventures of David Copperfield — No 1)

Chapter 1.

I am born.

Father dead — Gravestone into idle the house
Young mother — Tendony Weakness and Vanity

— Mrs History — The old wrongs
— Why rake among your bed?

Peggoty
Ham Peggoty

Chapter II.

I observe.

The things that come out of the blank of his infancy on
looking back. — Child at church — at this minute I see him
— The future father in law — with his damned black eyes " — &
First received in the shadow

Chapter III.

I have a change.

— The stranded boat.
— The life there.
— corespondent "father"
Black whiskers and black dog.

Dickens's plans for the first three chapters of *David Copperfield*.

story of which he fused a great deal of autobiography. The novel is a dramatization of all those painful elements in his childhood and youth, those experiences that had shaped him for good and ill. In its deepest levels it represents a gigantic effort to understand the forces that had made him and determined his character and his career.

In 1850 he founded *Household Words*, the weekly periodical that he thenceforth conducted with well-nigh despotic energy, having at last a magazine of which nobody could dispute his control. With the growing size of his family – there were now eight children – he had been seeking a larger home, and in the autumn of 1851 bought and moved into a larger dwelling in Tavistock Square.

His next novel, written in 1852–3, was *Bleak House*, that dark and furious storm of a story in which the Court of Chancery, the slum tenements of Tom-all-Alone's, the false charity of Mrs Jellyby and Mrs Pardiggle, the religious hypocrisy of Chadband, the class privilege of Chesney Wold, and the Parliamentary corruption of Coodle and Boodle are all symbolic devices for articulating the institutions of society into a vast system of vested interests and power.

This analysis of nineteenth-century society Dickens continued relentlessly throughout the entire decade of the 1850s, both at home and from the villa on the hills outside Boulogne that he rented for various periods. *Hard Times*, which appeared as a weekly serial in *Household Words* during the earlier part of 1854, makes a deadly attack on the world of mechanized industry and the rationalizations of political economy that used economic 'laws' to justify a callous exploitation of the labouring poor. *Little Dorrit* (1856–7) uses the Marshalsea Prison which had darkened his childhood as the symbol of a bleak system that makes society into one vast gaol that imprisons all humanity, from its governors and the aristocratic admirers of the financial wizard Mr Merdle down to the rack-rented slum-dwellers in Bleeding Heart Yard.

Everywhere, as Dickens now saw the world, venality and materialism blocked all fruitful endeavours at improvement. The Circumlocution Offices of all government departments stood massive as an invulnerable Chinese Wall to wear down the attacks of the reformers. In Parliament the dire influence of privilege had destroyed the potentialities of representative government and made it a gloomy failure. Wealth and industry savagely denied that they had any duty to their employees except to pay the wages established by the law of supply and demand and insisted that the welfare of the country depended on high profits and cheap labour. The selfishness of society's leaders condemned the masses to ignorance, misery, and squalor.

Dickens supervising a
rehearsal for *The
Lighthouse*, a play
by Wilkie Collins.

But not all of Dickens's time was darkened by these melancholy observations. He still enjoyed his mastery of his art, writing at breakneck speed, exulting in the comic portrayal of Flora Finching and the hammer-blows of his satire. In Paris he met Victor Hugo and attended luxurious dinners with Augier and Sandeau. Again and again he put on amateur theatrical performances, – of *Every Man in His Humour*, *The Merry Wives of Windsor*, Lytton's *Not So Bad as We Seem*, Wilkie Collins's *The Lighthouse*, – directing and managing the entire productions with tyrannical energy, and acting in them himself with dramatic power.

During one of his summers at Boulogne there was an exciting war to preserve a pet canary from two marauding cats. They would sneak into the house and hide away 'in the most terrific manner: hanging themselves up behind draperies, like bats, and tumbling out at dead of night, with frightful caterwaulings.' Outdoors the household blazed away at them with shotguns from ambushes in the shrubbery; 'the tradesmen cry out as they come up the avenue, "Me voici! c'est moi – boulanger – ne tirez pas!" ' – and no sooner had firing ceased in the front garden than a cat would enter 'in the calmest manner, by the back window'.

But none of these flurries of comedy were more than flickers in the darkening despair with which Dickens gazed on society. And mingled with his social disillusion was a deepening misery in his married life. For Catherine had not kept pace with her dynamic genius of a husband; as he rose higher and higher she was left behind. The brilliant circles to which he had the entrée found her dull, and often failed to include her in the invitations they showered upon Dickens. She was an ineffectual hostess and an indolent housekeeper. Dickens himself was obliged to deal with the butcher, the baker, and the greengrocer. From the time of their return from America, in 1842, Catherine's younger sister Georgina Hogarth, who then came to live with them, assumed the management of the household. The three older children, Charley, Mary, and Katey, were now growing up, but Georgina had one after another taken over the care of the six younger children, down to the baby, 'Plorn', who had been born in 1852. Catherine grew fat and red-faced, wallowed in self pity, and at the same time voiced jealous and resentful suspicions of even Dickens's most innocent attentions to other women.

David Copperfield's marriage to the hopelessly incompetent Dora undoubtedly mirrors one facet of these marital difficulties. 'There can be no disparity in marriage,' David reflects forlornly, 'like unsuitability of mind and purpose'; his misfortune in taking her as his bride he at last explains to himself as 'the first mistaken impulse of an undisciplined heart'. More and more, 'as with poor David', Dickens felt 'a vague unhappy loss or want of something', and, when he fell into low spirits, found himself lamenting 'one happiness I have missed in life, and one friend and companion I never made'. Despairingly he told his friend Forster, 'I find the skeleton in my domestic closet is becoming a pretty big one.'

In a pattern that had become recurrent when he was restless or unhappy, Dickens flung himself with furious desperation into the amateur production of still another play, this time Wilkie Collins's melodrama *The Frozen Deep*. Grinding rehearsals were followed by triumphant performances; the play was given both in London and in Manchester before enthusiastic audiences, Dickens tearing himself to pieces in the tragic role of Richard Wardour. But when the curtain fell for the last time he fell into deeper wretchedness than before. 'Low spirits, low pulse, low voice, intense reaction,' he groaned. ' . . . My blankness is inconceivable – indescribable – my misery, amazing.'

It was grimly ironic that as his married life was thus falling apart Dickens at last acquired the little rose-brick mansion that had been the dream of his Chatham childhood. Gad's Hill Place came on the market; on

14 March 1856, he bought it. Painters splashed brushes, carpenters hammered, plumbers delved at the drains; on 17 May 1857, there was a house-warming at which 'a small and noble army of guests' ate cold meat, and on 1 June the family moved in for the summer. But by this time his life with Catherine had become unbearable.

'Poor Catherine and I are not made for each other,' he confessed to Forster, 'and there is no help for it. It is not only that she makes me uneasy and unhappy, but that I make her so too – and much more so. She is exactly what you know, in the way of being amiable and complying; but we are strangely ill-assorted for the bond there is between us. . . . I am often cut to the heart by thinking what a pity it is, for her own sake, that I ever fell in her way . . .'.

As the tension between them mounted, a further twist of anguish came from the fact that suddenly Dickens found himself in love with a pretty young actress named Ellen Ternan, who had played in the Manchester performances of *The Frozen Deep*. He found a despairing relief pouring his feelings into one letter to a friend, pretending they were merely the restlessness of the artistic temperament and giving them a fairy-tale disguise: 'I wish I had been born in the days of Ogres and Dragon-guarded Castles. I wish an Ogre with seven heads . . . had taken the Princess whom I adore – you have no idea how intensely I love her! – to his stronghold on the top of a high series of mountains, and there tied her up by the hair. Nothing would suit me half so well this day, as climbing after her, sword in hand, and either winning her or being killed.'

Though Dickens tempestuously insisted that he had not broken his marriage vows, Catherine did not believe him. She was sure that Ellen Ternan had become his mistress, and wept bitterly. Her own family, except for her sister Georgina, angrily fanned her disbelief. Weeping, Catherine at last left the home she and Dickens had shared for so many years. Charley felt unhappy for both his father and his mother; Mary sided with Dickens; Katey fiercely sympathized with her mother. The two little boys who had not yet gone away to school were bewildered by the painful turmoil of their home. A separation agreement was gradually worked out. Catherine was to have a home of her own and an allowance from her husband. On 29 May, 1858, the separation became final.

Literary London boiled with the scandal. Dickens was bitterly criticized in the press. He felt as if his heart was 'jagged and rent and out of shape' – all the more so because, although he would not admit it, he knew that his own behaviour had not been stainless. In self-defence he issued a public statement in which he proclaimed his innocence and hinted at some of poor

Catherine's shortcomings. Technically guiltless of her suspicions he might be, but he knew that emotionally they were not without cause and that he had been far from chivalrous in thus addressing the world. Darkly contending with his self-justification was an unavowed sense of guilt.

But his readers were faithful to him. When that June he began in London a series of public readings from his works, he was greeted with roars of applause that were testimony to their loyalty and support. The London readings were a tumultuous success; they were followed during the autumn and winter by a triumphant tour of England, Ireland, and Scotland. Everywhere the extraordinary entertainment he had devised was more than a mere reading; it was a mesmeric feat of acting. He brought the characters of his stories to life by sheer histrionic brilliance. His audiences screamed with laughter at the comic scenes, thrilled at the drama, sobbed at the pathos. These readings were continued at intervals throughout the remainder of his life; the last of them he gave only three months before his death.

Resenting the sympathy and support that Bradbury and Evans had given Catherine in the breakup of his marriage, he severed his publishing connection with them and went back to Chapman and Hall. To punish Bradbury and Evans still more severely, he killed *Household Words* – in which they had owned a quarter share – and started another weekly on an almost identical plan, which he named *All the Year Round*. Here, in 1859 began *A Tale of Two Cities*. Within five weeks the circulation of the new magazine had trebled that of its predecessor.

Meanwhile Dickens had presented a second series of readings in London and later in the year undertook another provincial tour. During his brief intervals of leisure he stayed more and more at Gad's Hill; in 1860 he sold his house in Tavistock Square and, except sometimes for the spring months, resided entirely in Kent. He had achieved a pattern in his life that seemed like serenity.

It was more appearance, though, than reality. The adulation of his audiences excited and sustained him, but the constant railway journeys and the strenuous performances beneath the glare of gaslights were a strain under which even his energies began to wear down. And though he had at last prevailed over Ellen Ternan, his conquest did not bring him the happiness of which he had dreamed.

Great Expectations, which appeared in *All the Year Round* from December, 1860, to June, 1861, is significant; Pip's sufferings at the hands of Estella almost certainly reflect those of his creator. Pip's love is all anguished need, almost without tenderness, without illusion. The 'one friend and companion' for which Dickens so agonizingly longed still eluded him. When he saw *Faust* for the first time, at the Paris Opera in 1863, he found the story unbearably moving: 'like a mournful echo of things that lie in my own heart'.

He felt no happier when he looked around him at the world. The Crimean War, the Indian Mutiny, the American Civil War, the Fenian disorders in Ireland, the deep discontent with the régime of Napoleon III in France, which Dickens believed was leading irrevocably to an even more violent renewal of the French Revolution, the divisions between the people and the ruling classes in England – all left him weary, almost in despair. His readings were a relief and an encouragement; in them he was in communion with human hearts and human emotions in which he still believed.

In the intervals between his tours Dickens returned to Gad's Hill. Katey had married in 1860, but Mary was still at home. Dickens was troubled about his sons, none of whom showed any outstanding abilities or seemed to have inherited his capacity for industrious application. But he tried to start them in professional careers. Charley, the eldest, was in business. Two of his brothers desired to go to India and one to enter the Navy, and Dickens managed to obtain commissions for them. Still another wanted at first to be a doctor, then a farmer, then he didn't know what, and Dickens found him a position in a City mercantile house. The two younger were still at school, where the youngest was lonely and homesick. Dickens moved him to a smaller school, where he hoped the boy might feel happier.

With the approach of autumn Dickens's thoughts were turning purposefully to a new serial, *Our Mutual Friend*, which he began writing that winter. The first number came out in May, 1864, and sold 30,000 copies in the first three days after publication. But Dickens was not in good health; his writing went slowly. He developed coughs and was stethoscoped, rubbings were ordered for his chest. During Christmas at Gad's Hill his left foot swelled, with excruciating pains, and had to be treated with poppy fomentations. He refused to believe that it was gout, insisting that it was merely frost-bitten from long walks in the snow. He fell lame, and was often unable to bear putting on a shoe.

At the end of May he went to Paris for a week's vacation. Returning on the boat train from Folkestone Harbour on 9 June, he and Ellen were in a terrible accident. Coaches were flung upside down and smashed into a little stream; their carriage hung from the edge of the bridge to the bank below. Dickens clambered out, helped Ellen and another lady in the compartment to safety, then went up and down helping the mutilated, bleeding, and dying victims. When he had done all he could, remembering that he had with him the manuscript of the next number of *Our Mutual Friend*, he coolly climbed back into the compartment and retrieved it.

But the accident left him dreadfully shaken. His pulse was feeble, and at the slightest exertion he turned faint and sick. For a long while he could not bear the idea of railway travel. Trouble with his foot returned; his doctor told him that his heart was weakened. Nevertheless he decided on another series of readings, in England, Ireland, and Scotland. When the train jolted over switches or intersections, he often clutched the arms of his chair, his face whitened, and perspiration broke out on his brow. The stress was almost unbearable, but the performances were an anodyne to a restlessness and a need of affectionate contacts with his public that he could not forego. Everywhere the readings were a roaring triumph. But by the end, in May, 1867, Dickens was so exhausted that he felt hardly able to undress for bed.

Though his strength was almost gone, ignoring all advice, he promptly determined on an even more desperate undertaking. Repeated pleas had come to him that he read in America, with the most golden prophecies of fantastic earnings. Americans had long since forgotten their fury at *American Notes* and the satire of *Martin Chuzzlewit*; Dickens was assured that his reception would be one prolonged ovation. After a farewell dinner at the Freemasons' Hall in London, attended by all the notables of the literary, dramatic, and artistic world, on 9 November he sailed for Boston.

Everywhere he was greeted with a frenzy of enthusiasm. Boston went mad; in New York people stood in lines eight hundred long throughout nights of freezing weather to buy tickets; then came Philadelphia and Baltimore; then Washington, where the President, the Cabinet, and the Supreme Court came to hear him almost in a body. Dickens read strenuously through a series of one-night stands – through upstate New York and through cities in New England as far north as Portland, Maine. But he caught a bad cold with a hacking cough he was unable to get rid of, even with the aid of the 'Rocky Mountain Sneezer' of brandy, rum, and snow given him by the landlord of his New York hotel. At a final banquet at Delmonico's in New York, Dickens hobbled in with a bandaged foot and leg, barely able to walk, and was obliged to leave in agony as soon as he had made a speech of grateful farewell.

Financially the tour had outsoared all expectations. After deducting every expense Dickens cleared £20,000. But it had been bought at a fatal cost of pain and exhaustion; his body was twisted and wracked with the dreadful strain. The one-night stands, the glare and heat of the gaslights, the jolting on the long railway journeys, had brought him to the verge of a breakdown. Perhaps if he had given up any idea of further public readings his extraordinary vitality might even now have restored his strength. He could not bear, however, to surrender the excitement and the clamorous loving applause that had become the solace of his life. Before he sailed for home he had already agreed on a last tour of readings in England. He had broken down under the seventy-six he had given in the United States. Now he committed himself to a hundred more.

On the homeward voyage his unbelievable resiliency and the restful life of shipboard reanimated his vigour. He arrived bronzed and well-looking. He spent a peaceful summer at Gad's Hill. Barely, though, had the readings gotten under way in October 1868, than painful signs reappeared. After a reading at Manchester he admitted that he was hoarse and croaking all the next day. At the end of a month he suffered from nausea and sleeplessness. From Sikes's murder of Nancy, in *Oliver Twist*, he had devised a horrifying new reading which he gave with terrible exertion and gruesome effect. At every performance ladies in the audience fainted. Dickens's sleeplessness, nausea, and lameness became worse, there were effusions of blood from his bowels, he grew giddy and uncertain of his footing, he felt a strange weakness and deadness on his left side.

The indications of paralysis were plain, though Dickens refused to believe them. Twice he collapsed, but struggled on. At Liverpool in April, his doctor firmly insisted that the readings must stop at once. A distinguished specialist in London confirmed the judgement. Dickens, he said, had been on the brink of paralysis, possibly of apoplexy.

With his relentless determination, Dickens had managed to get through seventy-four of the hundred planned readings – two less than the number which in America had brought him so near collapse. He now refused to accept the verdict, and at last got the doctors to agree that he might venture on the platform once more – but only, they insisted, if the readings did not exceed twelve in number, involved no railway travel, and were deferred at least eight months until early in 1870. To these conditions Dickens reluctantly yielded.

In his heart, though, he knew that he had averted death only by a narrow margin. But he hardly cared. One by one his sons were worrying and disappointing him. Though the middle class had wrested power from the old landed aristocracy, privilege, inefficiency, corruption, and cruelty were everywhere deeply entrenched. What had become of all his shining early hopes for humanity? And yet he refused to surrender them; though he had lost all faith in men's rulers, he still believed in mankind. The darkness came flooding back, and then he resummoned his faith, whipped up once more his gusty enjoyment of the thronging variety of life.

Early in May he made his will. During the summer he entertained American visitors and began turning over in his mind the conception of another novel. It was to be in only twelve monthly numbers, not the usual twenty, and one clause in the contract, by Dickens's own desire, provided what financial adjustments were to be made if he was unable to complete it. In October he read the opening chapters of *The Mystery of Edwin Drood* to one of his American guests.

Throughout the late autumn and winter he remained quietly at Gad's Hill. On Christmas his left foot was again painful and had to be bandaged, but he was cheerful. In January he rented a house in Hyde Park Place, and on 11 January began the very last series of readings at St James's Hall. They were even more enormously successful, but his pulse rose ominously in the course of each performance, and during intermissions he had to lie on a sofa in his retiring room.

Woodcut of No. 5 Hyde Park Place, rented by Dickens from November 1869 to May 1870, where some of *Edwin Drood* was written.

At the last of them, on 15 March, there were thunders of appreciation that made the glittering chandeliers vibrate. Dickens looked out tremulously over the audience, striving to speak, tears rolling down his cheeks. It was the last time. This ferment of excitement that for twelve years had filled so much of his life, that had so often been almost all his life, was over. 'I now vanish evermore,' he managed to say, 'with a heartfelt, grateful, respectful, affectionate farewell.' Mournfully, his cheeks still wet, he kissed his hand, and limped from the stage.

The opening numbers of *Edwin Drood*, he was presently recording, '*very, very far outstripped every one of its predecessors*'. But he was destined to leave it only half finished. On 3 June he was back at Gad's Hill, rejoicing in the foliage and the perfume of the flowers. All day on 8 June he wrote away at *Edwin Drood*. The last page has a description of a bright sunlight day in Rochester: 'Changes of glorious light from moving boughs, songs of birds, scents from gardens, woods, and fields . . . penetrate the Cathedral, subdue its earthy odour, and preach of the Resurrection and the Life. The cold stone tombs of centuries ago grow warm; and flecks of brightness dart into the sternest marble corners of the building, fluttering there like wings.' The words are a fitting valedictory to the exalted, laughing, despairing, tormented, and triumphant career.

That night at dinner his sister-in-law Georgina was frightened by the look of pain on his face, and he admitted that he felt very ill. Suddenly he staggered up from his chair, and would have fallen if she had not managed to lower his body to the floor. 'On the ground,' he murmured faintly.

MR. CHARLES DICKENS'S
Farewell Readings.

Mr. CHARLES DICKENS has resumed his Series of Farewell
Readings at

ST. JAMES'S HALL, PICCADILLY.

The Readings will take place as follows:

TUESDAY EVENING, FEBRUARY 8, The Story of Little Dombey
(last time) and Mr. Bob Sawyer's Party (from Pickwick).

TUESDAY EVENING, FEBRUARY 15, Boots at the Holly Tree Inn;
Sikes and Nancy (from Oliver Twist); and Mrs. Gamp
(last time).

TUESDAY EVENING, FEBRUARY 22, Nicholas Nickleby (at Mr.
Squeers's School, last time); and Mr. Chops, the Dwarf
(last time).

TUESDAY EVENING, MARCH 1, David Copperfield (last time), and
The Trial from Pickwick.

TUESDAY EVENING, MARCH S, Boots at the Holly Tree Inn
(last time); Sikes and Nancy (from Oliver Twist, last
time); and Mr. Bob Sawyer's Party (from Pickwick, last
time).

TUESDAY EVENING, MARCH 15, FINAL FAREWELL READING,
The Christmas Carol (last time), and The Trial from
Pickwick (last time).

To commence each Evening at Eight o'Clock.

No Readings will take place out of London.

PRICES OF ADMISSION:

SOFA STALLS, 7s.;   STALLS. 5s.;   BALCONY, 3s.;
Admission - ONE SHILLING.

Tickets may be obtained at CHAPPELL & Co.'s, 50, New Bond Street.

A notice announcing Dickens's last series of Readings.

Doctors were sent for, but there was no hope. It was a paralytic stroke, an effusion of blood on the brain. Only four of Dickens's children were in England, but they arrived at Gad's Hill in the course of the next day. At six o'clock on the afternoon of 9 June Dickens's breathing grew fainter. At ten minutes past that hour he gave a deep sigh. Then he was gone.

The sorrow that rolled through the world was more than a testimony to Dickens's fame; it breathed the love he had kindled in even the humblest hearts. 'It is no exaggeration,' wrote Longfellow from America, 'to say that this whole country is stricken with grief.' 'My pen trembles between my fingers,' said a writer in the *Moniteur des Arts*, 'at the thought of all we – his family – have just lost in Charles Dickens.' 'The good, the gentle, ever friendly noble Dickens,' exclaimed Carlyle, ' – every inch of him an Honest Man!' But Carlyle's insight went deeper. Beneath Dickens's 'sparkling, clear, and sunny utterance,' he said, beneath his 'bright and joyful sympathy,' there were 'fateful, silent elements, tragical to look upon, and hiding, amid dazzling radiances as of the sun, the elements of death itself.'

It was true. Dickens's whole career, indeed, in its fusion of sympathy, high spirits, relish for the richness and variety of human nature, hatred of cruelty and injustice, his concrete awareness of actual human beings and their sufferings, and his insistence on weighing everything in terms of their living welfare, is singularly consistent. If in personal conflict he was sometimes bitter and unyielding, he could love with warm and generous love. And unlike those lovers of humanity who are so often unable to love real people but only an abstraction, it was men, women, and children whom he loved, with all their weaknesses and absurdities.

He laughed and wept and loved and hated; he could be desperately unhappy; he was never superior and indifferent. When he thought people evil it was hard for him to regard them as human; his heart could explain them only as monsters. The evil that they did he fought with unwavering hostility, attacking them with the weapons of caricature and burlesque, of melodrama and unabashed sentiment. His spontaneous sympathy with the fruitful and the creative enabled him to understand how human nature was crippled by exploitation and selfishness, and he fought his way steadily to an understanding of all those dark forces in society that blight men's health and happiness. The great roll call of Dickens's work on every page is a celebration of the true wealth of life.

Dickens's London

London was the heart and soul of the Dickens world; and although much squalor and great poverty prevailed in his day [8], he loved the intricate streets, the jumbled tenements, the little City churches, and not least the crowded and cheap lodging houses of London [1 and 5] better than the great public buildings and the mansions of the wealthy. When his family were in dire straits, they moved from home to home and from lodging to lodging; and the young Charles often had to make do on his own [4 and 14]. It was then that he first acquired the habit of walking the streets, first by day and later by night, until this became a necessary imaginative stimulus [11], which he greatly missed during his periods abroad. He was particularly attracted to London's river [9], which featured in books from 'Sketches by Boz' and 'Oliver Twist' to 'Our Mutual Friend' [16]. Dickens, despite his passion for reform, was temperamentally affected by the 'attraction of repulsion', and he found himself particularly drawn to the sordid areas of London, to the slums and cheap eating-houses, and even on occasion to the opium dens, to which he would sometimes conduct visitors and which provided one of the themes of his last novel. But the London of Dickens was a great deal more than a poverty-stricken metropolis. From his youth up, Dickens saw and enjoyed its healthier excitements and gaieties. As a boy he was addicted to the theatre [10], so much so that at one point he contemplated a theatrical career. Then, as a lawyer's clerk, he saw something of the fun and humour and recreations of the lower and middle classes ("Making a Night of It" in 'Sketches by Boz' must be based upon personal experience). As an increasingly prosperous author, he would enjoy a ride or walk in the gardened suburbs, especially Hampstead or Highgate, and visits to the gracious homes of friends. Of Dickens we can say that he loved and revered the traditional institutions of London even when he criticized and satirized them; and he enjoyed good company at a good inn [3 and 5] rather than the newer gin-palaces [12], which he regarded as corrupting. Even today, despite enormous changes, the London which feeds the imagination, and excites the interest of the world, is still largely the London of Dickens.

1 Cloth Fair. Once the abode of merchant princes this was in Dickens's day a group of tottering houses, let out to lodgers of every description.

2

2 St Bartholomew the Great, Smithfield. One of the surviving transcripts in Dickens's hand, when he was a shorthand writer at Doctors' Commons, concerned a quarrel in the vestry of this church.

3

3 The White Hart Inn, Southwark, the
scene of Mr Pickwick's first encounter
with Sam Weller.

4 Somers Town, where Dickens lived
from 1825-9.
☞ *overleaf*

5 The Oxford Arms, Warwick Lane,
dominated by St Paul's.

6 Market scene at Lambeth, New Cut,
an area referred to in *Sketches by Boz*.

7 Auction rooms in Leadenhall Street.

4

5

6

8

8 St Mary Overy's Dock, Southwark, a
slum area in Dickens's boyhood.
9 A dockside scene, evoking the
atmosphere of *Oliver Twist*. Dickens
remained all his life fascinated by
London's river.

10 Drury Lane. At the theatre here, the
young Dickens saw many famous
Shakespearean productions.

9

10

11

12

11 Bishopsgate: one of the landmarks
of the city, and familiar to Dickens both
in his boyhood wanderings and his later
night walks.

12 A scene at the gin distillery firm of
Octavius H. Smith, Thames Bank.
Sketches by Boz contains a realistic
account of a gin shop.

13

14

15

16

13 A wayside food-stall, patronized by a typical sweep of the day.

14 A corner of Covent Garden,
the site of many episodes in the novels.

15 A shop in the poorest part of the East End.

16 Thames bargemen. *Our Mutual Friend* opens with an unforgettable river scene.

Dickens's London

Christopher Hibbert

'What an amazing place' London seems to David Copperfield when he sees it in the distance for the first time from his uncomfortable seat in the coach that has taken seventeen hours to get there from Yarmouth. It excites his young imagination to such an extent that he pictures all his favourite heroes enacting their adventures there, and he imagines it to be fuller of wonders 'than all the cities of the earth'.

The excitement and the wonder were a memory of Charles Dickens himself. At the age of ten, just before Christmas 1822, he had left his childhood home in Chatham to join his parents in Camden Town. His father, a clerk in the Navy Pay Office, had been transferred from the Chatham dockyard to Somerset House and had already moved into a new house with his wife and the other children, leaving Charles behind to finish the school term. So Charles travelled to London alone, the only passenger inside the coach where the smell of the damp straw was to remain fixed in his memory for ever, eating his sandwiches in silence, eagerly and anxiously looking out of the window for his first glimpse of the town through the pouring rain.

The coach stopped outside the Cross Keys, Wood Street, Cheapside, and from there Charles was taken to the house in Bayham Street, Camden Town, which his father had rented for £22 a year. It was a small terrace house of four rooms, a basement and a garret, one in a row of forty which had been built in the year of Charles's birth; and the sight of its cheap brick front, its flat roof and the three blank windows that overlooked the street, its quiet, dreary, shabby-genteel surroundings, suddenly brought Charles face to face with the realities of life in one of those dismal suburbs which were spreading ever further outwards from Regency London. This was a very different place from the amazing magical city that Charles, like David Copperfield, had imagined. Opposite, to be sure, lived a Bow Street runner, but the washerwoman next door was a more characteristic neighbour.

At one end of the street there was a terrace of gloomy almshouses backing onto a burial ground, at the other, where the lonely road to Kentish Town began, there was a run-down eating-house; between them stood a row of little oil lamps which, lit by the watchman at night, threw a dully flickering glimmer onto the pavement. Behind Number 16, where Mr and Mrs Dickens lived with their six children and an orphan maid from the Chatham workhouse, there stretched a depressing wasteland of rank grass and rubbish dumps, nettles and dockweed, looking, as Dickens afterwards said, 'rather like a barbarous place of execution, with its poles and cross-poles erected for the beating of carpets'.

'There were frowzy fields, and cow-houses, and dung hills, and dust heaps and ditches,' he wrote elsewhere, having chosen Camden Town as a suitable place for the home of Mrs Toodle, Paul Dombey's wet nurse, 'little tumuli of oyster shells in the oyster season and of lobster shells in the lobster season, and of broken crockery and faded cabbage leaves in all seasons . . . posts, and rails and old cautions to trespassers, and backs of mean houses, and patches of wretched vegetation.'

Such frowzy fields and such dingy streets as Bayham Street could be found in numerous other suburbs north of the New Road from Paddington to Islington. Not only in Camden Town itself, but in Somers Town and Kentish Town, from Fulham in the west to Canning Town and Hackney in the east, row upon row of terraced buildings, factories, workshops, cottages, taverns and bakeries, were transforming the face of the London country-side, pushing the green fields farther and farther away from the heart of the City. The population of London had already risen to well over a million when Dickens arrived in Bayham Street; before he was twenty it had increased by almost a quarter, and thereafter continued to increase more rapidly than ever. Much of this increase was crowded into these new suburbs, into places like Walworth, 'a collection of back lanes, ditches, and little gardens' presenting the 'aspect of a rather dull retirement' where Pip is taken by John Wemmick to meet the Aged Parent in *Great Expectations*, and into such depressing areas as the Staggs's Gardens of *Dombey and Son*, 'a little row of houses, with little squalid patches of ground before them, fenced off with old doors, barrel staves, scraps of tarpaulin, and dead bushes, with bottomless tin kettles and exhausted iron fenders thrust into the gaps. Here the Staggs's Gardeners trained scarlet beans, kept fowls and rabbits, erected rotten summer-houses (one was an old boat), dried clothes, and smoked pipes.'

By the 1840s London's squalid suburbs had spread far beyond Camden Town and were already sprawling up the Finchley Road, where Harriet Carker lives in a neighbourhood which 'is neither of the town nor the country. The former, like the giant in his travelling boots, has made a stride and passed it, and has set his brick-and-mortar heel a long way in advance; but the intermediate space between the giant's feet, as yet, is only blighted country, and not town. Here, among a few tall chimneys belching smoke all day and night, and among the brickfields and lanes where turf is cut, and where the fences tumble down, and where a scrap or two of hedge may yet be seen' is Harriet Carker's house.

In 1848 Dickens made a journey on the Blackwall Railway and wrote to a friend of the ten minutes spent looking out of the carriage window at 'the tiles and chimney-pots, backs of squalid houses, frowsty pieces of waste ground, narrow courts and streets, swamps, ditches, gardens of duckweed, and unwholesome little bowers of scarlet beans'.

This was the kind of London landscape that he had first known as a child. He was not sent back to school after his arrival there, being kept about the house to look after his younger brothers and sisters, to clean the boots of a morning, and to go on such errands as arose out of the family's poor way of living. Left free to spend much of his time wandering about Camden Town and the neighbouring suburbs, he developed that taste for walking the streets of London which later became a passion, a kind of obsessive need. Even at this age he spent hours strolling about, looking into workshops, gazing at the goods on display in the markets, staring through the windows of chandlers' shops and eating-rooms, living in a strange world of his own.

Sometimes he would wander south of the New Road where there was a wholly different London from the one he knew, a London that had been altered out of all recognition since the New Road (afterwards renamed the Marylebone Road) had been completed in 1757 and had at that time marked the limit of the expanding town. South of Oxford Street the development of various family estates into squares and streets of imposing houses had begun in the early years of the century. First Hanover Square and George Street had appeared on land belonging to the Earl of Scarborough, a devoted adherent of the new royal house; then Burlington Street and Cork Street, Grosvenor Square, Grosvenor Street and Audley Street, Berkeley Square, Bruton Street and Hill Street combined to give to the area between Park Lane and the Earl of Cork and Burlington's vast Palladian mansion in Piccadilly a fashionable distinction that had formerly belonged to St James's Square, Pall Mall and Bloomsbury. After the middle of the century fashionable London began to extend north of Oxford Street, into the squares and streets built on the Harley estate and on the neighbouring estate of Henry William Portman; and a few years before Charles's arrival in London it had spread even further north, beyond the New Road and into Regent's Park, where John Nash's graceful sweeps of stuccoed terraces and crescents were still to many tastes a disconcerting novelty 'which damp and smoke must destroy in a season or two'.

Yet these new fashionable areas of London – so close to Bayham Street, so far removed from it in spirit – might scarcely have existed for all the mention that Dickens was to make of them in his novels; neither they, nor the grand works of George IV's architects farther south, nor the fine curve of Regent Street that cut across the red and brown brick of London like a yellow swathe, seem to have excited his imagination in the least. He was to live himself for several years in a large and handsome house in Regent's Park, but on the rare occasions when such residences are described in his novels they appear as blank and gloomy as Mr Dombey's house in that 'tall, dark, dreadfully genteel street' between Portland Place and Bryanston Square, 'a corner house with great wide areas containing cellars frowned upon by barred windows . . . a house of dismal state, with a circular back to it, containing a whole suite of drawing-rooms looking upon a gravelled yard . . . as blank a house inside as outside.'

Nearby, at the top of Oxford Street, are more such doleful houses in 'great streets of melancholy stateliness', as Arthur Clennam discovers one summer evening in *Little Dorrit*, 'wildernesses of corner-houses, with barbarous old porticoes and appurtenances; horrors that came into existence under some wrong-headed person in some wrong-headed time, still demanding the blind admiration of all ensuing generations and determined to do so until they tumbled down'. The smart, little houses in Mews Street, Grosvenor Square, were even worse, 'airless houses which went at enormous rents on account of there being abject hangers-on to a fashionable situation; and whenever one of these fearful little coops was to be let (which seldom happened, for they were in great request) the house agent advertised it as a gentlemanly residence in the most aristocratic part of the town, inhabited solely by the élite of the beau monde'. At Number 24 is to be found Mr Tite Barnacle, whose footman (his pocket flaps covered with large buttons bearing the Barnacle crest) ponders at irritating length over the cards of his employers' visitors.

Even in the streets leading off Park Lane, the atmosphere on any summer evening is depressing, starchy and close.

The shops, few in number, made no show. The pastry-cook knew who was on his books, and in that knowledge could be calm, with a few glass cylinders of dowager peppermint-drops in his window, and half-a-dozen ancient specimens of currant jelly. A few oranges formed the greengrocer's whole concession to the vulgar mind. A single basket made of moss, once containing plovers' eggs, held all that the poulterer had to say to the rabble. Everybody in those streets seemed (which is always the case at that hour and season) to be gone out to dinner, and nobody seemed to be giving the dinners they had gone to. On the door-steps there were lounging footmen with bright parti-coloured plumage and white polls, like an extinct race of monstrous birds; and butlers, solitary men of recluse demeanour, each of whom appeared distrustful of all other butlers. The roll of carriages in the Park was done for the day; the street lamps were lighting; and wicked little grooms in the tightest fitting garments, with twists in their legs answering to the twists in their minds, hung about in pairs, chewing straw and exchanging fraudulent secrets.

To Dickens, as a boy and as a man, London did not mean this fashionable world of grand houses and liveried flunkeys, it meant that part of the city the other side of Regent Street; and in later years it was the walks that he took as a boy through Somers Town and down Gray's Inn Lane, past Holborn and into the City that he most vividly remembered. From the end of Bayham Street you could see the City in those days with the dome of St Paul's looming through the smoke, a sight, so Dickens said, that served him 'for hours of vague reflection afterwards'; and he walked towards it 'like a child in a dream, inspired by a mighty faith in the marvellousness of everything. Up courts and down courts – in and out of yards and little squares – peeping into counting-house passages and running away', peering into Austin Friars, South Sea House and India House, staring at the men munching biscuits as they read the posters advertising the sailing of ships on Royal Exchange, watching the cooks in their white caps at work in the basement kitchen of the Mansion House until one of them caught sight of him at the grated window and called out through his black whiskers, 'Cut away, you sir!'

Once, he remembered, he summoned up courage to go into a cook-shop: 'I saw a pile of cooked sausages in a window with the label, "Small Germans, A Penny". Emboldened by knowing what to ask for, I went in and said, "If you please, will you sell me a small German?" which they did, and I took it, wrapped in paper in my pocket, to Guildhall.' Later, he wandered off to Goodman's Fields where he could not resist going into a theatre and he sat up in the gallery with sailors and 'others of the lowest description'.

Goodman's Fields were outside Aldgate, not far from Bevis Marks where Sampson Brass has his unsavoury office in *The Old Curiosity Shop*, an office which is 'so close upon the footway that the passenger who takes the wall brushes the dim and dirty glass with his coat sleeve', an office strongly impregnated with the smell of the second-hand wearing apparel exposed for sale in nearby Duke's Place and Houndsditch. Dickens spent a whole morning wandering through Bevis Marks, looking for a suitable house to describe as the Brasses' 'little habitation'; but even as a boy he knew this part of London well, for he passed through it often on his way to see his god-father, Christopher Huffam, a well-to-do 'Rigger to His Majesty's Navy' whom the convivial and socially pretentious John Dickens had met in the course of his duties. Huffam carried on business 'in a substantial handsome sort of way' in Limehouse where, in the old village, prosperous merchants still lived close to, or above, their counting-houses, with their servants and apprentices, as their predecessors had done since the Middle Ages.

Behind Huffam's comfortable house a jumble of warehouses, shipwrights' sheds, dockers' tenements, marine-stores, rag-and-bottle shops, sailors' cabins, ship-breakers' yards and ferry houses stretched in confused array down to the waterfront by Ropemakers's Fields. And it was here, walking

A side-street off Gray's Inn Lane, showing a house to let, still occupied in spite of its dilapidated condition.

View of Tyndall's Buildings, Gray's Inn Lane. The coffin of a pauper is carried unnoticed through the crowd.

along the creaking timber jetties and wharfs, standing on the dry docks between the warrens of ramshackle buildings, watching the oyster-boats and tenders, the lighters and colliers, the diving bells and windmill sails, that Charles was first gripped by that fascination with the London river that was to inspire so much of his work. With the smell of rotting hempen hawsers in his nostrils, and in his ears the never-ending sound of engines pumping in leaky ships, capstans clanking as they wound in dripping cables, dogs barking as they raced up and down the black lines of the colliers, steamships beating the water with their paddles, his mind was filled with wonder and curiosity.

Below him in the mud and slime were stranded boats and old hulks half knocked to pieces, rusty anchors, broken baskets and dregs of coal scum; and here at low tide the mud-larks scavenged for bits of iron and coal and

A child mud-lark preparing to sift through the 'sludge' of the Thames.

copper nails. They were either very old or very young, these mud-larks, for none but the weak or crippled would undertake such filthy work for so poor a return; many were about Charles's age, some much younger. They went down into the mud carrying old hats and rusty kettles, wearing a collection of rags stiff as boards, often cutting their bare feet on fragments of glass buried in the ooze. Some years later a journalist spoke to one of them who was nine years old. His father was dead; his mother went out washing for a shilling a day when she could find such work to do, which was not often. It was very cold standing in the mud. He had once had a pair of shoes, but that was a long time since. He had been mud-larking for three years, ever since he could remember and he supposed he would always be a mud-lark for that was all he knew how to do. He had been to a school once but had forgotten it. He had been there for a month; he could not read or write and did not think he could learn now even if he tried ever so much. He had heard of Jesus Christ but could not recall just what he was; his mother did not take him to church because they had no clothes. His mother came from Aberdeen; he did not know where Aberdeen was. He knew that this was London. England was in London somewhere, but he did not know just where. All the money he got – about a halfpenny a day – he gave to his mother; she bought bread with it. When he couldn't find anything in the mud, they lived as best they could.

Frightened as well as fascinated by the scenes and denizens of the waterfront at Limehouse, Charles confessed himself to be even more alarmed by the glimpses of London, 'strange in its glooms and flaring lights' that he caught through the window of the coach that took him home. Some of these sights were reassuring enough – 'the noisy, bustling, crowded streets, now displaying long double rows of brightly-burning lamps, dotted here and there with the chemists' glaring lights, and illuminated besides with the brilliant flood that streamed from the windows of the shops', the muffin-boy ringing his way down the streets, the beer-man going his rounds with a lantern in front of his tray, the sudden flare of light over a kidney-pie stand, a chimney-sweep with ribbons in his top hat, the swaying lamp of a waterman illuminating the big brass plate on his chest. But then, after the coach had rattled down Commercial Road and Leadenhall Street, up Cornhill, along Cheapside and Newgate Street, it turned into the swarming slums of St Giles and Seven Dials where 'wild visions of wickedness, want and beggary' arose in his anxious mind. In his first book, *Sketches by Boz*, and again in *Oliver Twist*, he was to paint an appallingly vivid picture of this district whose squalor was to remain almost unchanged from the days when Hogarth set the scene of his Gin Lane there in 1751 until in

1864 Dickens took Marcus Stone, the illustrator of *Our Mutual Friend*, there and showed him the taxidermist and bone articulator who had inspired the character of Mr Venus.

Of an evening this rookery was crowded with labourers in their working clothes, still covered in brick dust and whitewash, arguing with each other

The 'Rookery', St Giles – one of the most notorious of London's slums.

round the street posts, with drunken Irishwomen fighting to the shouts of encouragement from pot-boys, with half-naked children playing in the open drains or sitting in the gutter stupefied by a tot of the 'The Real Knock Me Down' which had been handed out to them from the garish interior of a nearby gin-shop. It was packed with 'dirty men, filthy women, squalid children, fluttering shuttlecocks, noisy battledores, reeking pipes, bad fruit, more than doubtful oysters, attenuated cats, depressed dogs', second-hand clothes shops, pawnbrokers' shops, shops full of birds and rabbits and old iron and kitchen stuff and mangles and advertisements for penny theatres, and with crumbling houses in which every room had a separate tenant and every tenant a family. In one small wretched hovel, whose broken windows were patched with rags and paper, there might be found a sweetmeat manufacturer in the cellar, a barber and a red-herring vendor in the front parlour and a cobbler in the back,

a bird fancier on the first floor, three families on the second, starvation in the attics. Irishmen in the passage, a 'musician' in the front kitchen and a charwoman and five hungry children in the back one – filth everywhere – a gutter before the house and a drain behind – clothes drying and slops emptying from the windows; girls of fourteen or fifteen with matted hair walking about barefoot. . . .

Scenes similar to this one in Seven Dials could be witnessed in several of London's other dreadful slums throughout most of Dickens's life until the great new thoroughfares of later Victorian times – New Oxford Street, Victoria Street, Southwark Street, Northumberland Avenue, Charing Cross Road and Shaftesbury Avenue – swept much of them away. There was Saffron Hill near Smithfield Market, where, in an upstairs back room near Field Lane, Oliver Twist is introduced to the sausage-toasting Fagin – and 'a dirtier or more wretched place' Oliver had never seen. There were the slums of Whitechapel, Rotherhithe, Houndsditch and Bethnal Green, Southwark and Spitalfields, where, as in St Giles, whole courts were inhabited by gangs of criminals, their women and their children; where holes were cut through walls and ceilings, into cellars and out of roofs so that a man wanted by the police might soon escape; where brothels, lodging-houses, rat-pits and skittle-grounds were entirely given over to the custom of criminals. There were also those numerous areas, less specifically criminal, where the poverty was abject and infamous. There were the streets running down to the river by Thames Street where Ralph Nickleby deposits his unwanted relations in an 'old and gloomy and black, sullen and dark' house; and the 'by-gone, faded, tumble-down' streets off Golden Square where Newman Noggs rents his garret, where the 'dingy, ill-plumed, drowsy' fowls that peck about in the kennels are 'perfectly in keeping with

Cross-section of a lodging-house in Field Lane, built over a sewer.

Scene in Wild Court, off Great Wild Street, showing a boy crossing-sweeper in the foreground.

the crazy habitations of their owners', and 'the very chimneys appear to have grown dismal and melancholy from having nothing better to look at than the chimneys over the way'. There were the rotting tenements of Tom-all-Alone's, foully stained and reeking, where Jo, the crossing-sweeper in *Bleak House*, lives, his body giving off so foul a stench that Lady Dedlock cannot bear him near her. And, worst of all, there was Jacob's Island, beyond Dockhead in Southwark, 'the filthiest, the strangest, the most extraordinary of the many localities that are hidden in London, wholly unknown, even by name to the great mass of its inhabitants'.

Jacob's Island was a noisome warren of decaying houses whose walls were crumbling down, whose doors were falling into the narrow streets, whose rotting floors were supported on piles driven into the stagnant marsh beneath, whose windows, windows no more, looked forlornly down upon every 'repulsive lineament of poverty, every loathsome indication of filth, rot, and garbage' that lined the banks of Folly Ditch.

It was here that the cholera epidemic that swept across London in 1832 began, and where, in 1848, cholera started again. Yet twelve years after *Oliver Twist* was published, 'in the year one thousand eight hundred and fifty,' as Dickens himself wrote in the preface to a new edition of his book, 'it was publicly declared in London by an amazing Alderman [Sir Peter Laurie, satirized as Alderman Cute in *The Chimes*] that Jacob's Island did not exist, and never had existed. Jacob's Island continues to exist (like an ill-bred place as it is).'

Stark and disturbing as is Dickens's description of this rookery, however, it seems almost discreet by comparison with Henry Mayhew's account of it in one of that series of articles from which developed *London Labour and the London Poor*, the first two volumes of which were published in 1851. Mayhew wrote of the disgusting graveyard smell of the place which made you feel sick as soon as you crossed the bridge, the heavy bubbles rising up in the slimy, greeny black water choked with rotting weeds and fish-heads, the swollen carcasses of dead animals ready to burst with the gases of putrefaction and the red effluent from the leather-dressers; he described what Dickens, with his care for the susceptibilities of his public, would never have felt able to do, the dark streaks of filth down the walls where the drains discharged themselves into the ditch, the open, doorless privies.

In describing the lower middle-class atmosphere of Lant Street, Southwark, in his previous book, *Pickwick Papers*, Dickens is more at his ease. He is able to display his descriptive genius without the inhibitions that so horrendous a locality as Jacob's Island imposed upon it:

Lant Street was colonized by a few clear-starchers, a sprinkling of journeymen bookbinders, one or two prison agents for the Insolvent Court, several small housekeepers who are employed in the Docks, a handful of mantua makers, and a seasoning of jobbing tailors. The majority of the inhabitants either direct their energies to the letting of furnished apartments, or devote themselves to the healthful and invigorating pursuit of mangling. The chief features in the still life of the streets, are green shutters, lodging bills, brass door-plates, and bell-handles; the principal specimens of animated nature, the pot-boy, the muffin youth, and the baked-potato-man. The population is migratory, usually disappearing on the verge of quarter-day, and generally by night. His Majesty's revenues are seldom collected in this happy valley, the rents are dubious, and the water communication is very frequently cut off.

Dickens, as a boy, had once lived in Lant Street himself in a house occupied by a good-hearted fat old man, his gentle wife, and a 'very innocent grown-up son', a placid, contented family later to become the Garlands of *The Old Curiosity Shop*. Charles had been sent to live with them because, when he was twelve years old, his father had at last been arrested for debt and incarcerated in the Marshalsea Prison; his mother and the other children had joined him there, but for Charles there was no room.

His mother had attempted to save the family from this fate by opening a school, as Mrs Micawber does in *David Copperfield*. She had persuaded her husband to leave Bayham Street and move to a more imposing house at 4 Gower Street North; but although a prospectus was printed and pushed through likely looking letter-boxes in the district, and although an impressive brass plate was displayed beside the front door advertising the presence there of *Mrs Dickens's Establishment*, not a single pupil was enrolled; and Charles became an ever more frequent visitor to the pawnshops of the neighbourhood and to a drunken bookseller in Hampstead Road whose hands shook so badly that he could scarcely get money out of his pocket.

So that he could make some sort of contribution to the family's finances, Charles had been sent out to work in a boot-blacking warehouse at 30 Hungerford Stairs just off the Strand, at six shillings a week for a twelve-hour day. This factory, which – like the houses in Bayham Street and Gower Street North – has long since been demolished, was down by the river close to the present Charing Cross Station. It was a forlorn, ramshackle, rotting building, and for the rest of his life Dickens could never forget the dirt and decay of the place, the sound of the creaking floors, the scuffling and squeaking of the old grey rats in the cellar, the smell of the cement which was used on the corks of the blacking bottles. For years afterwards he could not bring himself to go near Hungerford Stairs; when walking down the Strand he would always cross to the other side of the road to avoid the smell of Warren's warehouse; and if ever he found himself walking through the streets through which he had passed at night after visiting his family in the Marshalsea he could not hold back his tears.

Before moving to Lant Street, which was nearer the prison, he had been lodged with a 'reduced old lady' who took orphaned or unwanted children in to board at her house in Little College Street, Camden Town; and although it was a long walk from there to Hungerford Stairs and an even longer one back from the Marshalsea, over Blackfriar's Bridge, through Holborn and Bloomsbury and up Tottenham Court Road, he did at least have the opportunity of exploring more of London than he had time to do in the hour he was allowed off for lunch or the half-hour for tea.

Sometimes he would go to look wistfully at the toy bazaar in Soho Square or to the 'toy shop in Fleet Street to see the giants of Saint Dunstan's strike upon the bells', or to the fascinating tea-tray shop on the corner of Bedford Street and King Street and stare at the scenes painted on the trays. On other mornings he would walk down to the back streets of the Adelphi and look into the Adelphi arches, or sit on a bench outside the waterside tavern, the 'Fox-under-the-Hill', to watch the halfpenny steamboats chugging up and down the river between Salisbury Stairs and London Bridge, or he would go down to Scotland Yard to see the coal-heavers fill their wagons from the barges moored at the wharf, and, if he were lucky, he would catch sight of them dancing in their leather gaiters and aprons and coalies' hats, mugs of Barclay's best in one hand and long-stemmed pipes in the other, in the courtyard of the inn.

The inn he frequented mostly himself was the 'Swan' in Hungerford Stairs, a 'miserable old public-house', though the best he could afford. For after breakfast of 'a penny cottage loaf and a pennyworth of milk', or a piece of the cheap pastry (cheap because it was stale) sold at the confectioners' shops he passed of a morning in Tottenham Court Road, he had to be contented with a saveloy sausage or a bit of bread and cheese for his dinner; and it was only when he had been given some money by his godfather that he could afford to go to one of those pudding-shops and eating houses so common in the area of St Martin's-in-the-Fields that it was known as Porridge Island. Once he plucked up courage to go into Johnson's *à la mode* beef-shop in Clare Court, with his own bread wrapped up in paper to look like a book, and to order a plateful of larded beef; and once he went into the 'Red Lion' in Parliament Street and ordered a twopenny glass of the landlord's 'very best – the VERY *best*-ale'. But more often he was reduced to staring in a dismal reverie at the signs on the plate-glass doors of the coffee-shops in St Martin's Lane.

The old Red Lion Inn, which Dickens once visited as a child.

One of his favourite distractions was to go down to Covent Garden, which was later to appear so frequently in his work, and to walk, as Tom and Ruth Pinch do in *Martin Chuzzlewit*, along the rows of fruit and vegetables piled up like fortifications, down the side avenues where old women sat on up-turned baskets shelling peas, through the poultry markets where 'ducks and fowls, with necks unnaturally long, lay stretched out in pairs, ready for cooking', past live birds in coops and cages, 'looking much too big to be natural, in consequence of those receptacles being much too little', and 'rabbits, alive and dead, innumerable'. At night Covent Garden was a quite different place 'where', as Little Dorrit discovers when she goes to Arthur Clennam's lodgings there one midnight, 'miserable children in rags ... like young rats, slunk and hid, fed on offal, huddled together for warmth and were hunted about'. Towards the end of his life, Dickens decided that the spectacle of these children prowling about Covent Garden at night was 'one of the worst sights in London'. After one visit there in the early hours of the morning he wrote in *All the Year Round* in 1860 of the pathetic little creatures 'who prowl about this place; who sleep in the baskets, fight for the offal, dart at any object they think they can lay their thieving hands on, dive under the carts and barrows, dodge the constables, and are perpetually making a blunt pattering on the pavement of the Piazza with the rain of their naked feet.' Most of them, if not all of them, would soon be in prison.

Dickens's own experience of prison, even as a child, was not limited to the Marshalsea, that 'oblong pile of barrack building, partitioned into squalid houses standing back to back', where his father had been held and which for twenty-three years is the 'living grave' of William Dorrit. Dickens knew well, too, the other London prisons. He knew the Marshalsea's two neighbours in Southwark, Horsemonger Lane Gaol which was not abolished until 1879, and the King's Bench, Micawber's place of confinement, which survived until 1880; he knew the Fleet Prison where for the first time in his life Mr Pickwick turns away from a fellow human being, unable to stand the sight of a 'woman with a child in her arms, who seemed scarcely able to crawl from emaciation and misery'.

Most intimately of all, Dickens knew Newgate, the oldest and most notorious of the London prisons, rebuilt after its destruction in the Gordon Riots of 1780 and not pulled down until 1902. As a child he had gazed at its forbidding walls and huge iron-plated and spiked door; as a young journalist he wrote a long and effective account of it and its denizens for *Sketches by Boz;* as an essayist he described how he walked past it on his night walks and touched its rough stone, thinking of the sleeping prisoners within and glancing in at the lodge over the spiked wicket, 'seeing the fire and light of the watching turnkeys on the white wall'; and as a novelist he used it for scenes in both *Barnaby Rudge* and *A Tale of Two Cities*, sent Fagin to the condemned cell there, and showed Pip in *Great Expectations* being conducted round it by Wemmick at visiting time when a potman was going his rounds with beer, 'and the prisoners, behind bars in yards, were buying beer, and talking to friends; and a frouzy, ugly, disorderly, depressing scene it was'. Pip had seen the outside of the prison on a previous occasion when, overcome by the heat and musty smell in Mr Jaggers's office, he is advised to take a turn round the Smithfield meat market:

So I came into Smithfield; and the shameful place, being all asmear with filth and fat and blood and foam, seemed to stick to me. So I rubbed it off with all possible speed by turning into a street where I saw the great black dome of St Paul's bulging at me from behind a grim stone building which a bystander said was Newgate Prison. Following the wall of the jail, I found the roadway covered with straw to deaden the noise of passing vehicles; and from this, and from the quantity of people standing about, smelling strongly of spirits and beer, I inferred that the trials were on.

While I looked about me here, an exceedingly dirty and partially drunk minister of justice asked me if I would like to step in and hear a trial or so. . . . As I declined the proposal, he was so good as to take me into a yard and show me where the gallows was kept, and also where people were publicly whipped, and then he showed me the Debtors' Door, out of which culprits came to be hanged; heightening the interest of that dreadful portal by giving me to understand that 'four on 'em' would come out at that door the day after to-morrow at eight in the morning to be killed in a row. This was horrible, and gave me a sickening idea of London.

Dickens shared Pip's revulsion; but, although he hated Newgate and public executions, he was drawn to them both, as he was drawn to the slums and the *morgue*, 'dragged by invisible forces' as he put it himself, by the 'attraction of repulsion'.

He made several visits to Newgate in the course of his career; and in 1849 he was present at the public hanging of those two eccentric murderers, Mr and Mrs George Manning, on top of Horsemonger Lane Gaol, though he had already attended the execution of Courvoisier, and one, or perhaps two, beheadings on the Continent. There were thirty thousand other witnesses of the Mannings' last moments – for which Mrs Manning wore black satin and so banished that material from the London dress shops for almost thirty years – and Dickens, who rented a nearby roof for ten guineas, afterwards wrote to *The Times* of the immense crowd's inconceivable 'wickedness and levity'. 'You have no idea what the hanging of the Mannings really was,' he added to a friend. 'The conduct of the people was so indescribably frightful, that I felt for some time afterwards almost as if I were living in a city of devils.'

Shortly after Charles's twelfth birthday, his father came into an inheritance from his mother and was able to leave prison. He settled his family at 26 Johnson Street, a dirty, crumbling street between Camden Town and Somers Town, and sent Charles back to school at Wellington House Academy on the corner of Granby Street and Mornington Place in Hampstead Road. On leaving there, Charles went as an office-boy at ten shillings a week to a firm of solicitors, Messrs Ellis and Blackmore of 5 Holborn Court and later of 6 Raymond Buildings, Gray's Inn.

LIFE, TRIAL, CONFESSION &
EXECUTION
Of T. H. Hooker, for the Murder of Mr. J. De la Rue.

Dickens was now introduced to the London professional world of Kenge and Carboy, Dodson and Fogg, Snitchey and Craggs, Spenlow and Jorkins, to dark and dirty offices smelling of must and dust and unwholesome sheep, a smell 'referable to the nightly (and often daily) consumption of mutton fat in candles, and to the fretting of parchment forms and skins in greasy drawers', to government offices, stationers' shops and legal chambers where 'the dull cracked windows in their heavy frames' have 'a determination to be always dirty and always shut', to clerks who sit on high stools with quill pens behind their ears and seem to spend their time – if old – in wearily scratching away in crumbling ledgers, or – if young – in mixing seidlitz powders, lolling over their desks on which their initials have been carefully carved, and in relating their experiences of the previous evening at the oyster shop, the cider cellar, the music hall or theatre.

Dickens, himself, so he afterwards said – and so from a reading of his work it is not difficult to believe – 'went to some theatre every night, with a very few exceptions: really studying the bills first, and going where there

Broadsheet to commemorate a public execution, 1845.

was the best acting.' His taste was catholic, his appetite for the stage so great as to be indiscriminate. He was as enthralled by the great tragedian, William Charles Macready, as by the comic actor, Charles Mathews, whose funny stories, imitations, conjuring tricks and ventriloquism were amongst the main delights of London audiences. He was as likely to be found in the rowdy, nut-cracking, orange-peeling, beer-swilling audience at Astley's in the Westminster Bridge Road, clapping the clowns and acrobats, as at a Shakespearean production at one of the 'major' theatres, Drury Lane, Covent Garden or the Haymarket, which, until the passing of the 1843 Theatres Act, held a monopoly in 'legitimate' drama.

The law was not taken too seriously. If a 'minor' theatre wanted to put on a five-act tragedy it would merely provide the characters with a few not too incongruous songs to sing and call it a burletta; while over the 'private' theatres there was very little control at all. There were numerous 'private' theatres all over London – mainly off Gray's Inn Lane, in the purlieus of the City or in Catherine Street, Strand, patronized by

dirty boys, low copying clerks in the attorneys' offices, capacious headed youths from City counting houses, Jews, whose business, as lenders of fancy dresses, is a sure passport to the amateur stage, shopboys who now and then mistake their masters' money for their own, and a choice miscellany of idle vagabonds . . . The lady performers pay nothing for their characters, and, it is needless to add, are usually selected from one class of society.

For their characters the male performers paid a fee which was calculated upon the length or popularity of the part and the quality of the costume available; the best parts being bought for as much as £2, the more insignificant for half-a-crown or so, but in any event for a good deal more than the price demanded from the members of the impatient and critical audience.

Although these 'private' theatres often formed 'the chief nuisance of some shabby street, on the Surrey side of Waterloo Bridge', far more of a nuisance in Victorian London were the 'penny gaffs', the upper floors of shops where disreputable performers danced and sang to the accompaniment of a raucous band, where young men lit their pipes at the gas jets, spluttering on each side of the makeshift proscenium, or tickled the girls in the seats in front of them. These girls, some of them only eight years old, laughing at the obscene songs, delighting in the suggestive dances, clapped their hands and waved the feathers in their dirty bonnets in time to the music; then, when the last tune had been played, they joined the throng of prostitutes, bare-headed and in Adelaide boots, who crowded round the canvas curtains at the entrance calling out for customers.

For the truth of this particular aspect of Victorian London, for the

London of 'penny gaffs' and 'dolly mops', of brothels and the notorious night-houses of Spitalfields and Lambeth, we cannot turn to Dickens or, indeed, to any reputable Victorian novelist. We have to rely on such reporters as Henry Mayhew and such uninhibited underground writers as the indefatigable author of *My Secret Life*. Dickens's prostitutes are mere creatures of melodrama. Martha Endell has little to do with the reality of the estimated 80,000 women and girls who followed her profession in mid-nineteenth-century London.

Thousands of these prostitutes, many of them under thirteen, walked the streets at night, especially in the Haymarket area; thousands more worked in brothels, from the fashionable establishments in Oxendon Street and King's Place, St James's, to the rat-infested hovels down by the docks where, in certain courts off Bluegate Fields, every room in every house was given over to prostitution, where the smell of opium lay sweet and heavy in the air, and the only items of furniture to be found were damp palliasses and broken bedsteads. Bill Sikes's Nancy knows such places and so does John Jasper, the Cloisterham Cathedral choir-master who is introduced to the readers of *Edwin Drood* in the 'meanest and closest of small rooms', in the company of a Chinaman, a Lascar and a haggard old woman who has been 'heavens-hard drunk for sixteen year afore' she took to opium. So, too, although he believed that detailed reports of them should be confined to official reports and male conversation, did Dickens know such places.

As a lawyer's clerk with Ellis and Blackmore, and later with Charles Molloy in New Square, Lincoln's Inn; as a shorthand writer in Doctor's Commons; as a Parliamentary reporter and a roving journalist; and, finally, as novelist and editor, Dickens was an untiring investigator of every aspect of London life, seeking out the City's every secret, its every pleasure and vice, walking its streets by day and by night until he knew it as well as any man could hope to know it.

Sometimes with a companion but often alone, he went into tea gardens and gin palaces, into crowded fairs and empty City churches, into taverns where old men, wheezy and asthmatical, 'expressed themselves opposed to steam and all new-fangled ways, and held ballooning to be sinful', talking to turncocks and cab-drivers (all 'bottle-nosed red-faced men') and waiters (who, 'according to the immemorial usage of waiters in all ages', stand – like the one in *A Tale of Two Cities* – observing the guests while they eat and drink 'as from an observatory or watch-tower'.)

He went down to Greenwich for the fair and up to Camden Town to see how the railways were uprooting the northern suburbs:

... here a chaos of carts, overthrown and jumbled together, lay topsy-turvy at the bottom of a steep, unnatural hill; there, confused treasures of iron soaked and rusted in something that had accidentally become a pond. Everywhere were bridges that led nowhere; thoroughfares that were wholly impassable; Babel towers of chimneys, wanting half their height; temporary wooden houses and ragged tenements, and fragments of unfinished walls and arches, and piles of scaffolding, and wildernesses of bricks, and giant forms of cranes, and tripods straddling above nothing.

Work on the London and Birmingham Railway had begun in 1834, the year in which Joseph Aloysius Hansom introduced his 'Patent Safety Cab' into a city already crammed with carriages, carts, tilburies, phaetons, growlers, gigs and horse-drawn omnibuses. And within a few years the 'railway mania' was at its height, covering acre upon acre of London with iron rails, platforms, shunting yards and engine sheds, repair shops and ticket offices, refreshment rooms and coal bunkers, and displacing hundreds of thousands of its inhabitants. Almost twenty thousand people were obliged to abandon their homes by the building of the line from the London and Birmingham's depot to its terminal station in Euston Square alone; and most of them, unwilling to move far away, crowded into already over-populated areas nearby, adding yet another problem to the continuing tragedy of the London poor. Nor was this problem eased when the railway boom was over, for by then countless numbers of labourers, many of them Irish, had been tempted to come to London to find work in the 'Hungry Forties' (as, earlier, others had come to work as navigators on the capital's canals), and only a small proportion of them ever returned home.

A large number of these immigrants went to swell the thousands of those who earned their living in the London streets, those costermongers and muffin-men, cats' meat dealers and hot-eel boys, bone pickers and dog finders, organ-grinders and Punch and Judy men, keepers of breakfast-trolleys and coffee-stalls, of ginger-beer foundations and potato-ovens, those numberless casuals and vagrants that form so vital a part of the Dickens world. Some of these London street workers whom Dickens knew were employed by contractors, like the omnibus cad in *Sketches by Boz*, whose great boast is that he can 'chuck an old gen'lm'n into the buss, shut him in, and rattle off, afore he knows where it's a goin' to', and the labourers – men, women and children – who work up to their waists in refuse sifting the 'brieze' from the 'soil' on Mr Harmon's dust-heaps in *Our Mutual Friend*. But most of them, like Jo, the crossing-sweeper, and Silas Wegg, are self-employed, living from day to day and hand to mouth, their horizons limited by the 'cold, wet, shelterless, midnight streets'.

In these streets Dickens watched them, listening, remembering, observing

A London coffee-stall, from Henry Mayhew's *London Labour and the London Poor* (1860).

their companions and their background, transforming the reality into that uniquely imagined world of his novels at once so strange and so familiar. Whenever he felt that his inspiration was flagging or his ideas were running down he would stride forth from his house – at first from Furnival's Inn, then from Doughty Street, in the 1840s from Devonshire Terrace, later from an even larger house in Tavistock Square – walking very fast and usually into those parts of the town where people could be found. On a Saturday night, perhaps he would make for Leather Lane or Whitecross Street, the Brill or the New Cut, Lambeth, and push his way into the excited crowds milling round the stalls of a street market, where purple pickled cabbage and Yarmouth bloaters, old shoes and sugar-sticks were lit up by oil lamps or by candles stuck inside turnips or sieves, where costermongers sat under their carts, drinking purl, a mixture of beer and gin, and playing games with filthy cards from which the numbers had all but been effaced, where little watercress girls tried to sell the last of the bunches they had picked up that morning in Farringdon cress market, and where the stall-holders shouted themselves hoarse with cries of 'Ho! Ho! Hi-i-i! What do you think of this 'ere? A penny a bunch. Hurrah for free

A bone-grubber. Many of the unemployed were driven to collecting and selling refuse to keep themselves alive.

trade! Here's your turnips!' 'Come and look at 'em! Penny a lot. Old shoes!' 'Hot spiced gingerbread. Buy my gingerbread! Smo-o-oking hot. If one'll warm you, wha-at'll a *pound* do? – Wha-a-at'll a *pound* do?' 'Pick em out cheap 'ere. Live soles. Three pair for sixpence!'

It was all like a marvellous magic lantern, Dickens said; and he confessed himself unable to work for long without its stimulation. Often when abroad he felt that he had plucked himself out of his proper soil by leaving London, and that he would not be able to write anything more until he had refreshed himself by walking through its streets again. 'Put me down on Waterloo Bridge at eight o'clock in the evening,' he once wrote home to his friend John Forster from Italy, 'and I would come home, as you know, panting to go on. I am sadly strange as it is, and can't settle.' Later, in Switzerland, he wrote again of the 'prodigious difficulty' of writing in the absence of the London streets. Even in the country in England he could not get on for long without the excitement they afforded him; he was 'dumbfounded' away from them. 'The toil and labour of continuing day after day, without that magic lantern is IMMENSE! !' For the streets of London were the heart and the inspiration of the Dickens world.

A circular sent at Christmas by the 'regular Scavengers' to the citizens of their wards.

To the worthy Inhabitants of the Wards of Bridge, Candlewick, & Dowgate.

LADIES & GENTLEMEN,

You are humbly requested not to give your CHRISTMAS BOX to any persons but to us, who are the servants of Mr. BUTTERFIELD, the Contractor for these Wards ; and we most earnestly beg, that you will be so good as to demand an impression to be produced exactly similar to that in the margin of this bill, before you give to any one ; as many impostors have gone about, knowing the contents of our bills, and defrauded us of the bounty which would have been bestowed on us,

Your most obedient humble servants,

The regular Scavengers of these Wards.

Batchelar, Printer, Long Alley, Finsbury.

The Man of Letters

Dickens's literary career began when, as a schoolboy at Wellington House Academy, he contributed odd news items for the press, thus becoming what was called a 'penny a liner'; but he undoubtedly learnt much from his work as a reporter, first at Doctors' Commons and then in the House of Commons Press Gallery. By this time he was already contributing to 'The Mirror of Parliament' and 'The True Sun'. As an observant and gifted boy, left much on his own, he had acquired an intimate knowledge of London, and this provided the inspiration and material for the short Sketches he began to write, of which the first was published in 1833 in the 'Monthly Magazine' [1]. Collected into two volumes in 1836, these 'Sketches by Boz' proved a great success [2], and this success was crowned by the triumph of 'Pickwick'. Within a few months, Boz became the talk of the town, and within a few years he was a world-famous writer, adulated by the public and surrounded by admiring friends [4]. It is now recognized that Dickens, despite his enormous output, was a highly conscientious and methodical craftsman [5], with a feeling of obligation towards his readers [7], with whom he established a uniquely intimate relationship by reason of the serial publication of most of his books [6]. Later in life, he entered into a new and even more directly personal contact with his public through the immensely successful readings [8, 9, 10, 11 and 13], even going to the trouble of preparing special texts for such occasions [12], and declaiming from a desk constructed according to his own specifications [14 and 15]. Yet at the height of his fame as a novelist, he still hankered after his early career of journalist, first editing (though briefly) the 'Daily News', and then reaching a wider audience with his periodicals 'Household Words' and 'All the Year Round' [16 and 17]. At his death, Dickens was by far the most popular writer of his day; and although some of the professional critics tended at first to deny his artistry, the academic approach became steadily more favourable, while his public following never wavered. Today, a century after his death, his position as the greatest novelist of the English-speaking world, and perhaps the greatest of all masters of fiction, is acknowledged: for even though his pathos has not always survived the enthusiasm of his contemporaries, his comedy, with all its breadth and richness, exerts a perennial appeal.

1 Dickens delivers his first manuscript 'A Dinner at Poplar Walk', to the office of the *Monthly Magazine*, 'up a dark court in Fleet Street'.

2 The cover of a collected edition of some of Dickens's *Sketches*, bound up with others by Edward Calsall ('Quiz'), and collectively attributed to the latter.
3 The novelist's writing-desk, with some of the ornaments he habitually kept on it.
4 Montage showing Dickens with a group of his distinguished friends and contemporaries. *Back:* G. Macdonald, A. J. Froude, Wilkie Collins, Anthony Trollope. *Front:* W. M. Thackeray, Lord Macaulay, Lord Bulwer Lytton, Thomas Carlyle, Charles Dickens.

5 Notes and chapter-headings for the first number of *Little Dorrit*, showing the last-minute change from the original title *Nobody's Fault*.

☞ *overleaf*

6 Covers of the monthly parts of three of the novels and of *Sketches by Boz*.

7 A corrected proof of the announcement of the close of *Master Humphrey's Clock*, after the triumphant success of *The Old Curiosity Shop* and *Barnaby Rudge*.

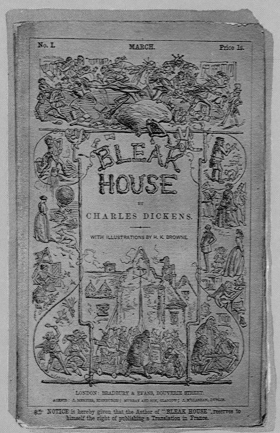

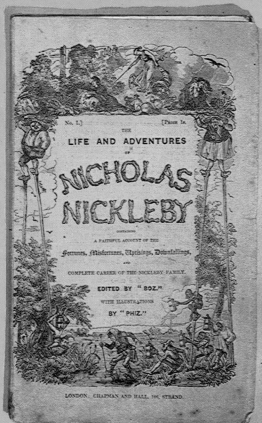

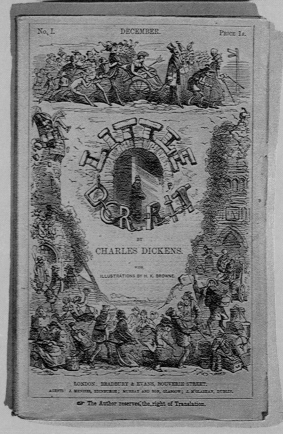

TO THE

READERS OF "MASTER HUMPHREY'S CLOCK."

DEAR FRIENDS,

NEXT November, we shall have finished the Tale, on which we are at present engaged; and shall have travelled together through Twenty Monthly Parts, and Eighty-seven Weekly Numbers. It is my design, when we have ~~accomplished that amount~~, to close this work. Let me tell you why.

I should not regard the anxiety, the close confinement, or the constant attention, inseparable from the weekly form of publication (for to commune with you, in any form, is to me a labour of love), if I had found it advantageous to the conduct of my stories, the elucidation of my meaning, or the gradual development of my characters. But I have not done so. I have often felt cramped and confined in a very irksome and harassing degree, by the ~~petty~~ space in which I have been constrained to move. I have wanted you to know more at once than I could tell you; and it has frequently been of the greatest importance to my cherished intention, that you should. I have been sometimes strongly tempted (and have been at some pains to resist the temptation) to hurry incidents on, lest they should appear to you who waited from week to week, and had not, like me, the result and purpose in your minds, too long delayed. In a word, I have found this most anxious, perplexing, and difficult ~~for me and~~ I cannot bear these jirking confidences which are no sooner begun than ended, and no sooner ended than begun again.

Many passages in a tale of any length, depend materially for their interest on the intimate relation they bear to what has gone before, or to what is to follow. I sometimes found it difficult when I issued thirty-two closely-printed pages once a month, to sustain in your minds this needful connection; in the present form of publication it is often, especially in the first half of a story, quite impossible to preserve it sufficiently through the current numbers. And although in my progress I am gradually able to set you right, and to show you what my meaning has been, and to work it out, I see no reason why you should ever be wrong when I have it in my power, by resorting to a better means of communication between us, to prevent it.

Considerations of immediate profit and advantage, ought, in such a case, to be of secondary importance. *They* would lead me, at all hazards, to hold my present course. But for the reasons I have just now mentioned, ~~and on account of many other difficulties connected with the movement of a story by such little levers with which it is unnecessary to weary you, but which, few have experienced them, I may venture to suppose few know better than myself~~ I have, after long consideration, and with especial reference to the next new Tale I bear in my mind, arrived at the conclusion that it will be better to abandon this scheme of publication, in favour of our old and well-tried plan, which has only twelve gaps in a year, instead of fifty-two.

Therefore, my intention is to close this story, (with the limits of which I am, of course, by this time acquainted,) and this work, within, or at about, the period I have mentioned. I should add, that for the general convenience of subscribers, another volume of collected numbers will not be published, until the whole is brought to a conclusion.

And now I come to an announcement which gives me mingled pain and pleasure pain, because it separates me, for a time, from many thousands of my countrymen who have given my writings, as they were myself, a corner in their hearts and homes, and a place among their household gods; pleasure, because it leads me to the gratification of a darling wish, and opens to me a new scene of interest and wonder.

Taking advantage of the respite which the close of this work will afford me, I have decided, ~~early in the spring of the year~~, to pay a visit to America. ~~It will be but a brief one;~~ ~~and~~ on the First of November, eighteen hundred and forty-two, I purpose, if it please God, to commence my new book in monthly parts, under the old green cover, in the old size and form, and at the old price.

I look forward to addressing a few more words to you, in reference to this latter theme, before I close the task on which I am now engaged. If there be any among the numerous readers of Master Humphrey's Clock who are, at first, dissatisfied with the prospect of this change —and it is not unnatural almost to hope there may be some—I trust they will, at no very distant day, find reason to agree with

ITS AUTHOR.

SEPTEMBER, 1841.

8

9

10

"WHENEVER HE FELT TOOTS COMING AGAIN, HE BEGAN TO LAUGH AND WIPE HIS EYES AFRESH; AND
WHEN TOOTS CAME ONCE MORE, HE GAVE A KIND OF CRY, AS IF IT WERE TOO MUCH FOR HIM."

11

large black wooden beads. Child being fond of toys, cribbed the necklace, hid it, played with the necklace, cut the string, and swallowed a bead. Child thought it capital fun, went back next day, and swallowed another bead."

Bless my heart said Mr. Pickwick what a dreadful thing! I beg your pardon, sir. Go on.

"Next day, child swallowed two beads; the day after that, treated himself to three beads and so on, till in a week's time he had got through the necklace—five-and-twenty beads Sister industrious girl, seldom treated herself to a bit of finery, cried eyes out, at the loss of the necklace, looked high and low for it necklace but, I needn't say, didn't find necklace. A few days afterwards, the family at dinner—baked shoulder of mutton, and potatoes child, wasn't hungry, playing about the room, when suddenly there was heard a devil of a noise, like a small hail storm. 'Don't do that, my boy,' said the father. 'I aint a doin' nothing'

12

14

13

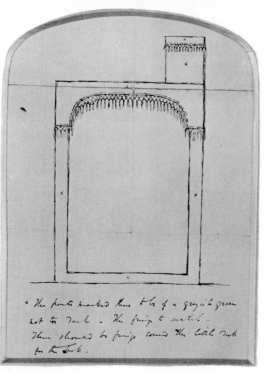

8, 9, and **10** Three artists' impressions of Dickens as public reader.
11 The response of the audience, with Dickens's own description in a letter to Georgina Hogarth underneath (9 December 1858).
12 Dickens's corrections to the special text he used for his readings.
13 Photograph of Dickens giving a reading.
14 The famous reading-desk.
15 The design for the desk, with Dickens's own directions underneath.

15

26, WELLINGTON STREET W.

Office of All the Year Round,

A WEEKLY JOURNAL CONDUCTED BY CHARLES DICKENS.

Late

N:o 11 Wellington Street North, Strand, London. W.C.

Wednesday Second may   1860.

My Dear Forster.

It did not occur to me in reading

16

17

16 The letterhead of the stationery of Dickens's weekly journal, founded in 1859 and successor to *Household Words*.

17 Cartoon inspired by *All the Year Round*.

The Genesis of a Novel: Great Expectations

Harry Stone

Pause you who read this, and think for a moment of the long chain of iron or gold, of thorns or flowers, that would never have bound you, but for the formation of the first link on one memorable day.

GREAT EXPECTATIONS

Wilkie Collins had great difficulty in naming his most famous novel, *The Woman in White*. This may strike us as strange, for the book seems to demand its title. But as Collins worked on his novel, and as the days and weeks went by, he could not find a name for it, and this not only disturbed him but also Dickens, who was his intimate friend and literary mentor. Dickens considered a book's title of utmost importance, and in this case he had a business interest in the name. The untitled work was to follow *A Tale of Two Cities* as a serial in Dickens's own magazine, *All the Year Round*. Furthermore, since *All the Year Round* used no by-lines, Collins's novel had to be announced and advertised primarily by title. But as the publication date loomed closer and closer, Collins could not settle on a title. He had long since written the unforgettable opening of his book, an opening which had sounded the major chords of his story. In that opening, drawing on his own experience, he had described how suddenly, in the dead of night, in the middle of an empty moon-blanched road, a 'solitary Woman, dressed from head to foot in white', had touched a startled stranger on the shoulder and changed his destiny. The episode was haunting, premonitory, central – Dickens thought the scene one of the two most dramatic descriptions in literature – but the days and weeks wore on and Collins could think of no name. Then, one evening, while Collins was lying on the grass and staring at the North Foreland Lighthouse, the title came into his head as swiftly and as unannounced as the real woman in white had come into his real life. He sent Dickens the name and asked for his reaction. Dickens replied immediately and settled the matter. 'I have not the slightest doubt,' he wrote on 16 August 1859, 'that The Woman in White is the name of names, and very title of titles.'

Collins could hardly have known why Dickens regarded The Woman in White as the 'name of names, and very title of titles'. Dickens himself was probably only dimly aware of the depth of his response. Yet even at that moment, *Great Expectations* and its 'Woman in White', Miss Havisham, were forming in his mind. Scarcely three months after Collins's novel concluded in *All the Year Round, Great Expectations* took its place in the same journal. That was the astonishing culmination: a Dickens novel that revolved, in part, around a persona similar to Collins's all-white figure, a

Portrait of Wilkie Collins, engraved in 1858, just before he began work on *The Woman in White*.

A scene from *The Woman in White* by Wilkie Collins.

figure that had called up very special and very different associations in Dickens's mind.

Those associations reached back to curious beginnings. The first faint premonitions of Miss Havisham had begun to take shape in Dickens's consciousness some thirty-five years earlier, and the strange unlikely history of Miss Havisham's gestation and of the genesis of *Great Expectations* is a fascinating untold tale.

Some of the crucial themes which became *Great Expectations*, and some of the everyday experiences which became Miss Havisham and ordained her fiery destruction, can be traced to the most casual happenstance of Dickens's early and late years. In the case of Miss Havisham this is surely a paradox, for she is often pointed to as a character who is totally unreal. She is too bizarre, runs the arraignment, too Dickensian; she is unbelievable. Whatever the validity of this judgment, one thing is certain: Miss Havisham is constructed out of everyday events. But there is another, still greater irony, and it is this: Dickens consciously suppressed the wilder, the more 'Dickensian' aspects of the everyday reality he drew upon.

That reality – 'the formation of the first link', to use Dickens's phrase – commenced with childhood. As a boy, Dickens had seen a strange lady wandering through the streets of London. The sight of this grotesque creature, and the romantic and tragic speculations he attached to her, sank into his memory and became an evocative part of his consciousness. Many years later, in 1853, in his magazine, *Household Words*, he wrote an essay about the indelible impressions of his boyhood. He called the essay 'Where We Stopped Growing', and in it he described the strange lady of his youth:

Another very different person who stopped our growth, we associate with Berners Street, Oxford Street; whether she was constantly on parade in that street only, or was ever to be seen elsewhere, we are unable to say. The White Woman is her name. She is dressed entirely in white, with a ghastly white plaiting round her head and face, inside her white bonnet. She even carries (we hope) a white umbrella. With white boots, we know she picks her way through the winter dirt. She is a conceited old creature, cold and formal in manner, and evidently went simpering mad on personal grounds alone – no doubt because a wealthy Quaker wouldn't marry her. This is her bridal dress. She is always walking up here, on her way to church to marry the false Quaker. We observe in her mincing step and fishy eye that she intends to lead him a sharp life. We stopped growing when we got at the conclusion that the Quaker had had a happy escape of the White Woman.

Here already are most of Miss Havisham's attributes: her externals –

'Pip waits on Miss Havisham', by Marcus Stone, an illustration from an early book-edition of *Great Expectations*.

bridal dress, all-white accoutrements, and ever-present staff (represented for the moment by an umbrella); her personality – cold, formal, conceited, eccentric, and man-hating; and her history – jilted and thereby frozen forever (she too has stopped growing!) in the ghastly garments of her dead love. But this White Woman – the White Woman of 'Where We Stopped Growing' – is not the simple figure of Dickens's boyhood. He had long since begun to surround the original image with fantasies of his own creation. What he had actually seen as a boy was an eccentric woman in weird white garments. The jilting Quaker, the walk to church, the white umbrella, the romantically provoked onset of madness – all these were added or magnified, as Dickens suggests, by his imagination.

His imagination may have embroidered or intertwined some of these motifs shortly after he turned nineteen, that is, several years after he had first seen the Berners Street White Woman. On the evening of 18 April 1831, at the Adelphi Theatre in London, Charles Mathews the elder, a great favourite of the youthful Dickens, opened in the twelfth of his annual 'At Homes'. One segment of the 1831 'At Home', a sketch entitled ' "No. 26 and No. 27" or Next Door Neighbours', featured a 'Miss Mildew', a character based upon the Berners Street White Woman. Miss Mildew, played by Mathews, was an eccentric old lady in white who had been jilted by her first love forty years earlier. On the day originally set for her marriage, Miss Mildew had donned her wedding garments, and every day since, in those yellowing weeds, she had made her way through London streets to a place bearing a startling name: the 'Expectation Office'. At the Expectation Office she inquires fruitlessly after her lost love. Her next door neighbour – a character played by Frederick Yates and also based upon a real-life London eccentric later described by Dickens in 'Where We Stopped Growing' – dresses all in black and constantly calls at the Expectation Office to collect a vast fortune that never arrives: another theme central to *Great Expectations*.

If Dickens saw this piece, he must have done so on opening night, for the sketch was withdrawn after its first performance. If he was present at that first performance, there is no doubt that 'No. 26 and No. 27' would have brought him instantly back to where *he* stopped growing; it would also have presented him, given the context of what he had seen as a boy, with an unforgettable linking of women in white and deluded expectations.

There is a reasonable chance that Dickens was present at that first performance. During his late teens he went to the theatre almost every night, and 'always', as he told Forster, 'to see Mathews whenever he played'. During this period too he thought of becoming an actor and memorized 'three or four successive years of Mathews's At Homes from sitting in the pit to hear them'. That Mathews had seized Dickens's youthful imagination there can be no doubt, but whether Miss Mildew and her evocative cluster of associations seized his imagination depends on whether Dickens was in the Adelphi audience on that April evening in 1831, and here the record, though suggestive, is inconclusive.

Many years later, however, another, more fantastic cluster of associations merged with Dickens's boyhood White Woman and helped shape Miss Havisham and the basic structure of *Great Expectations*. The second cluster of associations apparently entered Dickens's mind in 1850, that is nineteen years after Miss Mildew's brief life and three years before he wrote 'Where We Stopped Growing'. In 1850 Dickens launched a monthly supplement to the weekly *Household Words*. He called this supplement the *Household Narrative of Current Events*, gave it a departmentalized format, and sold it for twopence. In the first issue, that is, in the January 1850 *Household Narrative*, in the section entitled 'Narrative of Law and Crime', appeared the following paragraph:

An inquest was held on the 29th, on Martha Joachim, a *Wealthy and Eccentric Lady*, late of 27, York-buildings, Marylebone, aged 62. The jury proceeded to view the body, but had to beat a sudden retreat, until a bull-dog, belonging to deceased, and which savagely attacked them, was secured. It was shown in evidence that on the 1st of June, 1808, her father, an officer in the Life Guards, was murdered and robbed in Regent's Park. A reward of 300*l.* was offered for the murderer, who was apprehended with the property upon him, and executed. In 1825, a suitor of the deceased, whom her mother rejected, shot himself while sitting on the sofa with her, and she was covered with his brains. From that instant she lost her reason. Since her mother's death, eighteen years ago, she had led the life of a recluse, dressed in white, and never going out. A charwoman occasionally brought her what supplied her wants. Her only companions were the bull-dog, which she nursed like a child, and two cats. Her house was filled with images of soldiers in lead, which she called her 'body-guards.' When the collectors called for their taxes, they had to cross the garden-wall to gain admission. One morning she was found dead in her bed; and a surgeon who was called in, said she had died of bronchitis, and might have recovered with proper medical aid. The jury returned a verdict to that effect.

Reading about this eccentric white woman, Dickens must have recalled his own boyhood White Woman, and perhaps, if the association existed, Miss Mildew as well, for when he came to write about his Berners Street White Woman three years later in *Household Words*, he seems to have overlaid his early memories with details and associations from the history of Martha Joachim – that is, he projected upon his Berners Street White majority refuses to make one; Baron Rolfe, Baron Parke, and Chief Justice Wilde, dissented from the doctrine that the minority can bind the majority. The judgment of the majority of the bench was, that the judgment of the court below (the Queen's Bench) must be affirmed. So the monition of the Ecclesiastical Court to make a rate is now of operative force.

At the Middlesex Sessions, held at Clerkenwell, on the 22nd, William Anderson, a sharp-looking boy, aged fourteen, was indicted for *Robbery*. At about mid-day, on the 10th, he entered the shop of Mr. Cooper, baker, at Stepney, and asked Mrs. Cooper, who was serving behind the counter, for a halfpenny-worth of bread, at the same time laying down a penny. As she was about to give him the difference, he threw a handful of pepper in her eyes; and, jumping upon the counter, proceeded to help himself to the contents of the till, but becoming alarmed, he retreated, having got but threepence into his possession. Mr. Cooper pursued, and having overtaken him in Suffolk Street, he very coolly turned round, and presenting Mr. Cooper with the threepence, said, "It's only threepence, so it's not worth running for, and I gives in; but you wouldn't have nabbed me if it had been more!" He was then handed over to a policeman. But two days before this transaction, the prisoner had been liberated from Ilford gaol; where he had been imprisoned for highway robbery. He, and three others, having stopped a chaise on a turnpike-road; and one of them, not the prisoner, fired a pistol at the driver. They robbed the chaise and made off. The judge said this case presented a most extraordinary instance of juvenile depravity; and sentenced the culprit to imprisonment with hard labour for six months.

At the Mansion House, on the 28th, Alderman Humphery expounded a point in *Omnibus Law*, when a conductor of a Camberwell omnibus was summoned for having refused to admit a gentleman as a passenger into his omnibus. A few days before, at a quarter before five, the complainant went to the door of the omnibus, being desirous to be driven as far as Walworth, and requested the conductor to allow him to enter. The evening was extremely wet, but the conductor refused to admit the applicant, and excused himself upon the ground that all the seats were engaged, at the same time that there was abundance of room in the vehicle. The complainant represented the unfairness of the refusal, and determined to have the decision of a magistrate upon the subject. A gentleman who regularly takes a seat in the defendant's omnibus stated that the defendant was expected by his regular "whole of the way" customers to keep seats for them, especially in wet weather, during which alone the passengers to Walworth or the Elephant and Castle were disposed to ride. The conductor stated he considered himself bound to reserve seats for his regular "whole of the way" customers, and had acted accordingly. The Alderman admitted the reasonableness of the defence, but the law was positive on the subject. No seat could be reserved so as to prevent any applicant being refused admission into the omnibus. No penalty was inflicted.

An inquest was held on the 29th, on Martha Joachim, a *Wealthy and Eccentric Lady*, late of 27, York-buildings, Marylebone, aged 62. The jury proceeded to view the body, but had to beat a sudden retreat, until a bull-dog, belonging to deceased, and which savagely attacked them, was secured. It was shown in evidence that on the 1st of June, 1808, her father, an officer in the Life Guards, was murdered and robbed in the Regent's Park. A reward of 300*l.* was offered for the murderer, who was apprehended with the property upon him, and executed. In 1825, a suitor of the deceased, whom her mother rejected, shot himself while sitting on the sofa with her, and she was covered with his brains. From that instant she lost her reason. Since her mother's death, eighteen years ago, she had led the life of a recluse, dressed in white, and never going out. A charwoman occasionally brought her what supplied her wants. Her only companions were the bull-dog, which she nursed like a child, and two cats. Her house was filled with images of soldiers in lead, which she called her "body-guards." When the collectors called for their taxes, they had to cross the garden-wall to gain admission. One morning she was found dead in her bed; and a surgeon who was called in, said she had died of bronchitis, and might have recovered with proper medical aid. The jury returned a verdict to that effect.

In the Insolvent Debtors' Court on the 29th, Capt. Robert Talbot, of the Royal Artillery, having applied for his *Discharge*, the application was opposed by counsel on behalf of John Jeffreys. Jeffreys was the racket-keeper of the regiment, and Captain Talbot its treasurer; Jeffreys sued his Captain in the County Court for 5*l.* arrears of salary, and obtained judgment; thereupon he was dismissed from his appointment, and "forcibly ejected therefrom" by Captain Talbot and some other members of the regiment. He brought an action for the assault; and it came on for trial at the Maidstone Assizes, but was compromised on the advice of the Judge, by an admitted verdict for nominal damages only enough to carry costs; six counsel had been engaged. It appeared that Capt. Talbot's debts amounted to 700*l.*; 600*l.* in respect of his own costs and those of Jeffreys. Not being in possession of funds to pay this amount, he sought the benefit of this Court, almost exclusively, if not solely, for the purpose of relieving himself from the costs attendant on keeping up the legal ball with Jeffreys; and he admitted the arrest on which he was in custody was a friendly one, made with the above object. The Commissioner felt doubts as to receiving such a petition, and dismissed it after consulting with the Chief Commissioner.

At the Marylebone Police Office on the 30th, J. Gammage, master of a National School at Paddington, was charged with having *Cruelly Ill-used* a William Taylor, one of his pupils, a delicate little boy, 10 years of age. The witnesses examined proved the boy had been so severely caned for a breach of school discipline, that large wheals, from one of which blood flowed, were produced on his shoulders and sides. In reply it was alleged that the boy had behaved with great impropriety while in attendance on a lecture in the school, and required correction, and also that he was generally unruly; and a number of testimonials from clergymen, which set forth that the defendant was a man much respected, firm of purpose, and kind towards his pupils, were produced. The Rev. Mr. Boone spoke in the highest terms of the defendant, whose salary had recently, in consequence of his valuable services, been raised. The magistrate considered that the chastisement was of much too severe a nature, and inflicted a penalty of 40*s.* The amount was paid by the Rev. W. Boone, who considered it a very hard case.

NARRATIVE OF ACCIDENT AND DISASTER.

Accounts have been received of the *Loss of the Transport, Richard Dart*, with a lamentable loss of life. She left Gravesend on the 5th of April last year, for Auckland; besides the crew, there was a detachment of twenty-eight sappers and miners, under the command of Lieutenant Liddell, Dr. Fitton with his wife and child, Dr. Gale, Mr. Kelly, four soldiers' wives, and nine children. South of the Cape of Good Hope bad weather was experienced, and on the 19th of June the ship struck on the north side of Prince Edward's Islands. The waves ran terrifically high; the boats were filled and torn from the quarter, and the sea swept away forty-seven of the passengers and crew. Of these, the chief mate alone contrived to reach the rocks. The commander, four seamen, an apprentice, and four of the soldiers, took refuge in the mainmast rigging; and the wreck having been driven broadside to the shore, the mainmast went by the board, falling fortunately upon the rock, and the survivors crawled along the spar to the shore. The night was intensely cold, and there were frequent falls of snow; the sufferings of the unfortunate men were consequently most severe. They found on the shore a few blankets which had been washed from the wreck; but they were unable to obtain any provisions beyond a piece of beef, and they subsisted upon the raw flesh of birds. In the course of six or seven days they determined on exploring the island. One of the soldiers perished from the intensity of the cold and the want of proper nourishment, and after rambling about the island for no

A page from the *Household Narrative* of January 1850 describing the circumstances of Martha Joachim's death.

Woman the Martha Joachim-Miss Mildew syndrome of rejection and ensuing madness. Miss Havisham herself, who was not concvieed until 1860 – that is, not until almost ten years after the *Household Narrative* paragraph, and eight years after 'Where We Stopped Growing' – is indebted in yet other ways to the *Household Narrative* account of Martha Joachim. Miss Havisham, like Martha Joachim (but unlike the boyhood or the *Household Words* White Woman, and unlike Miss Mildew) is wealthy, is associated with crime and murder, undergoes an instantaneous breakdown caused by her suitor, becomes a recluse, surrounds herself with toylike mementoes of her past, and lives in a house with a walled garden. But Dickens – softening, as he so often did, life's own outrageous brand of 'Dickensian' exaggerations – left out such proto-Dickensian touches as the pampered bulldog, the lead-soldier bodyguards, and the splattering brains.

Selection and suppression, then, there surely is; and yet there is also a seemingly indiscriminate absorptiveness. Can scraps and bits such as these, we wonder, help shape, perhaps even help inaugurate, a great novel? And is it not curious that these trivially encountered and swiftly scanned details should become crucial parts of an artist's consciousness, or that years later they should be reproduced so faithfully, yet so wonderfully transformed? Perhaps there is no contradiction here. Perhaps herein lies the method and the power of art. In any case, Dickens was always a snapper up of unconsidered trifles; his genius made those trifles meaningful, and when an image or association held a special emotional charge for him – as the image of the White Woman had since boyhood – he unconsciously sifted out every scrap of consonant material scattered through his life, even as a magnet sifts out every scrap of iron scattered through a heap of dust.

That sifting was intensified by two reinforcing factors: by his lifelong fascination with the grotesque, and by his early introduction to the lurid delights of Gothic literature. In that terrific literature White Women abound. There are many famous late eighteenth- and early nineteenth-century White Women: Monk Lewis's white-veiled Bleeding Nun, for example, and his equally popular Fair Imogine who, 'arrayed in her bridal apparel of white', danced to damnation with the skeleton spectre of her jilted lover (both ladies were great favourites of the youthful Dickens); and the tradition of the deadly White Woman is with us still as Faulkner's ghastly Miss Emily and her dusty bridal chamber bear witness. At the same time, Dickens's woman in white is part of a separate but cognate syndrome that fascinated Dickens. For Miss Havisham is another of his daft, obsessed, disappointed, time-stopped females: Miss Betsey Trotwood in *David Copperfield* and Miss Flite in *Bleak House* are two earlier versions of this type. Given Dickens's sensibility, it is not difficult to understand why the paragraph about Miss Martha Joachim remained in his mind.

For reasons that are less clear, other portions of the January 1850 issue of the *Household Narrative* also stuck in his mind. The January issue deals, for example, with the transportation of convicts. In one section, a section eerily and crazily premonitory of the Magwitch-Pip relationship, a paragraph discussing the 'loathsome contamination' – the phrase is from the paragraph – of Australia by transported convicts, is followed by an account of how lowly emigrants to Australia, having buried their past, can expect to achieve wealth for themselves and social standing for their children. This theme had impinged upon Dickens's mind several times during these months. In March 1850, in 'A Bundle of Emigrants' Letters' (an article on emigrants to Australia that Dickens wrote for the first issue of *Household Words*), he had included one letter from a transported convict. '[My Master]', wrote the convict to his wife, 'is a rich Gentleman . . . and when you come ask for me as a emigrant and never use the word Convict . . .

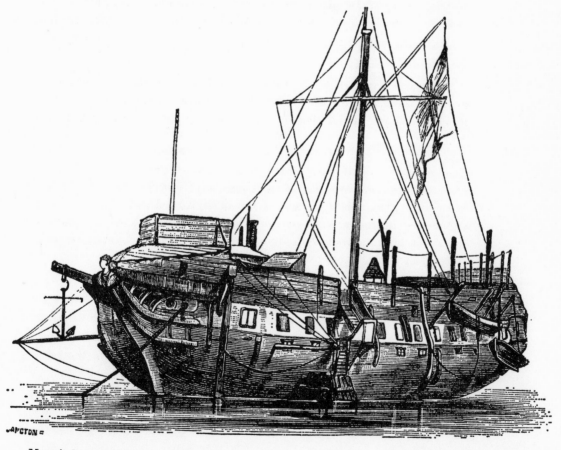

Magwitch escaped from a convict hulk such as this – a 'black Hulk . . . like a wicked Noah's ark'.

never let it be once named among you, let no one know your business.'
The account in the January 1850 *Household Narrative* quotes similar
letters. An emigrant daughter warns her father, who is about to join her,
not to 'say how you got your living at home' but to 'remember, you are to
be a gentleman if you come here; that is, you will be dressed as well as any
country farmer in Scotland – you will have the best food, a good horse to
ride on, and a farm of sixty acres to go to'. Here then, in matter-of-fact
compression, are some of the primary concerns and concatenations of
Great Expectations. One is struck by the analogies: one thinks of the crude
transported convict Magwitch, of how he hides his past, accumulates wealth
in Australia, and gives his surrogate son the trappings and prestige of a
gentleman; and one thinks also of Pip, the surrogate son, of how he buries
his lowly origins (in this he is like Dickens himself), shrinks from the returned Magwitch as from a 'loathsome contamination', and hurries, when
summoned, to the dress and food and appurtenances of a gentleman.

But perhaps the most extraordinary example of how happenstance and
association can help shape art occurs in yet another paragraph in the
January 1850 issue of the *Household Narrative*. Under the section entitled
'Narrative of Accident and Disaster', just a leaf removed from the Martha
Joachim history, appears the following paragraph:

An accident, fortunately not serious in its results, occurred on the evening of
the 7th at the residence of W. O. Bigg, Esq., of Abbot's Leigh. There was a large
party at the house, and during the night a *'German Tree,'* about five feet high,
with its branches covered with bon-bons and other Christmas presents, and lit
with a number of small wax tapers, was introduced into the drawing-room for the
younger members of the party. While leaning forward to take some toy from the
tree, the light gauze overdress of one young lady, Miss Gordon, took fire, and
blazed up in a most alarming manner. One of the lads present, whose quickness
and presence of mind were far superior to his years, with much thought and decision threw down the young lady, and folding her in a rug that was luckily close
by, put out the flame before it had done any serious damage beyond scorching
her arms severely.

Here, in brief, close enough to become forever entangled in Dickens's
mind with those other *Household Narrative* themes destined for *Great
Expectations* – with made gentlemen, transported convicts, hiding one's
past, jilted white-robed recluses, and his own boyhood White Woman –
occurs the accident, the rescue, and the wound that he will later attach to
his burning white woman and her rescuer when he comes to write *Great
Expectations*. For in *Great Expectations* Miss Havisham's gauzy white
dress blazes up when she approaches too close to a fire, Pip puts out the

flames by throwing her down and folding her in coats and a tablecloth that are luckily nearby, and Pip's hands and arm are severely scorched.

So much for this *Household Narrative* confluence of some of the central images and themes in *Great Expectations*. But Dickens's Woman in White teases us still. Why, we ask, did a convict and a made gentleman become entangled with the White Woman, why not some other equally available human events out of the scores recorded in that ordinary issue of the *Household Narrative*? Was the eccentric Berners Street White Woman of Dickens's boyhood somehow connected with the great secret of his early years – his apprenticeship in a blacking warehouse and his association with prisons and prisoners – and did the unexpected juxtaposition in the *Household Narrative* of a daft woman in white, convicts hiding their pasts, and made gentlemen merge with his own similar hidden associations and with his current position as a self-made gentleman? In other words, did the *Household Narrative* associations become meaningful because they reinforced vital configurations in Dickens's life?

I think this was the case. In fact, I think the key reinforcement may have been the *Household Narrative* statement that Martha Joachim had died in York Buildings. For York Buildings, strange to say, linked past and present, wild romance and grim reality. On the most elementary level, the linking was physical: 27 York Buildings, the house in which white-clad Martha Joachim dwindled into her maimed destiny, was only a few hundred yards away from 1 Devonshire Terrace, Dickens's current home and his home for the preceding eleven years. The macabre contrast of their separate yet intersecting lives would not have been lost on Dickens. He was always sensitive to such juxtapositions, and he was hypersensitive to time-stopped women in white. For eleven years he had passed and repassed York Buildings, for eleven years he had led his abundant life in nearby Devonshire Terrace, and all the while, unknown to him, blighted Martha Joachim, clad in white, had sat in the gloom of her York Buildings fortress, cut off from all the world. The *Household Narrative* had revealed this neighbourhood romance to Dickens. But the stunning revelation that a woman in white had immured herself for eighteen years in nearby York Buildings was only part of what made the episode unforgettable. Stranger still, and in some ways even more significant, York Buildings had older, more potent associations for Dickens: York Buildings was also the name of a street that had caused him to 'stop growing'.

The York Buildings I now refer to – York Buildings, Strand – was located just a few hundred feet away from the blacking warehouse in which

York Buildings, Mary-
lebone, where Martha
Joachim died in 1850.

Dickens had drudged as a boy: York Buildings and the streets surrounding York Buildings were his special haunt during that time. York Buildings was thus an inextricable part of those desolate and unforgiven days when his family was imprisoned in the Marshalsea, and he became, as he put it, a mere 'labouring hind', a 'small Cain'. The pain Dickens felt at this time merged with the bricks and mortar, with the streets and buildings, surrounding him. One can scarcely overestimate that identification. Until long after he was a grown man, until long after he had become the most famous writer in England, he could not re-enter that region.

For Dickens, therefore, the very name York Buildings was surcharged with blacking-warehouse and prison emotion. Coming on the name in the *Household Narrative* in a context that emphasized another old childhood association, the powerful association of the White Woman, he must have been strangely stirred by what he read. And when he realized that the York Buildings which hid this blighted recluse in white was the York Buildings which stood impassively only yards away from his own home in Devonshire Terrace, he must have been haunted by that unexpected melding of the old and the new, the fantastic and the familiar. York Build-

Devonshire Terrace, where Dickens was living in 1850.

ings probably served, therefore, as an emotional magnet that raised the intensity and influenced the pattern of his responses. It probably helped Dickens gather and then retain one of the great formative assemblages of *Great Expectations*, an assemblage composed of the hidden past and the echoing present, an assemblage that included the January 1850 *Household Narrative*, Martha Joachim, women in white, Berners Street, Devonshire Terrace, made gentlemen, imprisonment, servitude, the blacking warehouse, and his own secret childhood.

But the 'long chain' was only partly formed. In the late 1850s other links of 'iron or gold' were hammered into place. During the 1850s Dickens's imagination was increasingly haunted by the figure of a blighted woman in white, and during the same period he increasingly associated that figure with themes that were to dominate *Great Expectations*. His most striking anticipation of those tangled themes appeared in *The Lazy Tour of Two Idle Apprentices*, a series of five travel articles that he and Wilkie Collins wrote for the October 1857 issues of *Household Words*. Most of *The Lazy Tour* is by Dickens, and most of it is autobiographical; the series was designed to give a fanciful, highly personalized account of a trip he and Collins made to Carlisle, Wigton, Allonby, Lancaster, and Doncaster a few weeks earlier. In a section of *The Lazy Tour* by Dickens, a section set at the King's Arms Inn, Lancaster, Dickens interrupted his travel account to introduce a wild ghost story – I shall call the story 'The Bride's Chamber' – and this story, and the circumstances that produced it, shed additional light on the origins of *Great Expectations*.

The trip itself grew out of Dickens's need to escape into activity, an escape made necessary by one of the great emotional crises of his life. He had just returned from the distracting excitements of touring with his amateur theatrical company in *The Frozen Deep*, but now that he was home again and left to himself, he felt unbearably restless. The causes of his restlessness seemed beyond remedy. He was miserable in his twenty-year marriage with Catherine Hogarth, and he was in love with one of the actresses in *The Frozen Deep*, teen-aged Ellen Ternan. Yet a remedy of sorts was close at hand, for his restlessness was the onset of a storm of emotions which would cause him, a few weeks later, to separate from his wife. On 27 August 1857, with the storm mounting, he wrote to Collins in 'grim despair'. 'I want,' he said, 'to . . . go anywhere – take any tour – see anything . . . . We want something for Household Words, and I want to escape from myself.' At the same time he was confessing to Forster: 'Poor Catherine and I are not made for each other, and there is no help for it. . . . She is . . . amiable and complying; but we are strangely ill-assorted for the bond there is between us. God knows she would have been a thousand times happier if she had married another kind of man . . . I am often cut to the heart by thinking what a pity it is, for her own sake, that I ever fell in her way.' To Mrs Watson he later wrote additional confessions:

I am the modern embodiment of the old Enchanters, whose Familiars tore them to pieces. I weary of rest, and have no satisfaction but in fatigue. Realities and idealities are always comparing themselves before me, and I don't like the Realities except when they are unattainable – *then*, I like them of all things. I wish I had been born in the days of Ogres and Dragon-guarded Castles. I wish an Ogre with seven heads (and no particular evidence of brains in the whole of them) had taken the Princess whom I adore – you have no idea how intensely I love her! – to his stronghold on top of a high series of mountains, and there tied her up by the hair. Nothing would suit me half so well this day, as climbing after her, sword in hand, and either winning her or being killed. – *There's* a frame of mind for you, in 1857.

With these conflicting emotions – of feeling fettered to his complying wife, of blaming himself for her unhappiness, of longing to rescue an unattainable princess, and of yearning to escape from everyday realities – he set out for a two-week tour of Cumberland and the Midlands with Collins.

In the wild ghost story that Dickens wrote for *The Lazy Tour*, he combined the idea of destroying an unwanted wife – now a blighted bride in white – with other themes destined for *Great Expectations*: with a damning money nexus; with a passionate, impossible love; with a decaying, isolated and isolating mansion; and with the deadly sin of fashioning another human being to be an instrument of revenge. Obviously, a crucial transformation has occurred. Images and ideas which were originally brought together by chance juxtaposition or gross association – the Berners Street White Woman, the walled garden of Martha Joachim – have now been caught up in the gravitational field of the imagination. Early memories, later experiences, and *Household Narrative* facts, freed by time and distance, and summoned forth anew by consonant emotions, are being translated into romance.

'The Bride's Chamber', the story which exhibits this new melding, is soon told. A scheming, mercenary man, put aside by a tormenting woman for a moneyed suitor, and then, when the lady becomes a rich widow, again tormented by her and again denied her, this time owing to her sudden death, determines that since he allowed himself to be tormented for money, and since he was put aside for money, he will compensate himself with money. His plan is to rear and eventually marry the widow's daughter, Ellen, now ten, and his ward, and then to do away with her. The method of destruction he chooses is slow and terrible, but within the law – through long years of isolation, indoctrination, and psychological imposition, he destroys her ego and makes her a supine instrument of his will. She soon becomes compliant and fearful, and she performs a useless litany of propitiation; she constantly begs his pardon, pledges to do anything he wishes, pleads to be forgiven. At last, on her twenty-first birthday, he marries her, causes her to sign over her property to him, and then, while she begs to be forgiven, commands her to die. The isolated girl, deprived of any will or ego, constantly pleading to be forgiven, and constantly exhorted to die, proceeds in the course of time to do just that – the mercenary man has committed a murder which is no murder.

But for years he has been observed by a young man who has climbed a tree in the garden of the house and peered through a window into the Bride's Chamber. The young man has fallen hopelessly in love with Ellen, has received a tress of hair from her, but has felt incapable of rescuing her. Now, with Ellen dead, the young man confronts the husband and accuses him of murder. The husband, seized by a spasm of uncontrollable hate, dashes a billhook through the young man's skull, and buries the body under the garden tree. Years go by and the mercenary man, fearful of discovery, remains in his dark mansion, compounding and multiplying his purloined riches. But one night a bolt of lightning cleaves the garden tree even as the young man's skull was cleft, and scientists who later come to examine the strangely split tree and to dig around its roots discover the young man's body and the billhook in his skull. The husband is apprehended, accused, ironically, of murdering his wife as well as the young man, and hanged. But even in death the husband has no peace. Every night his unshriven ghost is haunted by his innocent victims; and periodically, in doomed attempts to disburden himself, he must tell his guilty tale to spellbound listeners – Dickens at the moment is one such listener – who sojourn in the precincts of the Bride's Chamber.

This brief summary of a Gothic tale emphasizes the improbable plot and ignores the elements that make the story memorable. Dickens characterized 'The Bride's Chamber' as 'a very odd story, with a wild, picturesque fancy in it'; he also called it a 'grim' story, 'a bit of diablerie'. Indeed, the power of the story, like the power of Dickens's letter describing his yearning to rescue an unattainable princess, lies in its fairy-tale intensifications of the most primary emotions. These intensifications are achieved by a host of touches and devices: by fairy-tale phrasings, formulas, omens, repetitions, correspondences, reversals, allusions, and the like, but most of all by the cunning use of profoundly evocative folklore motifs – the immured maiden, the garden tree, the token tress of hair, the tree-climbing suitor, the revelatory thunderbolt, the spellbound listener, the repeated confession of guilt, the unshriven and unshrivable narrator.

What concerns us here, however, is the way Dickens wedded these fairy-tale elements to the associations we have been tracing and to his current emotional state. *The Lazy Tour* is intensely and avowedly autobiographic; it records both the ambience and the events of Dickens's troubled flight away from self. Yet his personal revelations – and Dickens invariably revealed and concealed himself in his writings – are curiously, perhaps designedly, offhand, even lighthearted; his day-by-day account in *The Lazy Tour* of what he did and how he felt gives little hint that he was in the midst of the supreme sexual crisis of his life. 'The Bride's Chamber' is an exception to this generalization. Perhaps, in a kind of emotional economy, what he suppressed by effort of will everywhere else in *The Lazy Tour* (even the title feigns an insouciance he did not feel), he released through imaginative fabling in 'The Bride's Chamber'. In any case, whether consciously or unconsciously, he seems to have projected paradigms of his current emotions into his desolate little ghost story.

The white-clad bride is treated in two very different ways, both of which reflect Dickens's state. As a wife, the bride is destroyed by her husband; as the object of a forbidden love, she is secretly adored by her admirer. The husband's chief crime, the destruction of his wife's identity through the imposition of his dominating will, is a version of Dickens's current treatment of his wife, Catherine (Catherine also is a weak, self-effacing woman, soon to be put away); at the same time, the husband's crime is a version of Dickens's treatment of his 'Princess', Ellen (Ellen, like the Ellen of the story, is an inexperienced, teen-aged girl overwhelmed by a masterful, middle-aged man). In the story this destructive domination of another's personality is accompanied by massive externalized guilt. Dickens not only makes his protagonist a murderer, but requires that the villain's ghost be haunted through all eternity by the innocent creatures he has so grievously subdued. In other words, Dickens's tormented involvement with his wife and with Ellen – it is noteworthy that he cannot forbear naming the bride 'Ellen' – is partly reflected in the bride's enforced submission to the protagonist and in the protagonist's eternal contemplation of that ruinous submission. On the other hand, two other aspects of Dickens's emotional predicament are bodied forth in the two male adversaries of the story: Dickens the restless husband, in the middle-aged, unloving, wife-tormenting villain; Dickens the illicit adorer, in the young, passionate, disqualified lover. And fittingly, if one looks upon these adversaries as conflicting aspects of Dickens's emotional state, it is Dickens the husband who makes impossible or 'murders' Dickens the lover.

These emotional tensions underlie 'The Bride's Chamber'. But the emotions are wedded to images and themes that have been accumulating for years. The bride is more than a bride, more even than an autobiographical Dickensian bride, she is a version of the blighted spectre in white who had seized Dickens's youthful imagination. Here is how that white spectre appears in her new, ghost-story role:

When he came into the Bride's Chamber ... he found her withdrawn to the furthest corner, and there standing pressed against the paneling as if she would have shrunk through it: her flaxen hair all wild about her face, and her large eyes staring at him in vague terror.

.   .   .   .

There were spots of ink upon the bosom of her white dress, and they made her face look whiter and her eyes look larger as she nodded her head. There were spots of ink upon the hand with which she stood before him, nervously plaiting and folding her white skirts.

And here is the way his blighted, white-clad bride appears at the moment of her death: 'Paler in the pale light, more colourless than ever in the leaden dawn, he saw her coming, trailing herself along the floor towards him – a white wreck of hair, and dress, and wild eyes.'

The blighted bride lives in a blighted house – a gloomy version of the isolated house in which white-clad Martha Joachim had imprisoned herself; a remarkable premonition of the ruined mansion and ruined bride's chamber in which white-clad Miss Havisham would soon be immured. Here is a glimpse of this desolate precursor of Satis House: 'Eleven years she lived in the dark house and its gloomy garden. He was jealous of the very light and air getting to her, and they kept her close. He stopped the wide chimneys, shaded the little windows, left the strong-stemmed ivy to wander where it would over the house-front, the moss to accumulate on the untrimmed fruit-trees in the red-walled garden, the weeds to over-run its green and yellow walks. He surrounded her with images of sorrow and desolation.'

Added to this atmosphere of decay, imprisonment, and manipulation, and superimposed upon the figure of the blighted white-clad bride, is the corrupting influence of money. As in *Great Expectations*, the sin of valuing money more than men pervades and integrates the story. But the pecuniary similarities go further. In both works the destructive forces are set in motion when a projected marriage is broken off for monetary considerations. And again in both works the injured party destroys himself and all those around him in attempts to assuage his injury by monetary means. In 'The Bride's Chamber' the money nexus works with fable-like simplicity. The villain, who has been denied marriage owing to lack of money, seeks recompense through a marriage that will bring him money. Dickens underlines this mercenary equation by means of a refrain which recurs throughout the story: 'He wanted compensation in Money.' The refrain, in turn, is elaborated and counterpointed by dozens of images and episodes. The villain's awareness that the white-clad bride is dead is conveyed, for example, as follows: 'He was not at first so sure it was done, but that the morning sun was hanging jewels in her hair – he saw the diamond, emerald, and ruby, glittering among it in little points, as he stood looking down at her.' The implication, in terms of the fable, is clear. The villain now has his longed-for 'compensation in money', but his treasure, as this scene hints and as we finally see, is as illusory as the insubstantial jewels which glitter momentarily in his dead victim's hair. One is reminded of the glittering jewels which Miss Havisham hangs in Estella's hair. They too preach a message of false values and deluded longing. As poor Pip will discover to his endless dole, the fiery jewels in Estella's hair are fiery only in appearance; deprived of their reflected light, they are as hard and cold and pitiless as longed-for Estella herself.

The relationship between 'The Bride's Chamber' and *Great Expectations* is profound, but it is also limited. The two works have much in common: a blighted bride in white, a decaying mansion, a prisonlike bride's chamber, a money nexus, a preoccupation with crime, a focus on the sin of using another human being as an instrument, and a reflection of Dickens's involvement with Ellen Ternan. Yet the two works go their separate ways; each has its own logic and its own integrity. The brief ghost story with its pervasive supernaturalism and its folklore elements is no miniature *Great Expectations*. What is of special interest here is the way Dickens enlarged and refashioned old images and motifs. The Berners Street White Woman and Martha Joachim are now associated with larger considerations: with the manipulation of other human beings and with the corrosive effects of money. Places have been similarly transformed. The walled mansion of the *Household Narrative* is now more than a walled mansion: it has become the physical correlative of isolation, repression, and imprisonment. There is rearrangement as well as elaboration. Old themes have been joined in fresh configurations: commercial ethics, hopeless passion, and murderous aggression, brought together in naked conjunction, whisper of darker connections. A great centripetal force is silently working. The Berners Street eccentric, the *Household Narrative* news columns, the break-up of Dickens's marriage, and the other forces which shaped *Great Expectations* are being pulled into orbit; Pip and Magwitch, Miss Havisham and Satis House are waiting to be born.

But we are not done yet. Why – to probe still further into questions we cannot answer with certainty – why did Dickens begin *Great Expectations* some ten years after that fateful issue of the *Household Narrative* and some three years after the turmoil and the synthesis of 'The Bride's Chamber'?

Perhaps that commencement was shaped and heralded by the fact that the street frequented by the White Woman – Berners Street, Oxford Street – again entered Dickens's everyday life, again dramatically and unforgettably, a year or so before he began *Great Expectations*. For No. 31 Berners Street, Oxford Street was Ellen Ternan's residence in 1858 and probably in 1859 – a residence that Dickens himself seems to have procured for her, and a residence that Ellen and her sister moved to when Dickens sent Ellen's mother and Fanny Ternan to Italy. In any case, by virtue of this strange Berners Street conjunction and Dickens's latter-day visits to Berners Street, those motifs of self-wounding love which he would soon attach to the Estella-Pip node of *Great Expectations* – motifs which are versions of 'The Bride's Chamber' motifs of secrecy, forbidden passion, and social prohibitions – became merged still further with the cluster of associations surrounding his Berners Street White Woman and the January 1850 issue of the *Household Narrative*. In other words, in 1858 and 1859 the Estella-Pip cluster became further fused with the Magwitch-Miss Havisham cluster and with myriads of associations going back to Dickens's boyhood.

The 'long chain' – to use Dickens's metaphor again – was being hammered and beaten into shape; some of the great unconscious links at the centre of *Great Expectations* were now almost complete. The gestation of *Great Expectations* had gone on for thirty-five years. In the last years and months before Dickens sat down to begin his novel, the crucial associations that we have been tracing were intensifying and drawing closer together. Perhaps some stray stimulus – some chance remark or sight or sound – catalysed this highly charged constellation at the heart of *Great Expectations*. Perhaps some other influence – the publication, for example, of Collins's novel of a white-robed woman, criminals, and death by fire – quickened that waiting core. If Collins's novel supplied the final impetus, Dickens was responding in large part to his own creation, or more precisely to images and associations which *The Woman in White* shared with his own creation. For Collins's novel, with its monetary motivation, imprisoning mansion, victimized woman in white, manipulated identities, and murderous aggressions, was profoundly influenced by the ghost story Dickens had told less than two years earlier in their joint work, *The Lazy Tour*. Perhaps this consanguinity helps explain why Dickens called the sudden apparition of Collins's woman in white one of the two most dramatic descriptions in literature. At any rate, when Dickens read *The Woman in White,* he was reading an echo of what he himself had written, a recension of scenes and subjects that had stirred his imagination since childhood.

Such strange returns and coincidences engross and provoke us. But the heart of the matter eludes us still. We can look before and after, we can come close – very close – to the mystery of creation, but then we are forced to stop. The shaping process itself – the process that ultimately created *Great Expectations*, the process that selects, adds, orders, reshapes, and then finally brings forth, the process, in short, that transforms experience into art – that process goes on, as always, in silence and obscurity. The materials the imagination works on, the brute facts, even the fateful clusters of associations, are inchoate and primordial; suggestive though they are, they are the parameters, not the resolutions; they convey no rich insights, no extraordinary meanings, no reverberating contexts; they tell us of the anarchy of life, not the order of art. We value *Great Expectations* not for what went into it, but for what emerged from that humdrum given. We know the given all too well; we daily see the tantalizing gulf that separates it from art. In the *Household Narrative* as in life itself, the White Woman is no avenging vessel of fate, no godmother and no witch; the rude emigrant-father is no dark projection of his child's guilt, no fairy-tale instrument of his redemption; Miss Gordon's scorched arms are the result of an accident, they bear no witness to the searing consanguinity of sin; Miss Martha Joachim's white dress is a sign of her eccentricity, it is no infinitely varied, endlessly accreting reminder that she has married death in life.

These latter lessons, as they emerge in *Great Expectations*, the product of so strange and slow a genesis, are the province and the gift of art. For art allows us to see ourselves and sometimes to see into ourselves; art multiplies and magnifies, orders and clarifies. And in and through art, ever-remote, yet ever-powerful, the imagination works its will. The imagination need reject nothing; it can merge the hugger-mugger of journalism with the heart's desire and with the transient flotsam of life. It can fashion a new-old song from a weird Woman in White, an evocative 'title of titles', a would-be emigrant, a routine inquest, a York Buildings allusion, a Berners Street residence, a Christmas accident, an adored 'Princess', and a broken marriage – and it can make that song sing to all the busy world.

Social Conditions

Dickens's attitude to social problems differed markedly from that of later reformers, such as Shaw and the Webbs. Dickens was a man of the people, who, despite his unparalleled fame, remained faithful to 'the people governed' all his life. As a child and youth, he had personally observed the squalor and degradation in which many of his fellow men lived, and these early impressions never faded. From 'Sketches by Boz' to 'Edwin Drood', he dwelt repeatedly upon the darker aspects of social life, animated partly by 'the attraction of repulsion', and partly by a burning zeal for social betterment. Few writers have had such a direct influence upon the reform of particular abuses.

Dickens conducted his campaigns not merely through his novels but through a prodigious output of journalism. His attention was directed first upon conditions in London and then upon those of the industrial North, though there were certain problems of national dimensions, such as pauperism. He was painfully aware of the plight of the children of the poor [3], and of the cruelties to which they were subjected, whether in the course of employment [5 and 6], or in badly conducted schools [4]. He retained a horror of London prison-life from the days when he had visited his father in the Marshalsea, an institution which featured prominently in 'Little Dorrit' [7]. Of Newgate he wrote in 'Sketches by Boz' [9], of the Old Bailey in 'Oliver Twist', 'Great Expectations', 'A Tale of Two Cities' and 'The Old Curiosity Shop' [10 and 11], of the poverty-stricken area of the grim prison of Millbank in 'David Copperfield' [8] and of the misery and violence associated with unemployment and strikes [12 and 16]. Then there was his deep concern for those whom penury or vice had driven virtually outside society, the vagrants [13], and the growing criminal population [17], which lived in conditions rendered the more terrible because of the lack of sanitation [15] and the prevalence of drunkenness and its effects [14]. Finally he was concerned at the degrading influence of certain public spectacles such as hangings. It was the 'wickedness and levity' of the crowd at the execution of Mr and Mrs Manning [18 and 19] that impelled him to address letters to the press urging that such exhibitions should be discontinued. 'Dickens,' as Edgar Johnson writes in his chapter, 'opened the floodgates of his sympathy for all the neglected, unloved, and misused, all the innocent and suffering victims of society, all the prisoners of injustice and pain. Their cause became his cause.'

1 Coal-diggers in the Black Country, an example of the industrial conditions which aroused Dickens's indignation.

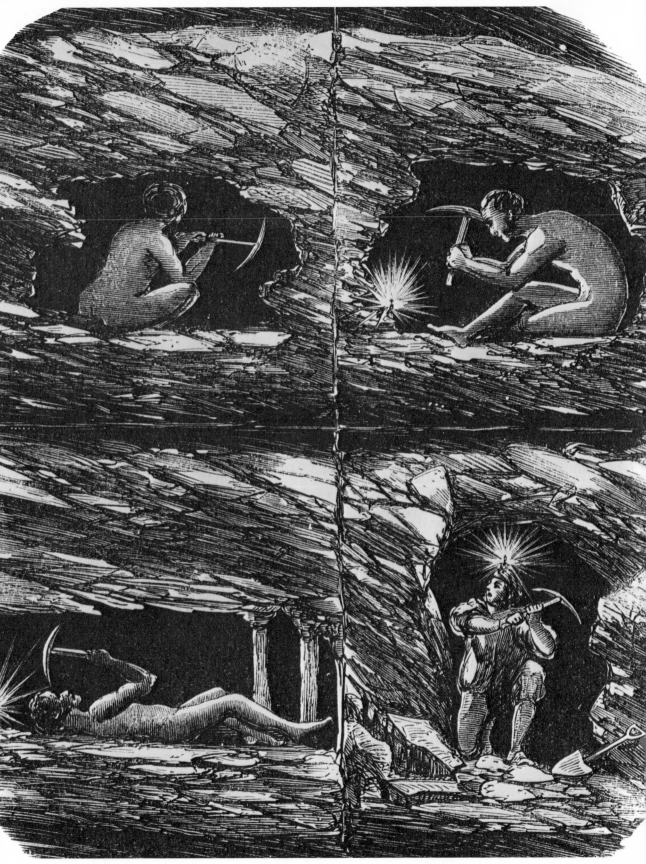

1

2

3

4

2 'Quilp's Wharf', illustration by
Cattermole from *The Old Curiosity Shop*.

3 A waif in the streets of London.
4 Page from an exercise-book belonging
to a boy from the school on which
Dickens is reputed to have based
Dotheboys Hall.

5 The death of a climbing boy in the
flues of a chimney, 1825, in conditions
such as those described in *Oliver Twist*.
6 The chimney cleanser designed by
Geoffrey Smart. Not until 1875 was
legislation enacted preventing the
employment of boys for the job.

☞ *overleaf*
7 'Little Dorrit leaving the Marshalsea',
by Phiz.
8 The fetter room at Millbank, showing
(a) handcuffs, (b) shackles for the legs,
and (c) iron rings for the waist.
9 The condemned cell, Newgate prison.
10 Drawing of the temporary galleries
in the Old Bailey.
11 The visitors' and the prisoners'
compartments.

7

8

9

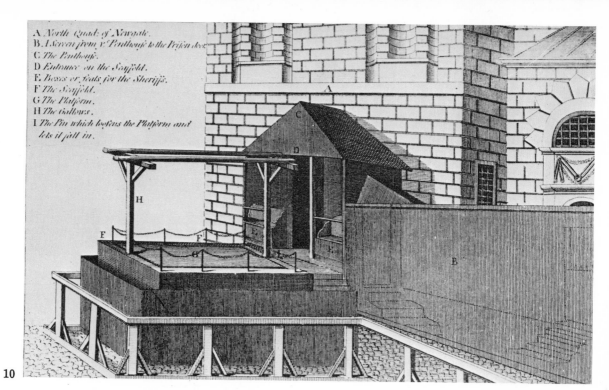

A. *North Quad. of Newgate.*
B. *A Screen from y.e Penthouse to the Prison door.*
C. *The Penthouse.*
D. *Entrance on the Scaffold.*
E. *Boxes or Seats for the Sheriffs.*
F. *The Scaffold.*
G. *The Platform.*
H. *The Gallows.*
I. *The Pin which begins the Platform and lets it fall in.*

10

11

J. PALMER

12

13

A LOOKING GLASS FOR DRUNKARDS

DRUNKENNESS LEADS TO

Murders, Rapes, Fires, Shipwrecks, Sabbath Breaking, Blasphemy, Seditions, Gambling, Fighting, Loss of Employment, Loss of Character, Beggary, Ignominy, & the Gallows.

14

12 'Procession of the Unemployed', from *The Old Curiosity Shop*.

13 'Visit to a tramps' lodging-house', London, 1858. Dickens investigated such places personally.

14 A warning of the dangers of drink, beneath which was printed a poem entitled 'Hard Times'.

16

15 'Flushing the Sewers'. It was not until 1857 that the Thames Conservancy was appointed to safeguard the purity of London's water.

16 Scene at the Spitalfields soup kitchen, 1867.

17 Jacob's Island, Bermondsey, starting-point of the cholera epidemics of 1849 and 1866, and mentioned in *Oliver Twist*.

18

19

20

Letters on Social Questions

Capital Punishment

To the Editors of the Daily News.

Gentlemen. We come now to consider the effect of capital punishment in the prevention of crime. Does it prevent crime in those who attend executions?

There never is and there never was an execution at the old Bailey in London, but the spectators include two large classes of Thieves; one clan who go there as the young & the other for the attraction and excitement of the spectacle; the other who mix in the crowd, make it a dry matter of business, and pick pockets. Add to these, the different, the drunken, the most idle, and abandoned & profligate, of both sexes — some morally ill-conditioned minds,

Dickens as Social Reformer

Ivor Brown

Reformers are of two kinds. There are the writers and speakers who expose evils and rouse public indignation. They create what is frequently called the climate of opinion and may put thunder in the air. Dickens excelled in his power to illuminate a scandal with his lightning flash of phrase amid the anger of his indignation. In this kind of agitation he was as much 'the Inimitable' as he was in his tumultuous presentation of the human comedy. His attacks on the callousness and corruption of the Victorian ruling class and its officials were sometimes so scathing as to embarrass those on his side who were trying to achieve social improvements by legal and administrative methods. They inevitably had to make use of stupid people and slow Parliamentary methods. It was necessary to practise some sufferance of dolts and even knaves. They had to collaborate with patience while Dickens used his freedom to castigate without stint.

There is the second type of reformer whose work is less spectacular but none the less essential. Collecting detailed evidence of scandalous conditions and drafting reports and new laws is not exciting; but it has to be done. For this kind of work Dickens was suited neither by occupation nor by inclination. He was too busy as a novelist, journalist, editor, letter-writer, and public speaker to apply himself to the drudgery of formulating clause by clause reformist programmes and measures, attending committees, and lobbying for support amid public apathy and discouragement, Parliamentary sloth, and factious opposition. He was several times invited to stand for a seat in the House of Commons and properly refused to do so. That was not his line and we may be thankful that he rejected all such approaches. If he had been harnessed to the team of Radical members and forced to listen to long debates, English literature would have been disastrously deprived. He drove ahead with his fiction based on fact while others planned and contrived to alter the facts. It was a fair division of labour. He knew his part and played it superbly.

There are various paths open to the critic of a cruel and unjust society. He can advocate violent overthrow of the existing régime, as did some of the Chartists. He can work through the constitutional means of legislation and Parliamentary action. He can turn to the other implements of power such as the trade unions. But to all these methods he was unsympathetic and sometimes actually hostile. Violence he loathed. His terrifying descriptions of raging mobs were not limited to the fury of the French in *A Tale of Two Cities*. His strictures in *The Old Curiosity Shop* on an English riot in the Midlands is ample proof of his social pacifism. Amid the screams of orphans and widows, Little Nell saw 'maddened men, armed with sword and firebrand,' rushing through streets full of rumbling coffins 'on errands of destruction to work no ruin so surely as their own.' If that was the product of Chartism's fanatical fringe, Dickens foresaw not an England reformed but an England smouldering in the flames of an inferno.

Of Parliament he was contemptuous. In 1846, when certain important improvements were being achieved, he wrote of 'The Great Dust Heap down at Westminster'. He may have had Mr Boffin's repulsive mounds of refuse and ordure already in mind when he used this image. That was no way in which to make allies and promote causes in the House of Commons where Ashley Cooper, who became the Earl of Shaftesbury in 1851, was steadily and splendidly at work. It was largely through the labours of that devoted man in the 'Dust Heap' that the hours of work in mines, mills, and factories were limited. His Lodging House Act of 1851, a measure of housing reform, was described by Dickens as the best piece of legislation that ever came from Parliament. Yet Dickens continued to deride the members of both Houses as snobs, sloths, jobbers and wastrel dandies. There were many such, but sweeping generalizations were unjust and tactless. There were some victories even at despised Westminster.

Dickens was far from approving of the old Combination Laws and naturally resented the persecution of trade unionists which continued when combination had been legalized. In 1834 there had been the conviction and transportation of six farm-labourers at Tolpuddle in Dorset for modest and innocent trade union activities. But in *Hard Times* there is more hatred of trade union tyranny than appreciation of what industrial organization could beneficially effect. His investigation of Lancashire, its staple industry, and the strike of the textile workers in 1854 has been criticized as hasty and superficial. Certainly it left him in two minds. He was of course sympathetic to the over-worked and under-paid men and women in the mills, but he despised the wind-bag Slackbridge as much as he loathed Gradgrind and Bounderby. He could see no future in singing 'England, Arise' if the proletarian choir were led by frothy, self-seeking rabble-rousers of the Slackbridge kind while independent men like Stephen Blackpool, a central figure in his story, were cruelly victimized by their fellows.

Trade unionism was shaking off the socialist idealism of Robert Owen whose plan for one monstrous Grand National Consolidated Trade Union had foundered. The idea, spread by some employers, that Owenism would produce an immoral chaos of atheism and free love was absurd. But there was no absurdity in the steadily increasing efforts of the new craft unions to 'agitate, educate, organize' in a more practical manner. The Amalgamated Society of Engineers, now so immensely powerful, was founded in 1851. That was the new model. Dickens could not be expected to realize that the future of working-class advancement lay partly in these developments. He saw both sides of the case and spoke with two voices. The picture of Slackbridge has been dismissed as one of his more grotesque caricatures, but he never drew a cartoon without some basis of fact. He knew that art is 'exaggeration à propos'.

That is no less true of the employers satirized. He was not wholly opposed to their belief that an industrial society must be competitive and that the prosperity of the owners and the workers is intricately involved. It was the creed of the philosophic Radicals, typified by James Mill, that free trade between nations and free contract between individuals with no interference by legislators or trade unions was the right economic policy for both parties. Dickens was not of that persuasion. He was a Radical reformist not a *laissez-faire* theorist. But in writing an article for *Household Words* in February 1854 he called the Lancashire strike 'a deplorable calamity' and 'a great national affliction', wasting energy and wages as well as wealth. He also lamented 'the gulf of separation which it hourly deepens between those whose interests must be understood to be identical or must be destroyed.' In that sentence, whose full implication he may not have fully realized, he was asserting the essential interdependence of capital and labour. He was never a socialist. State ownership means more power for the Civil Service and governing Boards which were continually exposed to his scorn.

It may be asked what did he, as a social reformer, demand. The answer is decency and generosity. 'Political economy', he wrote, 'is a mere skeleton unless it has a little human covering and filling out, a little human bloom upon it and a little human warmth in it.' By his insistence on the word 'little' he was making a moderate as well as a rather vague request. It was not one likely to make any impact on the Gradgrinds. But general shame at the existing industrial conditions was growing, and Dickens did much to stir the public conscience. He was mellowing the climate of opinion. *Hard Times* has not been thought one of his better books, except, of course, by F. R. Leavis and by John Ruskin, who was a rebel against the economists. But it was a further stimulant to the rejection of unfeeling individualism. Dickens could not solve the problem set by a capitalism which had the support of the 'Manchester School' academics on a high level while it satisfied the cupidity of ruthless employers on a lower one. But he could and did create awareness that the problem existed and he reached the complacent middle class who were happily ignoring it.

The Power of the Vote

Early in 1832 Dickens, then eighteen, became a Parliamentary reporter. He denounced nepotism in high places, but it is a curious fact that he got his first job in this profession as his uncle's nephew. That was on a publication called *The Mirror of Parliament* founded by his mother's brother, John Barrow. He soon was working also for a new evening paper called *The True Sun*. The presence of pressmen was regarded by many MPs as a tiresome intrusion; being unwelcome they were wretchedly accommodated, not in a place of their own, but jostling for room in the Strangers' Gallery. Dickens had to write with his paper on his knees; none the less he showed exceptional accuracy and speed and rapidly made a reputation with his diligence and skill.

He was there when the first Reform Bill was being passed under pressure and with threats of violence in many parts of the country. He was more disgusted by the slowness of Parliamentary procedure and the flood of verbiage than attracted by the prospect of a partially democratic Britain. If the scandal of the rotten boroughs were ended, there remained fixed in his mind the scandalous condition of the great 'Dust Heap'. The Mother of Parliaments was in his opinion a grossly incompetent housekeeper who pushed the abuses of the time under an antique and tattered carpet. What was most needed was a clean sweep at the centre of political power.

The idea of one man, one vote was in the air. The Chartists, led with peaceful intentions by Lovett of the London Working Men's Association and by Feargus O'Connor, who advocated forceful methods, put forward six demands: annual Parliaments, manhood suffrage, vote by ballot, equal electoral districts, payment of members, and the abolition of property qualifications for membership. The Reform Bill offered almost nothing to meet their campaign. But the nation was sufficiently satisfied with what it got, the franchise limited to householders with premises rated at ten pounds a year. Most manual workers were more cheaply housed and did not qualify. The country labourers were wholly excluded. The gainers were the urban middle class. Naturally the Chartists continued to pass resolutions. Since they were ineffective, there were threats of a general strike and of a march on London, but neither materialized. London was menaced with insurgence in 1842 and the citizens looked to their locks and shutters. They need not have worried. Only in Birmingham did the riots become dangerous. London went back to its business and Chartism faded out.

Dickens could not of course be enthusiastic about the first Reform Bill, whose range of enfranchisement was so limited. Even if the right to vote had been far more widely extended, he thought that Parliamentary methods,

Children at work in a
cotton mill. The small
child on the floor is
already deformed by
the positions adopted
during his work.

if they were not radically reformed, would be fatal to essential measures.
He was never fascinated with the idea of progress through the polls. In
1854 he wrote in *Household Words* that improvements in public health and
housing were more important than electoral reform.

Disraeli 'dished the Whigs' by coaxing the Tories into passing the
Reform Bill of 1867, which brought in two million new voters. Dickens was
then an exhausted man, over-strained by his strenuous dramatic readings
as dear to him as to his public, unhappy at home, plagued by a sense of
guilt, failing in health and shattered in nerve by the Staplehurst railway
accident of 1865. He was completing under pressure the twenty-six parts
of *Our Mutual Friend*, the darkest of his novels. He gave some greeting to
the new proposals which might, he thought, bring in more educated voters.
But he was not rejoicing at the prospect of a New Jerusalem. He was
apathetic to the cleverness of Disraeli, preferring among the Tories Sir
Robert Peel who had also outmanoeuvred the Radicals by making an end
of the Corn Laws and reducing the cost of living in very hard times. Peel
had had the courage to change his opinions on that issue, to the fury of
many Tories, including Disraeli. Another point in Peel's favour was

his reform of the Metropolitan Police, a force which Dickens admired.
In *American Notes*, 1842, he wrote of his attitude to democracy,

I do not remember ever having fainted away, or ever having been moved to
tears of joyful pride at the sight of any legislative body. I have borne the House
of Commons like a man and have yielded to no weakness but slumber in the
House of Lords. I have seen elections for borough and county and have never
been impelled (no matter which party won) to damage my hat by throwing it up
in the air in triumph, or crack my voice by shouting forth any reference to our
Glorious Constitution, to the noble purity of our independent voters, or the
unimpeachable integrity of our independent members.

The view that he was a democrat who did not believe in democracy was
supported by the cryptic aphorism made nine months before his death in a
speech in Birmingham. 'My faith in the people governing is, on the whole,
infinitesimal. My faith in the people governed is, on the whole, illimitable.'
The first clause could be and was taken to indicate his belief that self-
government would always be a failure. In a later explanation he denied
that. He quoted Buckle's opinion that 'lawgivers are nearly always the
obstructors of society instead of its helpers'. His difficulty was simply this.
The people had a right to elect their members of Parliament but lacked
the power to control them when elected. The people governing continually
betrayed the people governed. He had no contempt for the man in the
street but he despaired of the man in office. The ordinary person he thought
to be sound at heart but not always strong in the head.

The mob on the rampage was an abiding menace in his mind. On the one
hand there were the Veneerings climbing on the great 'Dust Heap' at
Westminster with the Barnacles clustered round them. On the other there
was the chance of social suicide through riot and looting with the Slackbridge type in vociferous command. The constant problem of democracy is
that of making politics ethical and reforms, ethical in intention, politically
practical. None was more aware than Dickens that we must count heads in
order to avoid breaking them. But the power-hungry politicians, so glib at
the polls, he thought shameless in their use of the voters' mandate. He
might have anticipated Walt Whitman's angry comment on 'The never-
ending audacity of elected persons'. What was the remedy? Benevolence
and more benevolence was the Dickensian demand. But it did not solve the
administrative problem. How is a statute to be given a heart? How was the
Civil Service to be civilized? Humphry House in his excellent book on *The
Dickens World* summed up the democrat's dilemma and concluded that
for a man of Dickens's temper and experience of life, politics remained 'a
permanent irritant that would not give him peace'.

The Barnacles

The man in Parliament needs the man in office. Administration is the essential sequel to legislation. The bureaucrat is accustomed to charges of obstruction and delay, but he can reply that laws are often badly drafted and easy to evade. The Civil Servant has a lot of tidying to do.

The early Victorian Whitehall was undeniably a fortress of sloth and jobbery. It was not only Dickens who arraigned in *Little Dorrit* the arrogant incompetence of the Tite Barnacles. He may have wondered how his father managed to hold a position in the Navy Pay Office and draw a pension after a career with intervals in prison for debt. But the easy-going Department which let John Dickens stay on was of minor importance. The major scandal was at the centre. The gross incompetence of the War Office during the Crimean War was exposed by the dreadful sufferings of the sick and wounded and by the practical protest of Florence Nightingale.

The sections of *Little Dorrit* came out in 1855 and 1856. The cluster of Barnacles is described in Chapter Thirty-Four. 'No building could have held all the members of that illustrious house.' Its principle stronghold was the Circumlocution Office; its equipment the Despatch-Box and the files in which Reports and Complaints were deposited and remained. At the head was Lord Decimus with a swarm of relatives in the 'Dust Heap' and a further swarm in the neighbouring government offices. They were unforgettably satirized as they dismissed enquiries, circumlocuted, declined to be 'precipitated' and met demands for 'something to be done' with a masterly display of 'how not to do it'.

It can be said that the onslaught of Dickens was made by an outsider in a temper, but the criticisms of Anthony Trollope came from an insider who had entered the Civil Service in 1834 and stayed there until 1867. In *The Three Clerks*, which appeared in 1858, there is an amusing and presumably accurate picture of bureaucracy drawn sharply by one who knew it intimately. The Offices of Weights and Measures and of Internal Navigation, with their senior members who arrive at eleven and leave at four and with their ignorant and idle juniors, are described in full. Entry was supposed to be by examination. Trollope said of *The Three Clerks* that readers would learn from his account of young Charley Tudor's acceptance how he himself was actually admitted into the Post Office. Charley had to do some copying to show that he could write. Nobody looked at the products of his pen. When asked about arithmetic he replied that he knew some of it. That partial knowledge was never tested. Thus he passed in. For members of a well-known family, Dickens's Barnacles and Stiltstalkings, the name sufficed for procuring an appointment.

Just before the Crimean War there had been a move to procure proper examination. An inquiry resulted in the Northcote-Trevelyan Report of 1853 which recommended the separation of administrative and clerical duties. The necessity for that was shown by the fact that at Dublin Castle the Under-Secretary was supposed to deputize for the Lord Lieutenant and advise on all criminal matters, while docketing incoming letters and seeing that stationery was not wasted. The report also made plans for entrance by genuine examination. That section of it was compiled in vain. The 'old gang' was not beaten yet. It was not till 1870 that Gladstone enforced the kind of competitive selection for which Benjamin Jowett, the Master of Balliol, and Trevelyan had argued. This brought in the best brains of the universities to replace the self-selected Barnacles.

In fighting the Circumlocution Office Dickens had a close friend and ally in Parliament, Henry Layard, a Radical member, who could speak up in the House as well as on public platforms about the iniquity of Civil Service sinecures and the cynicism of ministers who handed out the jobs. 'Can't you let it alone?', Lord Melbourne had said when reformers pestered him. One of the favoured was told that he could do in two hours the work that was supposed to take two months. The evil was not limited to the offices of state. In the Law and the Church huge salaries were allotted to favourites who left all the work to their clerks. When Layard addressed the Administrative Reform Association, he could supply the facts with a full knowledge of Whitehall and Westminster. Dickens was at the height of his powers when he created the almost factual fiction of the Barnacles and scourged the appointment system in *Household Words* as well as in *Little Dorrit*. But here as elsewhere results came slowly. Scorn is often described as withering, but the weed-killing process was faced with a dense and tenacious thicket of corruption deeply planted in and around the 'Dust Heap'. Considerable extirpation was at last achieved. Dickens had to work for posterity and his service to reform was often a legacy.

Prisons and Punishments

A gaol loomed over Dickens when he was still a child.

> 'Shades of the prison-house begin to close
>   Upon the growing Boy.'

Wordsworth had seen with his imagination the material world and the advancing years as forms of incarceration. Dickens had his young experience of the grimly enclosing walls and the castle of despair when, as a boy of twelve, he was alternating his walk to work at the blacking-factory with visits to his father in the Marshalsea. John Dickens was out of the debtors' prison in three months and the son was released from his drudgery in less than five. But both were abiding and searing memories in his life. He was a prison-haunted man from the apprentice years in journalism to those of the established master. Penal reform was urgently needed and found vigorous support from one who had been so closely acquainted with the follies and cruelties of the gaols.

The visit of 'Boz' to Newgate Gaol drove into the heart of darkness. When the mood of *Pickwick Papers* changed from the gaiety of the picaresque to the angry and sombre reporting of conditions in the Fleet Prison, he made his protest at the squalor of the broken lives. Twenty years later the horrors of confinement were to be the foreground and background of *Little Dorrit*, in which the gaol is a continuing symbol of a world in bondage to stupidity and greed. In this case some improvement came soon. This is attested by the note added to Boz's 'Newgate Sketch' in later editions.

The regulations of the prison relative to the confinement of prisoners during the day, their sleeping at night, their taking their meals, and other matters of gaol economy, have all altered – the construction of the prison itself has been changed.

Several of the antiquated and sordid buildings, so vividly described by Mr Hibbert in 'Dickens's London', were soon to vanish. The demolition of the Marshalsea began in 1842. (*Little Dorrit* was a back-dated book whose story started in the eighteen-twenties). In later editions of *Pickwick Papers* Dickens wrote that legal reforms had pared the laws of Dodson and Fogg. 'The laws relating to imprisonment for debt are altered and the Fleet Prison is pulled down.'

Pentonville was opened as 'a model gaol' in 1842. The prisoners were put in separate cells. Newgate was reconstructed with similar arrangements in 1857 and four years later a new block was added for women. Dickens had described the conditions as he saw them in his youthful work as a reporter. The state of those condemned to death was barbaric; owing to the number of capital offences there were many of them. The others, confined in 'wards', were not put to hard labour. They are described as loafing and left to rot in apathy, 'all idle, all listless'. The Pentonville methods, supposed to be humane, did not realize the good intention. Most of the inmates were accustomed to crowded homes in crowded towns. Solitude was something completely strange to them, a desolating and even maddening experience. They could not, as in a Newgate 'ward', corrupt each other. But they might find a new kind of hell in isolation. The horrors of solitary confinement were again exposed in the work of John Galsworthy three-quarters of a century later. His play *Justice*, produced in 1910, with its dreadful scene of the

frantic door-banging of the isolated men, had its effect. Mitigation followed. Once more a fiction, based on fact, altered the facts.

Imprisonment for debt is a major theme in *Pickwick Papers* and *Little Dorrit*. The system was absurd. When creditors took action the debtor was first removed to a sponging-house, an establishment kept by a bailiff or sheriff's officer. There he remained in some comfort for a short period in the hope that friends or relations would settle his affairs. If no money arrived he went to prison. Colonel Crawley in Thackeray's *Vanity Fair* was rescued by his wife from a sponging-house. He had not been suffering privation in Mr Moss's 'mansion in Cursitor Street'. There was 'a tably-de-hoty at half-past five with a little cards and music afterwards'. John Dickens

Prisoners at work on the 'silent system' at Holloway Prison: some at the tread-wheel, others picking oakum.

was removed by his son from a sponging-house, also in Cursitor Street, in 1834 and so escaped, through the generosity of Charles, from another spell in a debtors' prison.

If a gaoled debtor had money coming in, he could rent a room of his own and have food, drink and furniture brought in. For such a person the prison was a kind of compulsory lodging, shabby but tolerable. Mr Pickwick in the Fleet and John Dickens in the Marshalsea were thus accommodated. Those who had no money were massed together with nothing to do and very little to eat. They were scantily fed by charity. Outside the Fleet was a box, 'a kind of iron cage', for receipt of donations. There was no opportunity for a prisoner to earn money and pay his debts. He might dwindle

A debtors' prison, showing the interior and exterior of the 'grate'.

and decay for years while his creditors got nothing. Both parties were bound to lose. Reform of this nonsensical arrangement had to come. Debts over twenty pounds involved prison sentences until 1861 and gaoling for debt was not formally ended until 1869. The Dickensian revelations worked tardily, but they were effective in time.

In his attitude to punishment, deterrence was accepted as the governing purpose, but his general belief in 'benevolence' made him critical of the

penal severity which degraded more than it deterred. Capital punishment
he had long attacked but at the end of his life he accepted it in cases of
murder as a necessary safeguard of society. During his boyhood there had
been over two hundred capital offences, but there was a series of reductions
of this terrible total during his early life as a writer. In 1837, after the 'Boz'
account of Newgate, the number fell to fifteen. In 1861 the crimes leading
to the gallows were reduced to four, murder, treason, piracy, and arson in
naval dockyards and arsenals.

Until 1868 executions for murder could be public spectacles. Dickens
himself had seen two; a protesting critic had to know the facts of this
national disgrace if he were to denounce it effectively. In 1849 he was one

Public execution
outside Newgate, 1862,
with spectators
crowding windows and
rooftops of nearby
houses.

of a party who had paid two guineas a head for a place above the scaffold
in Southwark when Mr and Mrs Manning were the victims. He went, of
course, in order to strengthen his campaign against the demoralizing results
of such exhibitions. He saw the spectators and was appalled at their levity.
His letters to *The Times*, describing the sadistic rejoicing of a debauched
crowd including girls and boys, did not at once prevail despite the excitement which they caused. Once more the public conscience was slowly, but

at last effectively, moved. Two years before his death he knew that such a disgusting raree-show could never happen again.

Poverty and the Poor Law

In 1837 Dickens was working on *Oliver Twist*. The Poor Law of 1834 had recently stringently altered the treatment of poverty and paupers. It had rationalized an anarchy of muddled and wasteful relief. The philosophic Radicals and political economists approved of the new measure because it seemed logical. Dickens, as a popular Radical, thought it brutal and ridiculed its National Commissioners, its boards of guardians and their officials; the last of these were typified in the obtuse and callous beadle, Bumble.

The novel did more than satirize a species and plant the word Bumbledom in the language. It indicted a whole system of workhouse incarceration which the Act was putting into force and which, despite his attack, remained in force. Twenty-eight years after *Oliver Twist* he drew the picture of the outcast but stubbornly proud Betty Higden who would rather die than go into 'the House'. In a postscript to *Our Mutual Friend* he said

I believe there has been in England, since the days of the Stuarts, no law so often infamously administered, no law so often openly violated, no law habitually so ill-supervised. In the majority of the shameful cases of disease and death from destitution that shock the Public and disgrace the country, the illegality is quite equal to the inhumanity – and known language could say no more of their lawlessness.

Humphry House commented on this protest: 'No genuine attempt to meet his objections to the Poor Law was made until the appointment of the Royal Commission of 1905.' That Dickens toiled in vain was not wholly true; the handling of pauper children was not so abominable at the end of his life. But there was no major reform.

The measure of 1834 had been devised to end the scandal of a system which originated during the hard times and rising prices of the Napoleonic wars. This allowed workers to draw a dole for themselves and families varying according to the price of bread. This was paid for out of the local rates. It was obviously a subsidy to employers who could thus keep down wages at other people's expense. The ending of that injustice without a sufficient rise in wages meant bitter hardship for the poor. The able-bodied had to work in penury; if there was no food for their dependants they could go into the workhouses controlled by boards of guardians who were often chiefly guarding the tax-payers and determined to spend as little as possible on the inmates. In that they succeeded. The national burden of Poor Relief was rapidly reduced. The paupers paid for that by the miserable

RULES AND ORDERS,
To be observed by the Poor in this House.

IT is ordered by the Churchwardens, Overseers and Committee, that all Paupers resident in this Workhouse, do attend to the respective Employments allotted them on the Ringing of the Bell, (Sickness, &c. excepted,) the following Hours being appointed for their attendance, viz. from the 25th Day of March, to the 29th Day of September, from Six o'Clock in the Morning, until Six in the Evening, and from the 29th Day of September, until the 25th Day of March, from Eight o'Clock in the Morning, until Dark in the Evening, the usual Hours of Refreshment excepted; and it is strictly desired, that every Person, on leaving off Work, do wash themselves clean, and retire to the different Wards allotted for them, in a decent, orderly and becoming manner, and abide by all such reasonable and lawful Rules, as the Master or Mistress shall deem proper for the better Regulation of the House.

It is further Ordered, That all Persons not conforming strictly to the above Rules, or who shall idle away their Time in the Hours appointed for Work, on satisfactory Complaint being made to the Churchwardens or Overseers, the Allowance of the Person offending shall be stopped, (Bread and Beer excepted,) and in case of repeated Complaint, the Allowance of such Person to be again stopped, with the addition of Confinement, and if that fails to produce submission, then the Person so offending, to be taken before a Magistrate, and dealt with according to Law.

Rules of an early nineteenth-century workhouse.

accommodation and strictly regulated diet which awaited them if they 'went inside'. G. M. Trevelyan in his *English Social History* decided that 'Imperfect and harsh as was the Poor Law in 1834 it had been intellectually honest within its limits and contained the seeds of its own reform.' To the popular hatred of the Law Dickens was a powerful stimulant. He could not accelerate the product of the seeds.

In *Oliver Twist* it was alleged by Dickens that pauperism at all ages was reduced by the simple process of starvation. More deaths meant less cost. His picture was a caricature. The No. 1 Dietary authorized by the Commissioners in 1836 included meat, fifteen ounces a week, soup and cheese along with the daily ration of a thin porridge called gruel. Twelve ounces of bread were issued daily. It was dismal fare, limited and starchy. Oliver's famous request for a second helping of gruel made fictional history. What is not explained is how the boy survived the starvation described. The story needed him and so he had to keep alive – against all probability.

With more success Dickens denounced the sale of pauper children as chimney-sweeps. It was only by accident that Oliver escaped being one of 'the climbing boys' who were sent, often driven, up the flues by lighting a fire underneath them. 'It's humane', said the scoundrel Gamfield, Oliver's prospective employer. 'Even if they've stuck in the chimbley roasting their feet makes them struggle to hextricate themselves.'

Parliament fumbled with the problem of ending these wicked apprentice-ships. An Act passed in 1840 did not prevent evasion by employers. It failed and another Act was passed in 1864. Even so there had to be further legislation in 1875. No less horrible was the enslavement of apprentice children in the coalmines where, 'chained and belted and harnessed like dogs, crawling as they dragged heavy loads behind them', they presented an appearance 'indescribably disgusting and unnatural'. That was not the

Women at work in the mines, one using a harness to drag her load.

verdict of a campaigning novelist. It was the report of a Commission of Inquiry. In 1842, thanks to Ashley Cooper, an Act restricted the underground employment of boys. The age-limit was put at ten!

Mills and Factories

As a Londoner the young Dickens knew little of the new industrialism sprawling over and befouling those areas of the Midlands and the North which overlaid or adjoined the coalfields. The capital had its abundance of offices, shops, warehouses and craftsmen's premises where long hours of work were taken for granted. The London of 'Boz' and the novels is a jostle of lively individuals rich in what the Elizabethans called 'humours'. There was much self-employment by independent people. The town as Dickens saw it was not a swarming-ground of faceless 'hands' and mass-produced and regimented proletarians. That kind of existence, teeming round pit-heads and factory chimneys, he soon met and found repulsive.

With *Oliver Twist* behind him and an unknown affluence attained, he was free to travel. He took the coach to the Midlands, sampled the tranquillity of Leamington and Warwick, and then encountered the Black Country where the machinery clattered and the furnaces burned night and day. It was 'a mass of misery and dirt'. To the boy from the cherry-ripe Kentish landscape and the still semi-rural London suburbs, here was a vision of hell, and his record of the horror is stamped in ink and gall on the central pages of *The Old Curiosity Shop*. He went on to Manchester where he saw what were said to be the best and worst of the cotton-mills and declared them to be both alike. He wrote in a letter to Edward Fitzgerald that he had been 'disgusted beyond measure and meant to strike the heaviest blow possible for the unfortunate creatures in the factory towns'. Yet, except in his reaction to the Midlands, where an outbreak of mob-violence was as odious to him as was the system which evoked it, he did not for a long time produce the promised novel about industrial conditions. He knew that his readers expected the tragi-comical vein and the blend of laughter with tears and of satire with sentiment. At Manchester he had met squalor of which he did not write and kind hearts, those of the Grant brothers, who became his Cheerybles, of whom he did write. The horrors of the industrial vortex had so distressed him that he wanted time before he struck.

When he returned to journalism as, briefly, the editor of the *Daily News* in 1846 and, with continuity, in charge of his own creation *Household Words* in 1850 he kept his earlier promise of 'the heaviest possible blow'. The inadequacy of the Factory Acts was frequently his theme. The delayed attack was fierce when it came.

The Reform Parliament, many of whose debates Dickens reported, passed a Factory Act in 1833. This expanded the feeble protection of young people provided by the Cotton Mills Act of 1819. It restricted the hours of employed children. But boys, many of them subjects of the virtual slavery of the apprenticeship already described, could still begin work at the age of nine. Their day in mills and factories was limited – and it is hard to believe now – to thirteen and a half hours of which one and a half were meal-breaks.

A view of pits and furnaces in the Black Country, showing conditions such as those described in *Hard Times*.

Regulation is useless without vigilance to enforce it and previously the inspection of factories was only the spare-time and amateur occupation of magistrates and clergymen. Evasion by unscrupulous employers was easy and frequent. The Act of 1833 arranged visiting by competent officials who had a legal right of entry to working premises. In 1842 came Cooper's Mines Act, previously mentioned, and in 1845 the same champion of the victims of industry won a valuable series of reforms. His Act of that year forbade night work for women and contained rules for the safety, meal-times and holidays of the young. That these orders were wantonly disobeyed is shown

by Dickens's exposure of the disgraceful number of accidents in an article called 'Ground in the Mill' written for *Household Words* in 1854. Young and old workers were 'caught in the machinery and belting and smashed a hundred and twenty times a minute against the ceiling'. Two thousand deaths and mutilations were reported in a period of six months and it is likely that many more were never reported at all.

When Dickens founded *Household Words* in 1850 he was part-owner and so had a power which he lacked during his short and stormy editorship of the *Daily News*. He was his own master and could develop his own ideas. His policy was to win a large public. The *Daily News* had begun with a circulation of only four thousand. *Household Words* had soon reached a sale of one hundred thousand.

It was designed to mingle pleading for causes with writing that pleased. The doctrinal element was prudently kept small. The editor, able to call on the liveliest journalists and best writers of fiction, was not going to let his vast public feel that they were being swamped with humanitarian propaganda. He called his creation 'the gentle mouthpiece of reform' and demanded of his contributors 'brightness, more brightness'. His own articles were often far from gentle, but his editorial method gratified the middle-class magazine readers with its wide range of topics. Having been entertained they were more ready to be instructed on political and social issues. Attacking abuses can become a bore if the writers are obsessed with their own purposes and fall into monotonous preaching. Long before C. P. Scott said that 'the *Manchester Guardian* tried to make righteousness readable', Dickens had done the same for reform. He drove at the heart in order to plant the roots of radicalism in households for whom the fiction was cordial while the factual message was injected. Thus he continually assisted the campaigners who were slowly achieving reforms through legislation and administration.

When he tried to base fiction on industrial fact in *Hard Times* the theme overwhelmed the characters. He laboured over the book, whose length is only a third of that of his major stories. There was less of the usual leavening comedy. He had been to Lancashire and stayed briefly at Preston during a prolonged strike, but he could not catch the essence of the Northerners as he had so easily done with his Londoners. The vagrant circus folk have more reality than the men and women of the local mills. The events in the story are mysterious and Dickens seems to have been bogged down in his narrative, an unusual occurrence. There is a general indictment of drudgery among dirt, but there are no specific complaints about hours and pay. The workers, egged on by the implausible Slackbridge, are angry and vindictively intolerant of Stephen Blackpool who will not 'go with them' for reasons not explained. Blackpool, when asked by Bounderby to state his views about employers and employment and his remedy for his grievances, can only complain about muddle. He anticipates the remark of Sean O'Casey's Paycock that 'the world is in a terrible state of chassis'. The world is muddled, he is muddled, and so to some extent was the author, who could not believe in socialism because he distrusted state action and could not accept the capitalism of the time because of its ruthless methods.

In 1848, the year of European revolutions, the Ten Hours Act had been passed to the disgust of the *laissez-faire* philosophic Radicals and the fury of the Bounderby types. The Act applied to men as well as women. The appeasement did not last, as the Preston strike showed, but there was steady legislative progress in factory reform, modest by our standards but remarkable. The advance was gradual until the death of Dickens and faster after that.

The attack in *Hard Times* was more directed at a state of mind than at an economic condition. Gradgrind with his statistics which would prove anything, including the good fortune of the workers born into such a world of progress, is as much the enemy as the greedy bully Bounderby. To abolish the conception of men as units in an account book was the main purpose and the core of the message. They must be seen as human beings, not 'hands'. And how was that to be done? Dickens is back with his old salve, benevolence, which he shows to be as scarce among some trade unionists as among the worst employers. He could not find that virtue in economists and Civil Servants, nor did labour organizations provide more hope.

So, regarding such forms of socialism as then were mooted to be no cure, he could only drive away at the heart of the nation. It must be shocked and shamed into reform. The penetration was slow, but some things happened. The early Victorian age closed in the eighteen-sixties with more documented reports on work and wages, and with the useful statistics so much distrusted by Dickens. These did in his lifetime lead to extensions of the factory code. There were even Saturday afternoons free for sport. But Sundays remained a desolation of dreariness, an affliction which he had tried in vain to remedy. In 1836 he had attacked the extreme Sabbatarians in a vigorously written pamphlet called 'Sunday under Three Heads'. In the country he had happily seen cricket played on Sunday afternoons with the parson as its promoter. In the towns he watched the poor with nothing to do but loaf at street corners and get drunk on their day of leisure, while the rich kept their servants at work in the kitchens and stables and could drive out in their carriages with no frown from the bishops. This

Illustration from Burgess's *The Gin Fiend*.

was early Dickens and Dickens at his most trenchant in denouncing class-privilege and pious humbug.

The Fight with Filth

'Give them water, help them to be clean', said Dickens in a speech to the Metropolitan Sanitary Association in 1851. Victorian prudery and primness would not allow frank speaking. Dickens conformed to this delicacy. The plumbing, or absence of it, in people's houses is not described in the novels. There is no mention of the sanitary arrangements and drainage in the homes of his characters. He did not in his written and spoken campaigns for healthy living bluntly say, 'Abolish the stinking cess-pools round your houses and the dumps of dung in your streets.' But the readers and listeners must have known what he was talking about. They had their nostrils.

Water was the urgent need. Fouled water meant cholera and typhoid. There had been an epidemic of cholera in 1849. One of the principal plague-spots was Jacob's Island in Bermondsey, whose filthy condition he had described in *Oliver Twist* as the last refuge of Bill Sikes. There a viciously polluted stream, called the Neckinger, dribbled into the already polluted

Thames. One newspaper described this spot as 'the very capital of cholera'. Charles Kingsley, visiting this hell-hole of infection in that plague year, reported that 'the people had no water-supply but that of the common sewer stagnating under their windows, full of dead fish, cats, and dogs.'

The Fleet Ditch from the old 'Red Lion', showing the kind of open sewers which caused repeated cholera epidemics in London.

North London had the benefit of the clean New River, the creation of a capitalist 'projector', Sir Thomas Myddleton, in the reign of James I. This brought piped water from the Hertfordshire springs to Islington where New River Head is still the headquarters of the Metropolitan Water Board. But the Londoners of the river banks continued to draw on the Thames and the Lea and what they got was often disgusting. Dickens disliked official figures but in this case he could have quoted them with advantage. In an official report on Nuisances (July, 1849), it was disclosed that such sewers as there were pumped annually into the Thames more than seven million cubic feet of sludge on the northern bank and nearly two and a half million on the southern. The authorities on the latter side pumped 'puddle' not only into but out of the river, taking it from opposite the outfall of the Ranelagh sewer. Sludge was an evasive word. Defined as oozy mud in the dictionaries it included dung and offal of all kinds. Another polite term was 'residuum'. The report further stated that owing to the continued use of domestic cess-pools, the subsoil of London was 'sodden with seventeen million cubic feet of decaying residuum'.

The rich were by no means immune from the corruption of their air. The West End squares, where were the fashionable homes of the Dombey and Veneering class, stood over leaky sewers giving off repulsive smells. Close to Oxford Street there were cess-pools for two hundred and eighty-two houses on nine acres of ground. The lower tenements of the notorious Rookery in St Giles were sometimes flooded with their own sewage. An outbreak of fever in Westminster revealed on inquiry a network of cess-pools beside the Abbey. In Buckingham Palace itself Queen Victoria was the victim of wretched ventilation and the menace of drainage-smells. In addition to the cess-pools there were Mr Boffin's profitable mounds in many areas. On these garbage of all kinds was deposited and this was saleable for the manufacture of bricks and as manure.

'Money,' wrote Francis Bacon, 'is like muck, not good except it be spread.' In the mounds muck was money. The St Marylebone dust-heap was worth four or five thousand pounds a year in 1820. Humphry House explained that 'one of the main jobs of a dust-contractor in Early Victorian London was to collect the contents of the privies and the piles of mixed dung and ashes which were made in the poorer streets and the term was often used for decaying human excrement which was exceedingly valuable as a fertiliser.' In *Household Words* there was an article in July 1850 concerning the mounds and Dickens returned to the subject at some length in *Our Mutual Friend*. Before that, in *Bleak House*, he had decided that if people would not listen to argument they must be frightened. He warned

Christmas circular sent
by the 'Regular
Dustmen' of St Pancras.

TO THE WORTHY INHABITANTS OF

✧ ST. PANCRAS. ✧

North Division, No. 1 Ward.

LADIES AND GENTLEMEN,

We, the Regular DUSTMEN of this Parish, in the employ of JOHN
WALKER, Perfleet Wharf, Chalk Farm Road, humbly make application to you for

✧ A ✧ CHRISTMAS ✧ BOX ✧

Which you have hitherto been so kind as to give. We bring our Token—
Bronze Medal—" *St. George and the Dragon, Bank of Upper Canada*, 1857."

NO CONNECTION WITH THE ROAD SWEEPERS.

GEORGE MINCEY.   **THOMAS BARKER.**

☞ CAUTION.—As there are persons who go about with intent to defraud
and impose on you, be so kind as not to give your Bounty to any but those
who can produce the aforesaid Token.

PLEASE NOT TO RETURN THIS BILL.

the rich that 'the slime and pestilential gas' of the slum called Tom-all-Alone's would 'work its retribution through every order of society up to the very highest', and he made disease bred there far-reaching in its power to kill.

'Give them water, help them to be clean.' The repeated appeal was heard but ineffectively met. Foul pestilence could be more persuasive than good advice. A speaker for the London City Mission said that there were three great social agencies at work. One was the Mission; the others were 'Mr Dickens and the cholera'. Fear of the latter created a state of opinion in which the Public Health Act of 1848 was passed. It failed to achieve its objects because it only permitted local authorities to take action for the remedy of insanitary conditions. The nation had to wait for yet another cholera epidemic which came in 1866. Then evasion by sluggish local bodies was ended and compulsion introduced. Their administration had been far too long left to a tangle of boards and vestries which were often incompetent and dilatory. Some tidying of this anarchic confusion was achieved by the creation in 1871 of the centralized Local Government Board in Whitehall which at last became a powerful Ministry of Health in 1919.

An important event of 1855 was the institution for London of the Metropolitan Board of Works. During its life of thirty-three years, before its supersession by the London County Council in 1888, it greatly improved and expanded the main drainage system at a cost of six and a half million pounds. It also put the Thames under discipline; mud-flats and their squalor were replaced by the Embankments with their good riparian roads and solid and serviceable buildings such as that of St Thomas's Hospital opposite Westminster. Both the Victoria Embankment on the north bank and the Albert on the south were completed during the last four years of Dickens's life under the direction of one of London's great engineers, Sir Joseph Bazalgette. The Thames Conservancy was appointed in 1857 with many duties including maintenance of purity in the water. So, by 1870, the dark mysterious river of the novels, sometimes gay with its summer outings and more often gloomy and sinister, had lost some at least of its age-long employment as a poisonous drain.

When he was pleading to the Metropolitan Sanitary Association for a proper supply of water for the people he added, 'Give them a glimpse of heaven through a little of its light and air.' In the *Daily News* he had denounced the grotesque stupidity of the window tax. That was repealed in 1852. But no amount of glass could illumine a room in a fog-bound city. The horror of a 'London particular', as this sooty, suffocating plague came to be called, evoked the masterly opening chapter of *Bleak House* whose first section in serial form appeared just before the Smoke Nuisance (Metropolis) Act was passed in 1852. This put some control over factories. G. M. Young, in his *Portrait of an Age*, wrote, 'In the mid-fifties returning exiles were greeted by a novel sight. The black wreath over London was thinning. The Thames was fringed with smokeless chimneys.' This was being too kind to the limited progress made. The 'particulars' remained a potential curse for another century. Dickensian London was warmed by a swarm of domestic coal fires and none was more enthusiastic about 'the home fires burning' and the cordial blaze in the hearth than Dickens himself. The coverlet of smoke and soot was not mitigated until the coming of smokeless zones made possible by electric and gas-fires. But at least a householder in Dickensian London was no longer penalized for having a well-windowed house or shop. To that extent his calls for light and air had been accepted.

'The pessimistic reformer dwells upon the fact that souls are being lost while the optimistic reformer dwells on the fact that they are worth saving. The first describes how bad men are under bad conditions, the second how good they are under bad conditions.' Thus wrote G. K. Chesterton when considering the optimism of Dickens. It is a just tribute to a man who saw the progress of his desired reforms impeded and delayed by 'the people governing' and yet retained his belief in 'the people governed'. He never white-washed a poor scoundrel simply because he was poor and politically powerless. He was not a determinist who believed that the only sins are those of society. He never pretended that poverty and innocence went together. When villainy was to be depicted in black colouring he laid on the sepia whatever the rank of a cruel and corrupt rogue. But amid all the inhumanity of his time he never lost his faith in human nature. Some might think of his optimism as moon-struck and starry-eyed. But, as Chesterton pointed out in another essay, to look at a puddle on a dirty pavement is to see the moon reflected if the sky is clear and the lamps if it is not. To keep an eye on street-level does not mean dark despair.

Dickens had to accept the devious and dilatory stumblings of gradual reform instead of the steady march of improvement demanded by abominable conditions. The Fabian Socialists, middle-class people like Dickens himself, began their work fourteen years after his death. To the disgust of the revolutionary socialists they accepted 'the inevitability of gradualness'. Dickens could not have found them congenial company. Like the philosophic Radicals with their compilation of tabular data, the Fabians were devotees of statistics, reports, and blue books. They worked for the poor without meeting or liking them. With Bernard Shaw he could have laughed but could not agree, since Shaw despised 'the people governed' and was the least democratic of socialists. With Sidney and Beatrice Webb he could never have worked in collaboration; he would have acknowledged their good intentions but have thought them too close in their statistical studies to his Gradgrind and Alderman Filer. Yet it was a triumph of the Webbs and the Fabians to achieve at long last a drastic reform of the Poor Law which Dickens had denounced as infamous.

The raw material of social progress he provided with his anger and his imagination. Feelings, not figures, were his arsenal. It was the Fabian Shaw, once briefly a Marxist but soon 'lapsed', who wrote of *Little Dorrit* that it was 'a more seditious book than *Das Kapital*. All over Europe men and women are in prison for pamphlets and speeches which are to *Little Dorrit* as red-pepper to dynamite.' Shaw also said, wrongly of the novelist but rightly of the publicist, 'If Dickens's day as a sentimental romancer is over, his day as a social prophet and social critic is only dawning.' He added that the England of Thackeray and Trollope had gone but Dickens's England is 'the real England we live in'.

Horrified by violence and instinctively hostile to authoritarian rule, Dickens would have detested the results of the Marxist dynamite which exploded in eastern Europe and Asia. But in his gusts of laughter and in his majestic indignation he was the Victorian dynamo of reform. 'The Inimitable', he liked to be called. He was also the Unquenchable.

The suicide of a prisoner at the Model Prison, Pentonville, in 1865. Single cells, enforced silence at work and exercise caused many more suicides than before the prison was reformed.

Dickens Characters

Dramatic versions of Dickens's novels were always popular. Some were even made before the serialization of the story was concluded, and many received neither Dickens's authorization nor his approval. There were also unauthorized adaptations of some of the stories in 'Sketches by Boz'. Dickens was a strict judge in such matters, having been a student of the theatre from an early age. Although his characters have been called 'types', he was very careful to form an exact conception of what types they were to be, and he was ceaseless in his instructions to his illustrators. Years later, George Cruikshank was to claim that he had originated some of Dickens's best-known characters [12], but the claim was successfully rebutted in Forster's biography. We know that Dickens derived the name of Mr Pickwick from a well-known coach proprietor in Bath [24]. As the popularity of the novels increased, many of the characters assumed a kind of supplementary life of their own, and a 'Dickens industry' sprang up. Music [11], stained-glass [27], statuettes, china, table-linen, clothes – the familiar figures were to be found reproduced everywhere. Something of the universality of the Dickensian gallery of characters may be judged from the succession of famous actors who have played Dickens parts. One of the cleverest actors to specialize in the impersonation of the major characters was Bransby Williams [1 to 8], whose career started at the beginning of the century and extended into the television age. The world-famous names of Beerbohm Tree [13], Sir John Martin Harvey [17], W. C. Fields [19], Charles Laughton [26], Sybil Thorndike [18], Alec Guinness and John Mills [20] were associated with Dickens roles. Nor must we forget the distinguished producers, such as Stanislavsky, who have recreated Dickens stories [21, 22 and 23]. The Martin Harvey dramatization of 'A Tale of Two Cities' [17] under the title of 'The Only Way', made that novel one of the great Dickens best-sellers. Soon it was found that Dickens's novels, by reason of their construction and imagery, were easily adaptable to the cinema, and a series of famous stories was accordingly made into films. These were followed by new film versions [16] and by the enormously successful musicals, such as 'Oliver!' [14]. Even allowing for the variety of talent which has brought Dickens's characters to stage and screen, however, it remains true that one of the best actors of Dickens was Dickens himself; for in his famous Readings, he succeeded, by changes of expression and subtle alterations of voice, in giving the illusion of the presence of character upon character, thereby producing an impact on his audience unlike anything previously achieved.

Impersonations of Dickens characters by Bransby Willi
1 Grimwig and Fagin. 2 Fagin. 3 Bill Sikes.
4 Little Nell's grandfather. 5 Uriah Heep.
6 Daniel Peggotty. 7 Sydney Carton. 8 Wackford Squeers.

Oliver Twist

Brownlow

B.W.

BRANSBY WILLIAMS

Fagin

2

BRANSBY WILLIAMS
AS FAGIN IN OLIVER TWIST.

3

BRANSBY WILLIAMS
AS BILL SYKES.

4

BRANSBY WILLIAMS
AS GRANDFATHER IN THE OLD
CURIOSITY SHOP.

5

BRANSBY WILLIAMS

6

BRANSBY WILLIAMS
AS DAN'L PEGGOTTY

7

BRANSBY WILLIAMS
AS SYDNEY CARTON

8

BRANSBY WILLIAMS
AS SQUEERS IN NIKOLAS NICKLEBY

9 Phiz's preliminary sketches for
Mr Dombey.

10 Cattermole's illustration of Little Nell's grandfather sitting inconsolable by her grave.

11 Title-page of a waltz by Sir Dan Godfrey in 1871 on the theme of Little Nell.

☞ *overleaf: Oliver Twist illustrated.*

12 Cruikshank's original water-colour for 'Oliver introduced to the respectable Old Gentleman'.

13 Lyn Harding and Beerbohm Tree as Bill Sikes and Fagin.

14 Ron Moody as Fagin in the film musical *Oliver!*

15 A painting inspired by Beerbohm Tree's production of 1905.

16 Alec Guinness as Fagin in the Rank film of 1948.

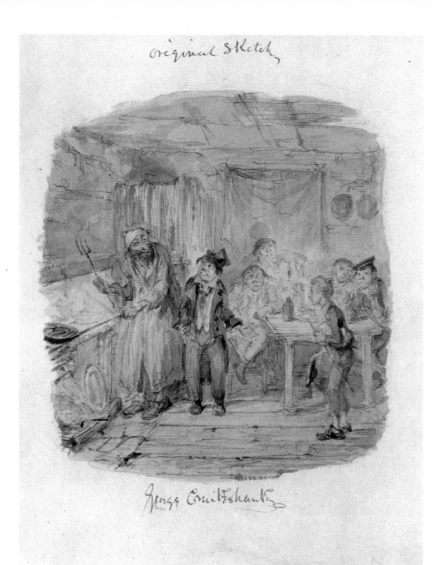

original Sketch

George Cruikshank

12

No. 354-J   MR. LYN HARDING & MR. BEERBOHM TREE   J. BEAGLES & CO. LTD.

13

14

18

19

17 M. Stuart and Sir J. M. Harvey in the dramatization of *A Tale of Two Cities* called *The Only Way*.
18 Sybil Thorndike as Mrs Squeers.

19 W. C. Fields posing as Mr Micawber beside Fred Barnard's drawing of the same character.
20 John Mills and Alec Guinness in the Rank film of *Great Expectations*.

21

22

23

21, 22, and **23** Scenes from a dramatization of *Cricket on the Hearth*, performed in 1918 at the Moscow Arts Theatre, with M. A. Chekhov as Kaleb and V. A. Uspenskaya as Tilly.

24

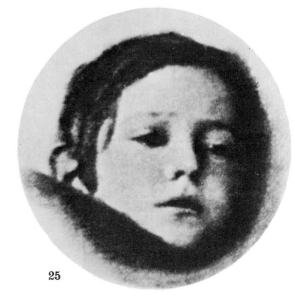

25

26

Paul and Florence Dombey.

27

24 Moses Pickwick, the Bath coach proprietor
from whom Dickens took the surname of his famous character.

25 The son of Dickens's sister, Fanny,
on whom Paul Dombey is supposed to have been partly modelled.

26 A scene from the Haymarket production of *Mr Pickwick* (Christmas 1929)
with Charles Laughton and Mary Clare.

27 A painting on stained glass of Paul and Florence Dombey.

Dickens and the Theatre

Emlyn Williams

Bleak House

From the moment when, like nine other people out of ten, I first encountered Dickens in the schoolroom, for years I thought of him as a favourite story-teller and a great writer of prose. But as nothing else; I assumed his dedication to the printed page to have been absolute.

Then, through biographies, I gradually became interested by an extraordinary second career which ultimately dominated his life as powerfully as did his literary output: so interested, indeed, that in 1951 I formed the idea of planning, as actor and adapter, a solo stage performance 'As Charles Dickens Presenting Scenes From The World-Famous Novels And Stories'. While embarking on the project, I felt impelled to examine Dickens's relation to the theatre, as writer, actor, and – above all – 'reader'. The more I delved, the more I realized the importance of my subject.

Charles Dickens, as surely as were Macready and Irving, was born with the theatre in his blood. And as over the years he sat toiling at his desk – bowed over a pen steadily forming, one after the other, a few million words – no amount of sedentary and remunerative hours could assuage a natural craving. For the footlights.

It was a craving from the moment he could walk: at the age of forty-seven he was to write nostalgically in a letter, 'I was an actor and a speaker as a baby.' Over the family into which that baby was born, the shadow of poverty lurked constantly, but they must have made a remarkably extrovert household who pushed the bills into a drawer and amused themselves. In an age where there was no button to switch on radio or television, amateur theatricals were part of family life, and of the Dickens family life as much as any – 'let's pretend!' And on the slightest provocation, Charlie would be lifted on to a table to sing duets with his sister Fanny, apparently acquitting himself with innate self-possession.

The record of make-believe and – later – theatre-going is continuous. His precocious novel-reading, as he tells us through his other self David Copperfield, 'enabled me to console myself by impersonating my favourite characters'. At six years old he was taken to see *Richard III*, when his heart 'leapt with terror' and he was left with indelible impressions; at eight he was taken to see Grimaldi, and the great clown would surely have been touched to know that he had enchanted a child so permanently that one day that child would (in the first flush of his own fame) edit his Memoirs.

In 1821, when he was nine and the family were uprooted and moved to London, his cousin James Lamert comforted the bewildered homesick child by making him a personal toy theatre which kept him engrossed for hours on end. One of the few facts of his attendance at Wellington House Academy is that he was a consistently leading light in school theatricals, making an enjoyable – and self-enjoyed – impression in 'A Miller and his Men'; and after he left school at fifteen, during his next five years as a London office-boy the tedious hours of paper-work were constantly lightened by the prospect of a 'night at the theatre'.

This could be typical of any pleasure-loving urban adolescent of the time: but this adolescent was taking a consistently growing interest in the art of the actor behind the footlights, particularly that of Mathews the Elder. It was an interest, indeed, strong enough to produce efforts more conscientious than those of many a young player already professional. At the end of the long drab day, on non-theatre evenings Charles would sit down and systematically learn long parts – and you have to be dedicated to do that, when a performance of those parts is presumably never to see the light of night! Then – 'I practised immensely (even such things as walking in and out, and sitting down in a chair) often six, seven hours a day.' Even allowing for double exaggeration, that is something.

It was during this season of the doldrums, he tells us, that he applied to Bartley, the stage-manager for Mathews at the Lyceum, for an audition, and (surprisingly) was granted it. However, he was forced to cancel the precious appointment because of 'a disfiguring illness', a bad cold mixed with raging toothache. As far as is known he never applied again, being obviously deflected by absorption in his new career of journalist.

There are invariably trivial incidents, in the lives of great men, which one has to speculate upon: if those incidents had taken a very slightly different turn, might they have been immensely decisive, for good and all? Suppose young Charles, light of foot and fresh of face (and that face symmetrical) had bounded in through the stage-door of the Lyceum Theatre, had stepped on to a vast deserted stage, and had regaled a delighted manager Bartley with an imitation of the great Mathews, complete with a graceful entrance through an imaginary door and an accomplished sit-down on a chair, as rehearsed? With his tenacity and preparation, and his known talent for mimicry, he might easily have made a strong impression and signed a long contract. What might have been his future? He was slight and of medium height, which in those stereotyped days would have automatically precluded him from the great romantic parts. At the same time, his physique and personality were not grotesque enough to put him in line as a great buffoon. He would most likely have made his mark as impudent lackeys and engaging dandies, a mark which could never have been a profound one. But enough to keep him in the profession.

Would a lifelong dream have been satisfied, at the cost of immolating vastly more important talent?

Illness, in any case, had settled the matter. Journalism presented itself as a temporary occupation, and the instinct to play to an audience was dissipated in high-spirited home charades and sing-songs.

But the theatre still tugged. At the age of twenty-four, having made up his mind to give up Parliamentary reporting and become a full-time 'writer', he made the leisure, in between his commitments, to dabble in dramatics. On his honeymoon in 1836, he amused his bride, and himself, by writing a farce: *The Strange Gentleman*, a stage version of a short piece of his own. This was first performed at Furnival's Inn 'before a few confidential friends literary and musical', when it had enough success for plans to be immediately made to present the piece professionally at the new St James's Theatre. There, in spite of indifferent notices – 'This will blast his reputation as a periodical writer' – *The Strange Gentleman* had a good run, to be followed by another gay piece, *The Village Coquettes*. But there is every reason to believe that Dickens looked upon all this as extra-curriculum diversion, for he was already making substantial contracts for novel-writing; 'Boz' was established and he was already hard at work on *Pickwick*.

And the career was set: a steady stream of books. As Dickens put it himself, in *David Copperfield*, he 'wallowed in words'. And in 1842, we see being set the typical pattern he was to follow for some years, of work-hobby, work-hobby: the hobby being 'theatricals'. On his first visit to North America in that year, a back-breaking experience for a celebrated young author, he suddenly found time, at Montreal, to stage and act in three plays.

Judging by the titles, they can hardly have taxed any intelligence – *A Roland for an Oliver*, *A Good Night's Rest* and *Deaf as a Post* – but a farce, as anybody in the theatre knows, is the most difficult and intricate form of entertainment an actor or director can tackle. The idea of acting with, and directing a group of amateurs – 'army officers and their ladies' – in three such pieces would daunt many a professional. But such was Dickens's enthusiasm and natural flair that he revelled in the whole adventure, devoting to the smallest detail of stage-management the same energies he gave to influencing the illustrators to his books.

This outlet was to be used over and over again: an energetic one, but Dickens's energies, through his middle years, seemed inexhaustible. In between – and even during – *American Notes*, *A Christmas Carol*, *Martin Chuzzlewit*, *Dombey and Son*, *David Copperfield* and *Bleak House* – he turned to acting as another writer might have sought relaxation in fishing or gambling. And every time he played, he continued to take such pains with the direction of the whole amateur venture that by the end the

Private Theatricals.

COMMITTEE,

Mrs. TORRENS,   Mrs. PERRY.
W. C. ERMATINGER, Esq.   Captain TORRENS.

THE EARL OF MULGRAVE.

STAGE MANAGER—MR. CHARLES DICKENS.

QUEEN'S THEATRE, MONTREAL.

ON WEDNESDAY EVENING, MAY 25TH, 1842,

WILL BE PERFORMED,

A ROLAND FOR AN OLIVER.

MRS. SELBORNE. — — — — *Mrs Torrens*
MARIA DARLINGTON. — — — *Miss Griffin*
MRS. FIXTURE. — — — — *Miss Ermatinger*

MR. SELBORNE. — — — — *Lord Mulgrave*
ALFRED HIGHFLYER. — — — *Mr Charles Dickens*
SIR MARK CHASE. — — — *Honorable Mr Methuen*
FIXTURE. — — — — *Captain Willoughby*
GAMEKEEPER. — — — *Captain Granville*

AFTER WHICH, AN INTERLUDE IN ONE SCENE, (FROM THE FRENCH,) CALLED

Past Two O'clock in the Morning.

THE STRANGER. — — — — *Captain Granville*
MR. SNOBBINGTON. — — — *Mr Charles Dickens*

TO CONCLUDE WITH THE FARCE, IN ONE ACT, ENTITLED

DEAF AS A POST.

MRS. PLUMPLEY. — — *Mrs Torrens*
AMY TEMPLETON. — — *Mrs Charles Dickens!!!!!!!!*
SOPHY WALTON. — — *Mrs Perry.*
SALLY MAGGS. — — *Miss Griffin*

CAPTAIN TEMPLETON. — *Captain Torrens*
MR. WALTON. — — *Captain Willoughby.*
TRISTRAM SAPPY. — *Doctor Griffin*
CRUPPER. — — *Lord Mulgrave*
GALLOP. — — *Mr Charles Dickens.*

MONTREAL, May 24, 1842.   GAZETTE OFFICE.

Playbill for production staged by Dickens in Montreal in 1842. His wife was
surprisingly successful as Amy Templeton in *Deaf as a Post*.

A sketch of Dickens as 'Bobadil'.

company had a surface polish and accomplishment that made it indistinguishable from a professional one.

In 1845 he appeared in *The Elder Brother* by Beaumont and Fletcher, and in Jonson's *Every Man in his Humour:* in the latter he played the taxing leading part of Bobadil, 'revelling in the braggadocio of the Captain's character'. The year 1848 saw him as Falstaff in *The Merry Wives of Windsor*, and in 1850 he threw himself heart and soul into a 'Charity Performance for Impoverished Authors' of a play specially written by Bulwer Lytton, *Not So Bad As We Seem*, given at Devonshire House with the blessing of the Duke himself; this was followed by a fair-sized provincial tour. Dickens played 'Lord Wilmot, a fop' and apparently his bearing was 'too rigid, hard and quarterdeck-like for such rank and fashion'.

This was followed by *Mr Nightingale's Diary*, a farce he had himself knocked together with Mark Lemon. In 1855, he considerably enlarged his play-acting scope in Wilkie Collins's *The Lighthouse*, playing the serious part of the lighthouse-keeper. Mrs Cowden Clarke wrote of his performance that it was 'a wonderful impersonation, very imaginative, very original, very wild'. In 1857, in a 'private production' at Tavistock House, he played – again a most important part – in Collins's *The Frozen Deep*. This was his last recorded appearance as a play-actor.

I inadvertently use the expression 'play-actor' because by 1857 Dickens was already involved in a form of acting nothing to do with plays.

Before turning to that most salient aspect of his brim-full life, there seems one pertinent side-question to be considered. Why, if Dickens had the theatre so much in his blood that he was determined to be involved in 'theatricals' as often as possible – why did he not train his magic pen to write for the theatre? One automatically discounts his frivolous pot-boiling contributions to the party spirit – *The Strange Gentleman* and such charade-like burlesque improvisations as *O'Thello* – why did he never sit down and write, out of his own head, 'a Play, by Charles Dickens'?

He never did, even when circumstances would seem to be turning his mind that way. It is on record – in his first preface to *A Tale of Two Cities* – that while he was playing in the Collins drama *The Frozen Deep*, he 'conceived the main idea of this story. A strong desire was upon me then to embody it in my own person.' In other words, he had the idea of a play with Sydney Carton as the central character. But he never wrote it, it became another novel. A great one, but the play might have been great too. Why did he not?

The answer is simple: the play, written in London in the year 1857, could not have been great. Dickens was one of those men of genius who, however powerfully urged on by that genius, have yet to be – at some point – thwarted by the character of the age into which they have been born. He had, at all costs, to express himself dramatically: but the medium he would choose for that expression must perforce allow him to be true to himself, to give scope for sweeping eloquence, imaginative humour, chilling morbidity – all the unique qualities we know. And instinctively he knew, without even wondering about it, that writing for the theatre of his day could never give vent to all he was bursting to give.

The first three-quarters of the nineteenth century constituted the feeblest era of the British theatre: so feeble, indeed, as to be moribund. The official stages of Covent Garden and Drury Lane offered a series of classics of varying quality, interspersed with 'new' plays which were already musty, being painstakingly stilted imitations of those classics. As for the free-lance theatres, they found themselves given over to a pit dominated by mindless gaping sightseers as opposed to playgoers; and intelligent people constantly expressed their puzzlement that they themselves, who demanded the highest standards in the books they read, would settle into a box cheerfully accepting beforehand the fact that they were about to witness an inept and vulgar spectacle not above the intelligence of a prurient potman in Long Acre.

It seemed to occur to nobody that the current theatre ought to aim at the same high standards as current literature. Even the most gifted authors, faced with the chance to make money by creating a piece for a London playhouse, were observed deliberately to lower their sights and write down to their putative public: an attitude which led to such successful rubbish as Bulwer Lytton's *The Lady of Lyons*, and caused Douglas Jerrold, a gifted and witty man, to perpetrate such fashionable stuff as a farrago of sentimentality called *Black-eyed Susan*, and to allow his *Rent Day* – which could have been as formidable and bold a work as *Hard Times* – to disintegrate into facile twaddle. Theatres were so vast that not only was it pretty impossible for the players to display subtlety of expression and gesture, there was no place either for detailed characterization in the writing. The *dramatis personae* of plays were as stereotyped as those of any medieval mystery: the hero was white of heart – brave, noble, chivalrous, a saint – and the villain black: snarling, cruel, treacherous, a devil. The heroine was a simpering symbol of purity, the farmer simple, slow and endearing, the lawyer fawning and unscrupulous – strokes bold but meaningless.

Melodrama, farce, comic opera, operetta, burletta – burletta, operetta, comic opera, farce, melodrama: the nomenclature recurs with maddening regularity, and most presentations plagiarized one from the other. No, the theatre of his time and place was not good enough for Charles Dickens the writer. It is tantalizing to guess, if he had been born a hundred years later, what his position would be in the present-day theatre. I would wager it would be that of the major British playwright.

'Nature intended me,' said Dickens once to Bulwer Lytton, 'for the lessee of a National Theatre. Have pen and ink spoiled an actor-manager?' And to Mrs Cowden Clarke, who had acted with him in *The Merry Wives of Windsor*, he declared just as plaintively, 'I should like to be going all over the country and acting everywhere. There is nothing in the world equal to seeing the house rise at you. . . . One sea of delighted faces, one hurrah of applause. . . . ' As the endless grindstone labour at his desk gave painful monthly birth to one masterpiece after another, the letters of appreciation were warm to the touch, as were the hand-clasps of strangers who stopped him in the street. But after all that work, it did not seem enough. He wanted much more. 'A sea of delighted faces . . . '

On 3 November 1844, in Genoa, he leaned back from his desk with a sigh of relief: yet another finished. *The Chimes*. To the printer as usual. But first . . .

He had an idea. That he would ask his mentor John Forster to invite a few close friends one evening to Forster's house in Lincoln's Inn Fields, where the author would read aloud to them his latest work.

Just to see.

Dickens can have had little idea what seed would now be planted, or of the tree into which the seed was to grow. But something was impelling him, even if he did not fully understand its gist – driving hard enough to persuade him to leave his wife and family behind in Italy, make a hair-raising winter journey over the Alps by sledge, return to London, and arrange the 'little party, Monday December 2 at 6.30'. Ten male friends, all distinguished men, including Carlyle, Douglas Jerrold and Maclise, who made a sketch of a scene he cannot have known would be of historic interest. It can only have seemed, beforehand, the harmless indulging of a popular author in an eccentric whim.

'High up in the steeple of an old church, far above the light and murmur of the town, and far below the clouds that shadow it, dwelt the Chimes I speak of . . . ' For years to come, the sitting-rooms of a thousand English-speaking homes were to vibrate with Dickens's words as one member of the family read aloud to the assembled rest, who sat absorbed to hear – to see, almost – the words spring into new life. A *speaking* life. Imagine,

then, the thrill of hearing those words come from the lips of their creator. '... Had Trotty dreamed? Are his joys and sorrows but a dream, himself a dream? The teller of this tale a dreamer, waking but now? ... So may the New Year be a happy one to you, happy to many more whose happiness depends on you!' For Dickens's friends it was an experience, but for him it meant far more. A blessed release, from what he called 'an unspeakable restless something'.

Back through the snow to his family and the inevitable desk. He may have harked wistfully back to the ten rapt faces – hardly enough to form a sea, but rapt – but any stirring of any sort of plan, however vague, stayed well in the back of his mind.

For nearly two years. By 1846, it was becoming increasingly clear to the most successful novelist of his day, extravagant and encumbered with family, that he could hardly hope to extricate himself from financial cares by his pen alone. He was by now bold enough to write to Forster, in black and white, 'I was thinking that a great deal of money might possibly be made by one's having readings of one's own books.' Forster, conven-

Drawing by Maclise of Dickens's first reading in 1844, to a group of friends in his rooms at 58 Lincoln's Inn Fields.

tional to a degree, dismissed the idea as unseemly: for a man in Dickens's exalted position, it savoured of literary prostitution. The subject was dropped. It took seven years for it to come up again – seven years of monthly part after monthly part – but come up again it did, as it had to do. In 1853, Dickens broached the matter in a craftily worded way – 'Surely there could be no indignity in reading aloud publicly for a worthy charitable cause, *taking no remuneration?* Where would be the harm?' Forster, indeed, could not find any, though he would have been glad to; and on the evening of 27 December 1853, in Birmingham Town Hall, in aid of the Birmingham and Midland Institute, Dickens – aged forty-one – gave his first public reading from his own works: *A Christmas Carol.* He faced an audience of two thousand people. Two evenings later, *The Cricket on the Hearth.* Another two thousand. The 'sea of faces' at last.

In December of the following year, 1854, after intense concentration on the grim *Hard Times,* Dickens celebrated with a second 'bout' of benefit readings of the *Carol,* at Sherborne, Reading and Bradford. At Bradford Town Hall the crowd was so great that two rows of seats had be to arranged on the platform, behind Dickens: success could go no further, and the future could not be ignored, not by Forster or anybody else. A new career was looming up, a second one that could be infinitely exciting: the chariot of success would gallop the heavens harnessed not to one golden steed, but to two. It would take time – several years – but it would be done.

There was the occasional charity performance, as if to keep his hand in periodically – a sort of annual letting-off of steam. 4 October 1855, in Folkestone, the *Christmas Carol,* in aid of a local educational project; December, the *Carol* again at Peterborough and Sheffield, in aid of their respective Mechanics' Institutes; 31 July 1857, the *Carol,* in Manchester, in aid of a fund to help Douglas Jerrold's widow, followed in the next months by two performances of Wilkie Collins's play *The Frozen Deep* in the same cause, at the Free Trade Hall in the same city.

In this Dickens played a juicy leading role, but after the *Carol* less than a month before, it is not hard to imagine his feelings. It was one thing to appear in an efficient but essentially superficial melodrama, on a stage cluttered up with scenery and surrounded by actors and actresses of varying merit, several unable to cope with the acoustics of a vast auditorium – and another thing to stand alone on a bare stage, communing with an absorbed audience by means of magic words created, for all time, by himself and by none other. Frustrating . . .

But he had made a great success in the play – Wilkie Collins wrote that 'he literally electrified the audience' – and these performances, solo and accompanied, were followed by a wretched reaction: bouts of depression which caused him to write to Collins, 'In grim despair and wretchedness . . . I want to escape from myself. Anywhere – take any tour – see anything . . . ' Then *Little Dorrit* engaged all his attention.

1858 was the decisive year. Agreeing to give one night of the *Carol* for the London Hospital for Sick Children, he again brought up to Forster the idea of giving public readings for his own financial benefit. Gad's Hill, he insisted, had to be paid for. And there were personal problems of the most pressing kind, which he felt could be eased only by this solution. 'I must do *something*,' he wrote to Forster, 'or I shall wear my heart away.'

Finally Forster – muttering 'cheap-jack' – grudgingly agreed. The charity reading at St Martin's Hall was to be followed by a series of sixteen nights 'for his own profit'.

From the moment the project was mooted, success was assured: the charity performance was sold out, people booked immediately for the series, and the charity audience themselves flocked to rebook. It was a tide neither Canute nor Forster could have stemmed. In the twelve years between 1858 and the last reading, in London, on 15 March 1870, three months before his death ('From these garish lights I now vanish for evermore, with a heartfelt farewell . . . ') he was constantly, while writing, going on a reading tour or planning one.

And 1867 saw a tour of the eastern United States which was sensational.

Cartoons from an American newspaper published during Dickens's second trip to America.

(Dickens's farewell to Hamerica'.)   (Hamerica's farewell to Dickins)

There were 423 (paid) readings in all, bringing in an estimated total income of £45,000 (then, of course, a staggering sum) which amounted to more than half the total value of his estate at his death. It had been a momentous decision.

Authors have read aloud in public before Dickens, and since – Thackeray, Mark Twain – but the Dickens phenomenon is unique. And is worth examining, from the aspects first of stage presentation, then of performance, then of text. How did he set about it?

The presentation had perforce to be simple, and for that very reason it was important that it should be unobtrusively perfect. The background was not difficult – simple draperies and/or screens of a warm dark colour, pleasing but not distracting from the actor (the protagonist of this adventure must in the end be named 'actor', and nevermore tame 'reader').

The actor's position? Simple – centre stage, clearly lit from gas battens some twelve feet above him, and three feet in front. Should he sit? Easier for him, obviously, but somehow the nature of the occasion, and the pyrotechnics which might be involved, called for command: a standing position throughout. And that called for something on which to rest the book. An ordinary table? Too low, and too dull for an audience to look at throughout an evening.

Preparing all this – hit and miss – Dickens must have sat down with drawing-paper and pencil, and thought. The result is a unique piece of furniture, most easily described as a 'desk' – which is still to be seen, shabby and denuded, but still fascinating – under a glass case at the Dickens House. When I embarked on my Dickens venture I had the desk copied in every detail by a theatre master-carpenter, so I know the article well. It is a small table on four slim stems, considerably longer than ordinary table-legs, so that the flat top is at the actor's navel when standing. On the audience's right, screwed into the flat top, an oblong block: on the table's left, a few inches below the flat top, a narrow shelf for water-carafe, tumbler, handkerchief for moist brow, and room for the nosegays which were periodically sent round by female admirers. At the foot of the desk, at floor level and part of it, a two-inch-high wooden rail connecting all four legs. (In the well-known *Punch* drawing of the last reading, the illustrator has placed this rail, mistakenly from memory, nine inches up from the floor.) The front of the desk is, at the top, blocked in and attractively arched; the whole, including legs and rail, is covered in a rich maroon velvet, matched by maroon fringe along the base of the arched top.

Throughout long tours during which I was to spend hours standing at the replica of this desk, I was to remain conscious of, and thankful for, the fact that Dickens had invented this affair with such craft. The oblong block on the actor's left was there not only to rest his elbow on when holding a book – not only to lean on for intimate effects (which also composed a good picture) – but *to rest the whole body*. As for the rail at ground level, it was mercifully at his service any time a leg began to protest; he had merely to rest that foot on the bar and transfer weight to the other leg. Which meant that he would be less tired after two hours at the desk than after twenty minutes in a bus queue. The desk is as useful as it is decorative, the invention of a true man of the theatre.

The performance. Above, I mention 'holding a book'; which brings us to an important question to which there seems no satisfactory answer. One can hold a book because one needs it to read from, or an actor can hold it for effect, while he remains free to turn his face wherever he wishes. The question is, did Dickens read from the printed page, or had he 'swotted'? If so, how *much* of his part had he learned? Some? Or all? His existent prompt-books are liberally sprinkled with stage-directions as to voice and gesture, but there are no indications of helps to memory.

And neither of the books devoted to his career as a 'Reader' (*Dickens as a Reader*, W. C. M. Kent; *Pen Photographs of the Dickens Readings*, Kate Field), expansive and complimentary as they are, clear up this question in any way. Neither do surviving letters and comments. This is particularly frustrating when such welcome information is replaced only too often by the hysteria of adulation, unreliable to say the least. It would seem, for example, from pieced-together contemporary reports, that when Dickens audiences, owing to their uncontrollable mirth ('screams of laughter') were not falling about – sometimes literally, apparently, as in one city several persons had been seen to roll to the floor – they were sobbing, audibly. One would think indeed, from these blurbs, that Dickens's public was seldom in a normal position of recumbent attentiveness. What happened if he got to a town where nobody sobbed and nobody rolled, but just watched and listened?

Through the letters and comments, there are vague references to the actor having been 'word-perfect'. But for a performer to become that, throughout an evening on his own, requires hours of concentration, hours which an author of even Dickens's Promethean energy could ill have spared from the piled-up demands of his publisher. (And I interpolate here, that anybody who thinks that a performer who appears in public to speak words of his own devising, knows them automatically by heart because they are his own, is mistaken: speeches are more difficult to learn for the very reason that they are already familiar and cannot make a completely vivid impact.)

The question is important because on it depends the variety and flavour of the whole performance. We do know that for the Peterborough charity performance, Dickens was persuaded by a well-meaning but misguided Mrs Richard Watson to present himself to the audience behind a contraption tall enough to hide all but his head and shoulders: could this have been because he was still reading from his book, and she felt that the fact should be made as little obvious as possible? We know too, that this absurd idea was quickly dropped, and that the 'desk' was then designed as a permanency. Dickens had not only been an actor, off and on, all his life: he had been a particularly volatile one, expert at quick switches of characterization, changes depending greatly on unhampered use of arms, legs, hands, feet. Mrs Watson's suggestion must have made him feel intolerably cramped: his whole body *must* be visible, and free.

And he must have sensed, even more quickly, the value of his eyes. While an actor is reading from a book he can still use his hands, but his eyes are firmly hooded; if Dickens really had to depend on the written words before him and had his look fixed on them – with his markedly elastic face and eloquent expression, must he not very soon have chafed to feel his eyes tethered to the printed page?

Again there is no record of his having undergone the routine combined chore of all actors and their families and friends: being 'heard in the part'. ('Cued', as Americans more sensibly put it, except that in this case there were no cues!) We know of no patient secretary or daughter, and there were several at hand, who sat and patiently corrected him as he plodded through sentence after sentence. Did he discover, from one reading to the next, that he was beginning to half-know certain passages, and then felt able (a daunting thought!) to ignore the book and get the words roughly right without it, paraphrasing where necessary? The idea of an author fooling about in such a way – and this was one who placed words in a sentence as a composer places notes – seems most unlikely.

I prefer to think, in view of no concrete evidence one way or the other, that very early on, probably after the frustrating Peterborough episode, Dickens lay down his pen, gritted his teeth, lit the midnight candle, tied the wet Sydney Carton towel round his neck, sat down and 'learnt his part'. I hope that one day proof will be forthcoming that he did.

The text of the readings. These (sixteen pieces in all, over the years) are available in print, and from a close study of them, line by line, two things emerge. Both are contingent on the fact that his world renown was of a magnitude difficult to evaluate in our day. In an age when the act of reading was the unchallenged distraction all over the globe, he was the most popular storyteller. It was an age, too, when the physiognomy of celebrities was still unpublicized enough for their appearance in public, 'in the flesh', to be a major sensation. Even allowing for the journalistic exaggerations mentioned above, Dickens's performances must have had an extraordinary effect. (Even Paris succumbed: 'Blazes of Triumph!' he wrote himself, 'When Little Emily's letter was read, a low murmur of irrepressible emotion went about like a sort of sea. . . . When Steerforth made a pause, they all lighted up as if the notion fired an electric chain . . .'). He was a legendary figure, a verbal magician who, speaking with his own voice words of his own from books which his audience knew by heart, hypnotized that audience from the moment he appeared. The only modern parallel would have been Churchill, at the end of the Second World War, touring America declaiming his war speeches. Dickens could do no wrong.

The first thing that emerges is that the books were so well-known that before the great man stepped on to the stage carrying one of them, he had not needed to adapt his material more than was minimally advisable. 'Mr Bob Sawyer embellished one side of the fire, and Mr Ben Allen embellished the other.' No need to describe Bob or to remind the audience what his job was or where he lived. Everybody knew. 'All this time I had gone on loving Dora more than ever.' Who was Dora? No need to explain. Everybody knew.

The second realization to be derived from a study of the text is to me the most important facet, psychologically, of the whole phenomenon: the text sheds special light on Dickens's atitude while choosing and preparing it, one peculiarly ambivalent. That is, the attitude of the author in him towards the actor, and of the actor in him towards the author.

In short, the actor was bent on acting. For the simple reason that he was an actor who, except for maddeningly short and intermittent bouts of performing in plays, charades, and the joyful domination over dinner-tables as the overdressed bejewelled 'Great Inimitable', had been repressed all his life. By the author. And now the actor was going to use the author.

Right from the beginning of his acting side-career, he had displayed the propensity to 'impersonate' characters in as versatile a manner as possible, as opposed to a performer's deeper instinct to seek to charm an audience with the speaking of fine words: as we have seen, in his day, outside Shakespeare there was no scope for that. All comments on his 'theatricals' confirm this – amazing mobility of expression, bravura use of voice up and down the register, 'an actor to his fingertips' – all culminating, in 1851, in the farrago *Mr Nightingale's Diary*, in which he impersonated an ancient crone in quavering search for a lost child, a testy hypochondriac, a waiter, a senile grinning sexton, and two other parts: an actor in search of six characters, and finding them too, all in one play. 'He proceeded from one to the other, with marvellous rapidity.' A field-day for an amateur who longed to be a professional: and it must have been a day – looking back – which represented a significant sign-post on the road leading to the readings.

And there they all are, *in* the readings – all the characters he had been born to bring to stage life, with every amazing trick of voice and gesture in the histrionic repertoire: he had trained his voice to acquire such a rich variety of intonation, all within a single sentence, that the Kate Field memoir gives several alarming-looking graphs reproducing examples of this. There they are, the piping child, the gruff cheap-jack Dr Marigold, drunken Mrs Gamp, the shrill dwarf, dear bluff Peggotty, the piercing screams of poor Nancy, the terrifying bass tones of Bill Sikes – they follow one another in a dazzling procession of sheer virtuosity.

All very fine, and the audiences ate out of his hand. But to me, Dickens the actor – and without having seen him, let us grant that he was as extraordinarily gifted as he may well have been – Dickens the actor did not do full justice to Dickens the author, in the material he chose to perform: I am emboldened to give that opinion after a long and arduous search through the entire Dickens canon, for my own stage material. To me, Dickens the actor chose to ignore the richest and most exciting vein in the whole treasure-cave: the descriptive writing. He neglected Dickens the man of literature.

The first time it struck me forcibly that Dickens comes to 'speaking life' when read aloud was when I once accidentally read aloud a passage from *Bleak House:* the paragraphs leading up to the Tulkinghorn murder. The lawyer is taking leave of Lady Dedlock.

'Your ladyship, I am going home.'
She bows her eyes rather than her head, the movement is so slight and curious; and he withdraws . . . He passes out into the streets and walks on under the shadow of the lofty houses, many of whose mysteries are tucked up within his old satin waistcoat. The high chimney-stacks telegraph family secrets to him; yet there is not one voice in a mile of them to whisper, 'Don't go home!'

How thrilling that would sound, surely, spoken from the stage!

When the moon shines very brilliantly, a stillness seems to proceed from her: even on this great wilderness of London, there is some rest. Its steeples and towers, and its one great dome, have the grey ghost of a bloom upon them . . .

Every noise is merged, this moonlight night, into distant ringing hum, as if the city were a vast glass, vibrating . . .

What was that? Who fired a gun? Where was it?

The few foot-passengers start, stop and stare about them. Terrified cats scamper across the road; the church clocks, as if they were startled too, begin to strike – the hum from the streets seems to swell into a shout . . . But it is soon over . . .

Then to the great climax: dawn in the lawyer's chambers, and the painted Roman pointing down from the ceiling 'at an empty chair, and at a stain upon the floor . . . at Mr Tulkinghorn, lying face downward, shot through the heart.' Beyond any doubt, Dickens the actor would have achieved a triumph for the author who had written that. He chose instead a piece of Grand-Guignol which was apparently ghoulishly effective enough to terrify his audience out of its wits, but surely cannot be classed with the above. The murder of Nancy, from *Oliver Twist*.

The girl rose to undraw the curtain. 'Let it be,' said Sikes, 'there's light enough for wot I've got to do.' The robber sat regarding her, with dilated nostrils and heaving breast; and then, grasping her by the head, placed his heavy hand on her mouth. 'Bill, Bill!' gasped the girl, 'I – I won't scream or cry – not once . . . Bill, dear Bill, you cannot have the heart to kill me – Bill, Bill, for God's sake, for your own, for mine, stop before you spill my blood!' . . . The housebreaker grasped his pistol . . . and beat it twice with all the force he could summon, upon the upturned face . . . Nearly blinded by the blood that rained down, she breathed one prayer for mercy to her Maker . . .

Is there any comparison between the two?

Then there is the novel which Dickens the actor does not seem to have even considered for inclusion in his programmes: *A Tale of Two Cities*.

It was the best of times, it was the worst of times; it was the age of wisdom, it was the age of foolishness; it was the spring of hope, it was the winter of despair . . . Monseigneur could swallow a great many things with ease, and was supposed, by some sullen minds, to be rather rapidly swallowing France . . . It is likely enough that in farmyards near Paris, there stood rude carts, bespattered with mire and roosted in by poultry, which the Farmer, Death, has had already set apart to be his tumbrils of the Revolution . . .

What a word to finish a sentence on! One would think that Dickens, framing that sentence aloud in his study, would have said to himself, 'But in public, this cannot fail!'

And even in the body of the versions he did choose to present, there is considerable evidence that the performer was inclined to turn a deaf ear to the verbal beauties of his original. In the preparation of stage extracts from gargantuan books, a surely vital process should be the editing – what to leave in and what to eliminate. Over and over again, in comparing closely the text of the readings with that of the novels, one finds that Dickens made the most puzzling decisions both ways, as if he had not taken time to weigh one passage against another. It would seem that the 'hours of preparation', which are insisted on by several chroniclers, were spent more in front of the looking-glass rehearsing gestures and vocal experiments than sitting down refining the text.

It was a temptation, of course, not to take too much trouble when he must have realized, immediately, that his audience would take anything from him in the way of words, because he was the author. Otherwise, how could he have got away with such bookish superfluities as 'Little Paul lived on, surrounded by this arabesque-work of his musing fancy', or 'Having brought affairs to this happy termination, and having ascertained, to his satisfaction, that Squeers was only stunned . . . when Nicholas had cooled sufficiently to give his present circumstances some reflection . . . ' et cetera, et cetera? And yet he omitted, from his opening passage from *Dombey and Son*, a sentence which remains one of the most effective (*theatrically* effective at that) which he ever wrote. The father contemplates his new-born child. 'On the brow of Dombey, Time had set some marks; while Son was crossed with a thousand little creases, which the same deceitful Time would take delight in smoothing out with the flat part of his scythe, as a preparation of the surface for his deeper operations.' How could he have left *that* out, and left in little Paul's musing arabesque-work? Not fair, one almost hears oneself mutter – again not fair to a great writer!

It seems apposite to add one final comment, again based on a detailed examination of Dickens's novels. It is that if he had lived a century later, an immense new field would have opened before his creative eye. For if ever there was a theatre-man with a cinematic mind, this was he. Which is obviously why his books so often make fine films, where legitimate dramatic adaptations have failed.

Lady Dedlock's moonlit journey is one of many examples.

She hurries down a side-stairway, muffled in a cloak; hurries into the garden, crosses it, and hurries out – by a side-gate – into the darkness of a side-street. The gate shuts upon its spring with a clash . . . Mr Tulkinghorn, nearing the foot of the great Dedlock staircase, takes out his watch. There is a splendid clock in the hall; with its sharp clear bell, it strikes: and ticks on again. He passes out into the streets and walks on, in the shadow of the lofty houses . . . With the blazing shoplights lighting him on, the west wind blowing him on, and the crowd pressing him on, he is pitilessly urged upon his way . . .

Again, in *A Tale of Two Cities*, the description of the Marquis's journey to his château, and to his death, reads like an inspired shooting script: a series of marvellously suspenseful tracking-shots culminating in a shock close-up.

The shadow of many overhanging trees . . . The light of a flambeau, the great château, two stone sweeps of staircase, stone urns, stone flowers, stone faces of lions and of men . . . The sound of an owl . . . Monsieur the Marquis, with his flambeau-bearer before him, proceeds to his own apartment . . . Jalousie-blinds are closed, so that the dark night only shows in horizontal lines of black. Raising his glass to his lips, he moves his head, abruptly. 'What was that?' The servant turns. 'It is nothing.'

Then the dawn, the carol of the birds, doors and windows thrown open, horses in the stable, dogs pulling at chains . . . Then, suddenly, the ringing of the great bell as the camera tracks in at the open window and reveals the mask-like profile of the murdered Marquis. Fade-out.

Surmise is always a temptation. Yes, in our day Dickens would surely have established himself as a great film-maker as well as a playwright.

But surmise tinged with regret must give way to the reality. Let us settle for what we already have, for good. A shelf of books. And they, surely, are assets enough.

Caricature of Dickens as various characters from the novels.

The Illustrators

The range of subjects, situations and characters dealt with by Dickens's illustrators is enormous. No less than sixteen artists collaborated with him over the years. They produced in all nearly nine hundred drawings, decorations and vignettes, showing in their various ways profound differences of style and technique, as well as of mood. What, for instance, could be more unlike the vivacity of Phiz's steel engravings for 'Pickwick' than the staid and inanimate woodcuts produced from Luke Fildes' illustrations for 'Edwin Drood'? Or the grotesque humour of Cruikshank's drawings for 'Sketches by Boz', and the pastoral melancholy of Samuel Palmer's 'Pictures from Italy'?— perhaps the least characteristic, though certainly among the most appropriate of all the illustrations for Dickens's works.

Dickens was exacting to a degree in supervising his illustrators' progress, criticizing their work, more often constructively than adversely, from start to finish [8 and 9]. Of utmost importance to him were the artists' preliminary drawings to establish the appearance of the characters [6, 7, 10-13]. These would be followed by more detailed sketches [14] placing them in their settings, which again would be submitted to Dickens for his intimate scrutiny; and finally came the finished engraving [15], though even this was not always approved unreservedly by Dickens, who occasionally required minor changes to be made when a plate had to be re-etched to replace one that was worn out.

The illustrations shown here are not meant to reflect the full extent of the huge and heterogeneous body of work produced to illustrate Dickens. The intention is to emphasize certain salient features such as the breadth of Phiz's range, exemplified by his illustrations for 'Pickwick' [16 and 20] and those of the more dramatic scenes in 'Dombey and Son' [17]; the inferiority in general of the 'extra' or unauthorized illustrations published without text, or for that matter without the sanction or approval of Dickens [21]; and the work of later illustrators [22-25] who have re-interpreted in their own way some of the classic scenes and characters originally created by Cruikshank, Phiz and others.

☞

Dickens and four of his illustrato

1 A sketch of Dickens by George Cruikshank.
2 John Leech by Sir John Millais.
3 Self-portrait of Cruikshank.
4 Anonymous engraving of Phiz.
5 Portrait of Luke Fildes by H. Furniss.

1

2

3

4

5

6 Preliminary drawing by George
Cattermole for the duel scene in
Nicholas Nickleby.
7 Cruikshank's first sketch of Noah
Claypole and Charlotte (*Oliver Twist*).
8 and 9 Dickens's letter of complaint
about one of the illustrations in *Oliver
Twist*, and the rejected 'fireside' plate.
10 Preliminary drawing by Leech for
The Battle of Life.

My dear Cruikshank.

I returned suddenly to town yesterday afternoon to look at the latter pages of Oliver Twist before it was delivered to the booksellers, when I saw the majority of the plates in the last volume for the first time.

With reference to the last one. Rose Maylie and Oliver. Without entering into the question of great haste or ~~as well~~ any other cause which may have led to its being what it is — I am quite sure there can be little difference of opinion between us with ~~refer~~ respect to the result — may I ask you whether you will object to ~~doing~~ designing this plate afresh and doing so at once in order that as few impressions as possible of the present one may go forth?

I ~~feel confident~~ feel confident you know me too well to feel hurt by this enquiry, and with equal confidence in you I have lost no time in preferring it.

8

9

10

☞ *overleaf*

11 and **12** Preliminary drawings by Cruikshank for 'Fagin in the Condemned Cell'.

13, 14, and **15** Three drawings showing the development of Cruikshank's illustration for 'The Burglary'.

Mr & Mrs Bumble & wife

Rose & Nancy

Noah & Fagin

woodcut.

First idea & Sketch for
Fagin in the Condemned
Cell—

George Cruikshank

The Cell—

George Cruikshank

Fagin in the Condemned Cell.

14

15

16

17

16 An early version of 'Mrs Bardell
faints in Mr Pickwick's Arms' by Phiz.

17 One of Phiz's 'dark plates' for
Dombey and Son.

18 19

20

21

18 and **19** 'Nicholas instructs Smike in the art of acting' by Phiz, together with the steel from which the impression was taken.

20 and **21** Phiz's illustration, 'The Fat Boy awake again', from *Pickwick Papers*, and an unauthorized drawing by T. Onwhyn of the same subject.

22

23

24

25

Later illustrators.
22 Fred Barnard (*Bleak House*).
23 Arthur Buckland (*The Old Curiosity Shop*).
24 Edward Ardizzone (*Nicholas Nickleby*).
25 Barnett Freedman (*Oliver Twist*).

Dickens and his Illustrators

Nicolas Bentley

No author ever gave greater inspiration to an illustrator than Dickens. To the richness of his imagination were added personal encouragement and criticism, as well as detailed descriptions of scenes and characters. This does not mean, though, that the artist's job was always easy.

From childhood we grow up with the idea that an illustration is simply a picture of something the author has described. If that were so, Blake's illustrations for *The Divine Comedy*, or Picasso's for *Lysistrata* would not exist. Illustration is more than mere 'pictorial elucidation', as the dictionary says. It is, or should be, a contribution in its own right to the reader's appreciation of the text.

The artists who originally illustrated Dickens – and there were sixteen altogether – were mostly of a fairly pedestrian order, but two of them, Cruikshank and Phiz, may be said to have made distinctive contributions to the understanding and enjoyment of Dickens.

The sixteen who illustrated Dickens's works in his lifetime contributed between them nearly 900 drawings, vignettes and graphic initials; and this does not include illustrations commissioned by piratical publishers in America, or the innumerable folios of 'extra' or unauthorized illustrations without text which were brought out by publishers and artists eager to climb on the bandwagon of Dickens's fame.

Who can say to what extent his happy conjunction with Phiz contributed to Dickens's early success? That he would have made the grade in any case, with or without illustrations, is obvious, but whether he would have made it so quickly in a collaboration less effective or less congenial is another matter. One is reminded of Surtees, who for twelve years wrote humorous sketches with only modest success until 1853, when Leech appeared on the scene as the illustrator of *Mr Sponge's Sporting Tour*, and Surtees's reputation rocketed. Much the same thing had happened when *Pickwick Papers* first appeared as a serial in 1836.[1] Only a few weeks earlier, *Sketches by Boz* had been published in book form and had been remarkably successful. In spite of this, *Pickwick* at first hung fire until the appearance of Sam Weller in the fourth of the monthly parts. And it was in this issue that Phiz's illustrations were seen for the first time.

Dickens had begun his career with a very considerable advantage. *Sketches by Boz*, published in February 1836, was illustrated by the best-known humorous artist of the day, George Cruikshank. His likeness, as well as that of Dickens, may be seen in a number of the illustrations. By his own account – without which it would certainly be difficult to recognize them – they are the two aeronauts in the balloon ascent on the title-page. More obviously, they are to be seen as two of the ushers in the illustration for 'Public Dinners', Cruikshank on the right with black whiskers and a white waistcoat, Dickens in the centre of the picture. Dickens is also shown in 'Early Coaches', as the young man buying a ticket; in 'A Pickpocket in Custody', walking behind the Bow Street runners; and in 'Making a Night of It', where he is sitting on the right in 'The Slips at the City Theatre'.

Cruikshank illustrated only one of Dickens's novels and that was *Oliver Twist* (1838). Why it was that he did not illustrate any of the others is something of a mystery.[2] Possibly he was too busy, for when Dickens's career began Cruikshank's was already in full swing and his reputation

'Public Dinners' by George Cruikshank, an illustration to *Sketches by Boz*.

was at its height. After the success of the *Sketches* and the far greater success of *Oliver Twist*, he would seem to have been the obvious choice as the illustrator of *Nicholas Nickleby* (1838). But in the meantime, Phiz's association with Dickens had become firmly established in the public's mind by *Pickwick Papers*; so perhaps Dickens's publishers, Chapman and Hall, and no doubt Dickens himself, may have thought it best to let the association with Phiz continue: an arrangement, incidentally, that was a good deal less expensive than employing Cruikshank.

Another reason may have been that Dickens, who had chafed at what he thought to be Cruikshank's slowness in delivering some of the illustrations for the *Sketches*, foresaw a possibility of friction developing between them. Cruikshank was full of ideas and also extremely conceited. He may well have shown signs of wanting to dominate their partnership – a situation to which Dickens would certainly not have consented – and had in fact suggested to Chapman and Hall at one stage that he should make certain changes in the second series of the *Sketches*. Dickens, when this was reported to him, replied with a note of justified sarcasm that he would have been glad to have preserved such 'emendations as "curiosities of Literature" '. It is significant of the way in which their relations might have developed that Cruikshank in his old age, when Dickens was dead, claimed in a letter to *The Times* that he himself had originated the idea of *Oliver Twist* and supported the assertion with a considerable amount of detail. However, later research makes it seem certain that there was no foundation for this claim.

Whatever the reason for Cruikshank's collaboration with Dickens coming to an end, posterity is certainly the loser. In the fertility of his imagination, in the acuteness of his eye for the small conceits as well as the larger imperfections of mankind, and in his enormous technical skill, few other English satirical artists have equalled Cruikshank. We are so used to the characters drawn by Phiz that it is difficult to imagine or accept other interpretations of them. Yet how much more memorable some of them might have been if they had had the vigour and intensity which Cruikshank gave to every one he drew. His characters may be lacking in grace or dignity, as they often are; they may seem slovenly, eccentric, even weird; but there is nothing sentimental or demure as there often is in Phiz's characters. Chadband, Clennam, Jaggers, Miss Murdstone, Miss Flite and Miss Podsnap, were each in their various ways subject to the passions, to the pleasures, to the alarms and frustrations of life; each cherished or reluctantly harboured secrets, or displayed eccentricities of mind or conduct all of which, as described by Dickens, often seem a little larger than life, but which life as often shows to be scarcely exaggerated. These subtle enlargements, which serve to underline their truth to nature, are seldom realized by Phiz, but give Cruikshank's characters a remarkable liveliness and unmistakable individuality. In *Oliver Twist*, the sweep to whom Oliver narrowly escaped being bound apprentice, Mrs Corney, Mrs Sowerberry, and Blathers and Duff, the Bow Street runners, are not only creatures of flesh and blood; they have strong and distinct personalities. Whereas Phiz's lesser characters often become mere caricatures of types; such, for instance, are the Misses Pecksniff, Mr Mantalini, and Mrs Gummidge; but every face in a crowd by Cruikshank is that of an individual.

It is no disparagement of Phiz to rate the work of Cruikshank higher than his in the pantheon of Dickensian illustration. Cruikshank was for one thing infinitely more experienced and more versatile and there was also from time to time an element of savagery in his work, the effect of which was beyond anything that Phiz might have achieved, as in the more sordid episodes in *Oliver Twist*. Though Phiz might well have illustrated other scenes with equal success, the more horrific episodes, such as Sikes's 'Last Chance' or 'Fagin in the Condemned Cell', would never have had the black ferocity that Cruikshank gave them. Phiz, on the other hand, excelled in scenes which, without being actually horrific, are full of menace, such as the picture in *Bleak House* of 'Tom-All-Alone's' or 'Making off' in *Little Dorrit*.

Although Phiz was never the equal of Cruikshank in draughtsmanship, no alliance between an author and an illustrator was ever more fruitful than that between himself and Dickens. As Chesterton remarked, 'They were as suited to each other and to the common creation of a unique thing, as Gilbert and Sullivan. No other illustrator ever created the true Dickens characters with the precise and correct quantum of exaggeration'.[3]

That the two came together was more by accident than by design. Robert Seymour, the artist whom Chapman and Hall first chose as the illustrator of *Pickwick Papers*, committed suicide after making seven drawings in all for the first and second of the monthly parts. For the third part two drawings were made by R. W. Buss, but Chapman and Hall found them disappointing, and so did Dickens. Buss, incidentally, was the father of a Victorian as distinguished in her own sphere as Dickens was in his, but a lady of whom he would have found it hard to approve – Frances Mary Buss, whose pioneer work in promoting education for girls did much to dispel the impression that her sex was bird-brained, cloying and fragile, which was Dickens's ideal of womanhood, epitomized in Dora Spenlow.

A number of artists were eager to succeed Buss, among them Leech and Thackeray. For what reason they were turned down in favour of Phiz (not then known as such, but by his baptismal name of Hablôt Knight Browne) is not clear. Both of them were already on the way to becoming well known, whereas Browne, who was barely twenty-one, had scarcely been heard of. Possibly it was the technical experience he had gained as an engraver's apprentice that tipped the scales. Whatever the reason, the choice was a happy and fruitful one. Of the thirteen novels that followed *Pickwick*, all but the last four were illustrated by Phiz, who drew altogether over five hundred illustrations, title-page vignettes and wrapper designs.

Like many humorous artists, Phiz found in his talent for caricature a compensation for weakness in draughtsmanship. He never learnt to draw with the same subtlety as, for instance, Keene, Leech, or Richard Doyle, and his weakness in this respect gives some of his work a tentative appearance in comparison with theirs. His figures especially often have a stiffness and at the same time a fragility that are quite distinct from the deliberate exaggeration of certain traits or features. Obvious examples of this weakness are to be seen in the illustrations to *Sketches of Young Gentlemen* (1838), written by Dickens but published anonymously. These admittedly are early drawings; nevertheless they are scarcely recognizable as being by the same artist who illustrated *David Copperfield* (1849) or *Little Dorrit* (1855).

Even in these later works, however, traces of this weakness persist. In *Copperfield*, Mr Spenlow, introducing Dora to David ('I fall into captivity'), is drawn so feebly as to make his right arm appear badly deformed. The figure of David himself carving an unrecognizable, though clearly described, leg of mutton ('Our housekeeping'), is equally inept. And in *Little Dorrit*

'A Sudden Recognition, Unexpected on Both Sides' by Phiz, an illustration to *Nicholas Nickleby* (1838).

Tattycoram, discovered weeping by Miss Wade ('Under the Microscope'), is no more than a disjointed lay figure.

In spite of this handicap, none of Dickens's illustrators, not even Cruikshank, were as successful as Phiz in interpreting the sinister as distinct from the barbarous side of Dickens's imagination. In what are known among bibliophiles as 'the dark plates', he achieved an effect quite different from that of his other work. An early example of this effect is the illustration called 'On the Dark Road' in *Dombey and Son*, in which Carker is fleeing from Dijon in the night. The horses clattering over the rough road, the anxious figure looking back from the carriage, the streaks of dawn on the distant horizon, the clump of sodden reeds in the foreground are all overshadowed by a velvety gloom that seems to charge the whole scene with menace.

A much more elaborate process was involved in producing these dark plates than in making an ordinary engraving, but its use was justified by the results that Phiz achieved, notably in *Bleak House*, in which the best of these plates appear, and in *Little Dorrit*.

In the academic tradition within which Phiz worked, sound draughtsmanship was highly important. Though he never mastered it completely, with time and experience his work achieved a good deal more assurance than it possessed at first. Both in composition and technical skill the illustrations for *Dombey and Son* (1848) are far superior to those for *Nicholas Nickleby* (1838). The jumbled and fragmentary effect of the scene, for instance, in which Mr Squeers collars Smike at Newgate is quite unlike some of the elaborate but much more harmonious designs for *Dombey*.

'Coming Home from Church' by Phiz, an illustration to *Dombey and Son* (1848).

Crowded scenes such as 'Coming home from Church' or 'Mrs Dombey at
Home', in spite of their abundant detail, have a unity of design and a
command of perspective that are often lacking in Phiz's earlier work, even
up to the time of *Martin Chuzzlewit* (1844).

For these improvements, Phiz's perseverance and his own sensibility
were no doubt responsible. But improvements in characterization, facial
appearance, gestures, and deportment, may well have been due to a
considerable extent to Dickens, who from the very beginning showed a
keen, not to say masterful, interest in the illustrations for all his works.
He knew precisely the effect he wanted and did all he could to see that the
artist produced it. At the ripe age of twenty-six he did not hesitate to take
Cruikshank to task, indifferent to his reputation and the fact that he was
twenty years older, for what he considered to be a bad illustration for
Oliver Twist. The now familiar drawing of 'Rose Maylie and Oliver', the last
in the book, a pious and undistinguished picture of them, is a substitute
for an earlier attempt at the same subject known as the 'Fireside' plate, of
which only a very few copies appeared before it was withdrawn. Dickens's
letter to Cruikshank on the subject was tactful but firm:

> I returned suddenly to town yesterday afternoon, to look at the latter pages of
> 'Oliver Twist' before it was delivered to the booksellers, when I saw the majority
> of the plates in the last volume for the first time.
>
> With reference to the last one – Rose Maylie and Oliver – without entering into
> the question of great haste, or any other cause, which may have led to its being
> what it is, I am quite sure there can be little difference of opinion between us
> with respect to the result. May I ask you whether you will object to designing
> this plate afresh, and doing so *at once*, in order that as few impressions as
> possible of the present one may go forth?
>
> I feel confident you know me too well to feel hurt by this enquiry and with
> equal confidence in you, I have lost no time in preferring it.

Dickens's disapproval of the drawing may have been instigated by
Forster, his attorney and self-appointed agent, for Forster's views,
especially in matters likely to affect his protégé, were firm and often
arrogant. He had previously written in his usual high-handed way to the
publisher, Richard Bentley, about this drawing, and another:

> . . . I allude to Mr Cruikshank's plates at pp. 216 and 313 . . . these must not
> really be allowed to remain an instant. I have had some difficulty in persuading
> Mr Dickens to restrict the omissions to these two, which, as they stand now, are
> a vile and disgusting interpolation on the sense and bearing of the tale . . .[4]

It is hard to see how such epithets as 'vile' and 'disgusting' could be
applied to the rather insipid 'Fireside' plate, or to believe that Dickens was

aware of its being so described. His criticisms were as a rule particular rather than general. They arose not from vague sensations of dislike or disapproval, but were the response of his visual imagination, which, as is clear from his descriptions of personal appearances and physical surroundings, was unusually vivid. Compared with that of Thackeray, George Eliot or Trollope, in whose works visual imagination is also a significant and important factor, that of Dickens may seem more easily excitable, less subtle and more highly coloured, but it was also exceedingly precise. It was not in a spirit of disappointment that he often gave advice to Phiz and other artists, but in order to amplify his descriptions and to give such help as he could towards their interpretation. As Arthur Waugh pointed out:

. . . he has left abundant testimony, in the form of counsel, comment, and written approbation, to his intense interest in the plates while they were being executed and his enjoyment of them when finished. Indeed, in many instances he may be said to have collaborated in their composition, supplying elaborate descriptions of details and insisting on alterations and improvements.[5]

Such alterations and improvements are referred to frequently in his letters to Phiz. Writing at the time of *Pickwick* about a preliminary sketch for the drawing of 'Mrs Leo Hunter's Fancy Dress Déjeuné', Dickens points out that:

. . . it would be better if Pickwick had hold of the Bandit's arm. If Minerva *tried* to look a little younger (more like Mrs Pott, who is perfect) I think it would be an additional improvement.[6]

Again, with reference to Mr Pickwick's 'First interview with Sergeant Snubbin', Dickens remarks:

I think the Sergeant should look younger, and a great deal more sly, and knowing – he should be looking at Pickwick too, smiling compassionately at his innocence. The other fellows are noble – [7]

On a sketch for 'Mr Winkle's Situation when the Door blew-to', Dickens says:

Winkle should be holding the Candlestick above his head I think. It looks more comical, the light having gone out.

A *fat* chairman so short as our friend here, never drew breath in Bath. I would leave him where he is, decidedly.[8]

It is significant of the relationship between Dickens and Phiz that Dickens's judgement of the illustrations counted for far more than Phiz's own opinions, and yet they remained on excellent terms until Phiz was thrown over. Preliminary sketches of all his chief characters were indispensable to Dickens and had to be approved by him before Phiz was allowed to go ahead. In the case of Mr Dombey, for instance, no less than twenty-nine pen and ink sketches of him in various attitudes were made before Dickens was satisfied that his own intimate and exact conception of Mr Dombey's character had been realized.

In spite of Dickens's meticulous attention to detail, mistakes crept into the illustrations now and then. No doubt these were due partly to the speed at which Phiz had to work. The pressure involved in the system of publication in monthly parts was extremely heavy and it would hardly have been surprising if more mistakes had occurred. Nowadays it is possible to reproduce an illustration many thousands of times without loss of fidelity to the original. In Dickens's day a rapid deterioration of the plates occurred during long runs, and to avoid this it was necessary for the artist (not, as nowadays, the blockmaker) to produce two, three, or sometimes even four duplicate plates, or 'steels' as they were called, of the same subject. Often, especially in the early books, Phiz made minute alterations to the second or subsequent steels, or marked them in some way to show that the steel was not the original one. In Mr Pickwick's 'First interview with Sergeant Snubbin', the first steel, but not the second, shows a roll of legal parchment on the floor; and in the picture of Nicholas Nickleby's 'First visit to Mr Bray' the figure 'III', etched below the footstool on the right in the third steel becomes 'IIII' in the fourth. It is partly by means of these minute variations that it is possible to identify the issues to which the monthly parts belong, those of the first issue – out of perhaps two or three of the same part – usually being the most sought-after and therefore the most valuable.

For Phiz this method had the disadvantage of requiring him to spend a considerable amount of time in the drudgery of engraving an illustration, not once but often two or three times, leaving him little time in which to produce his drawings for the next monthly part, to get them approved by Dickens, and to etch the steels for them. To prepare and etch four steels usually took about ten days. It did not help matters that Dickens was often behindhand in delivering his copy to the printer, or that he was sometimes abroad. *Dombey and Son* was begun while he was staying at Lausanne and the delay involved in sending the preliminary drawings there for Dickens to see, and in his returning them with the usual flow of comment and suggestions, meant that Phiz had to work at top speed in order to keep up with the publisher's schedule. Pressure of this kind is not helpful to the production of an artist's best work and it is noticeable that the drawings in the earlier part of *Dombey* are inferior to most of the others.

The schedule imposed by the requirements of part publication made it impossible to provide against accident or delay. Consequently, when Phiz became ill during the course of *Nicholas Nickleby*'s monthly appearances,

the issue for the month when he was indisposed went to press without
illustrations, but with a notice promising that four instead of the usual two
would appear in the following issue. *Nickleby*'s popularity was such that
the monthly run necessitated the engraving of fourteen steels in all for
these four drawings. It has been calculated that Phiz probably had not
more than twenty-eight days in which to do this and therefore, besides
having to prepare sketches for later issues, he must have completed one
steel every forty-eight hours for a period of almost a month.

Though, not surprisingly, Phiz overlooked details here and there,
Dickens, who almost certainly saw and approved proofs of each plate before
it went to press, cannot be absolved from responsibility for some of the
mistakes that occurred. It is odd that he should not have noticed, for
instance, such an obvious howler as the transposition of Captain Cuttle's
hook from the right to the left arm in the title-page vignette of *Dombey and
Son;* or, perhaps more surprisingly, that in the corresponding vignette of

'The Boffin Progress'
by Marcus Stone, an
illustration to *Our
Mutual Friend* –
'surely the worst
Dickens illustration
ever perpetrated'.

David Copperfield Mr Peggotty's boat is, to go by the text, the wrong way
up, with its keel forming the roof-tree. Again, in *Barnaby Rudge* the decorative initial P at the start of Chapter 31 is reversed, and in *Martin Chuzzlewit*'s title-page vignette the handbill fixed to the signpost was at first

headed 100£, a mistake (if it was a mistake; sterling values were still occasionally shown in this way) that was altered in later editions of the novel.

Phiz was not the only artist to make mistakes. Cruikshank in the frontispiece for *Sketches by Boz* ('Election for the Beadle') omitted from Spruggins's placard the all-important reference to 'the twins' that made Spruggins at one time the favourite candidate. In 'The Pawnbroker's Shop' the words 'Money Lent' on the glass door panel are the right way round instead of being reversed, as they would have been in order to read them from the street; and in 'Horatio Sparkins' the linen-draper's price ticket shows the sum of $\frac{1}{2}$d instead of $\frac{3}{4}$d after the 'dropsical' figure 7. Marcus Stone in 'The Boffin Progress' (*Our Mutual Friend*), surely the worst Dickens illustration ever perpetrated, gives the Boffins's carriage only three wheels; and Luke Fildes shows the egregious Mr Jasper in *Edwin Drood* playing a piano that has no pedals, as one of its date certainly would have had.

What was it that made Phiz, in spite of his being an indifferent and unpredictable draughtsman, the ideal illustrator of Dickens? The answer lies partly in his own temperament and partly in that of Dickens. By comparison with the ebullient and extrovert characters who were among some of Dickens's other friends, Phiz was much more subdued and docile. It was no doubt his willingness to accept Dickens's suggestions without question and his instinctive inclination to play second fiddle that appealed to Dickens. As they continued to work together, so did their mutual understanding of each other develop, Phiz adjusting his approach, and ultimately his technique, with increasing subtlety to suit the changes of mood demanded by the story, Dickens deliberately providing the kind of stimulus calculated to bring out the best in Phiz.

There is one notable lapse, however, in Phiz's steady improvement under Dickens's aegis, and this was not altogether Phiz's fault. It was decided with the publication of *Master Humphrey's Clock* (1840–2), in which were to appear first *The Old Curiosity Shop* and then *Barnaby Rudge*, that the stories should be brought out in weekly instead of monthly parts and that the illustrations, instead of being each on a separate page, should appear in the text. For technical reasons these changes meant that steel engravings would have to be abandoned and wood-blocks used instead. They also meant, incidentally, that another artist would be needed besides Phiz to keep up the supply of illustrations, and George Cattermole was chosen as his running mate. Wood-engraving was a process that was neither congenial to Phiz nor flattering to his work. However skilful the wood-engraver's interpretation of his design, the end-product was at one remove from his original and the coarseness and intractability of the process by comparison

with the subtlety of steel-engraving tended to emphasize the weakness of
his drawing. It is a pity that *Barnaby Rudge* in particular, which with its
turbulent action and vivid characterization should have given Phiz one of
his greatest opportunities, resulted in some of his feeblest work.

Cattermole, on the other hand, produced some delightful illustrations
with a particular emphasis on the physical and architectural surroundings
described by Dickens. Cattermole was by training an architectural
draughtsman, and later became a painter and illustrator of historical
scenes. Ruskin, in a judgement left unconfirmed by posterity, saw in him
'signs of very peculiar gifts, and perhaps also of powerful genius'. Applied
to his work simply as an illustrator of Dickens, perhaps this is not so wide of
the mark, even though his drawings were rather uneven in quality. At any
rate, Dickens, without intending any disparagement of Phiz, found
Cattermole's vision as near to his own as the most hopeful or most exacting
author could wish. Concerning the head-piece for the first weekly part of
the *Clock*, a painstaking but not, one would have thought, a particularly
inspired interpretation of the scene, Dickens wrote to Cattermole: 'I cannot
tell you how admirably I think Master Humphrey's room comes out . . . I
had not the faintest idea of anything so good . . .' He was equally apprecia-
tive of the drawings for *Barnaby Rudge*, which included by far the best of
Cattermole's illustrations for the two books. His drawing of the Maypole
Inn at Chigwell, an ornate, Jacobethan hotchpotch that bore little relation

'The Maypole Inn' by
George Cattermole, an
illustration to *Barnaby
Rudge*.

to the real inn, which was still standing, filled Dickens with delight. 'Words cannot say how good it is,' he wrote. 'I cannot bear the thought of its being cut and should like to frame and glaze it in *statu quo* for ever.'

In spite of Dickens's warm admiration for Cattermole, their association, though not their friendship, ended with *Barnaby Rudge*, perhaps because it was felt that his work was less suited to the contemporary scene than, as Waugh says, to 'the restoration of bygone times'.

A Tale of Two Cities, the only other novel for which he might have seemed a natural choice, appeared in 1859 and at that time Dickens's loyalty to Phiz had not yet evaporated.

Martin Chuzzlewit, published like Dickens's preceding novels in serial parts, was to his astonishment and deep distress less successful than anything he had written so far. In the middle of writing it, as though to challenge the public by a display of his virtuosity and to show that he could still provide what was expected of him, he produced in a few weeks, besides the monthly instalment of *Chuzzlewit*, the first of the five stories later to be included in *Christmas Books – A Christmas Carol*. Phiz had not enough time to draw and engrave the illustrations for this as well as for the instalment of *Chuzzlewit* and the job went to John Leech, whose work Dickens much admired.

Although this was the occasion of their first meeting, they had been in contact indirectly at the time of *Pickwick*. After Seymour's death, Cruikshank, not knowing that Phiz had just been appointed to succeed him, suggested to Chapman and Hall that Leech would be the man to do so. And so it must have seemed; yet Leech's illustrations for *A Christmas Carol* are disappointing. They have nothing like the vivacity, the sharp sense of character, or the comic inventiveness of his illustration for Hood or Barham or of his work in *Punch*. The reason is no doubt, as he confessed to Forster over his drawings for *The Battle of Life*, the fourth of the *Christmas Books*, that he was not altogether happy about the 'conditions' imposed on him by Dickens in his choice of subjects and depiction of details. But Dickens was well pleased with the drawings, and to each of the subsequent *Christmas Books*, except *The Haunted Man*, Leech contributed most of the illustrations.

The artists who provided the rest were an oddly assorted lot, of whom only two, Richard Doyle and John Tenniel, were exclusively illustrators. Doyle contributed to *The Chimes* (1844) *The Cricket on the Hearth* (1845) and *The Battle of Life* (1846), Tenniel to *The Haunted Man* (1848). The other artists were Clarkson Stanfield, a marine painter, Daniel Maclise, a painter of historical subjects, Frank Stone, a water-colour artist (all three were close friends of Dickens's, which no doubt counted in their favour), and Landseer, who drew a single illustration of Boxer, John Perrybingle's dog, in *The Cricket on the Hearth*. Almost all their drawings, with the exception of Doyle's (not that he was here at his best) are laboured and some are frankly quite unworthy of their subject, even though the *Christmas Books* are by no means vintage Dickens. None seem to have been inspired, except to some extent *The Chimes*, by a passionate conviction such as animates parts of *Nickleby* and *Bleak House*, nor have they the natural effervescence of *Pickwick* and much of *Copperfield*. *A Christmas Carol* was thrown off in a moment of reaction following the initial failure of *Chuzzlewit* and the others were produced in the hope that they would repeat the *Carol*'s success. But neither in conception nor characterization are they in the same class as the greater novels. Scrooge, Tiny Tim, Trotty Veck and Tilly Slowboy are perhaps the best-known of their characters, but they are puppets by comparison with some of Dickens's true originals. Scrooge is hardly more than a symbol of avarice, and Tiny Tim simply a masculine counterpart of Little Nell, and equally tiresome in the artificiality of his pathos.

But once again Dickens with his instinctive knowledge of his public had judged its mood exactly. The sales of *A Christmas Carol* were prodigious. Unfortunately, his insistence on its being published in a format far more expensive than was necessary cut its profits severely. Faced with a sudden need to economize, he decided to embark on a plan that he had had in mind for some months – to take a long holiday abroad, and in July 1844 he arrived with his family in Italy, where he stayed for the best part of a year, most of the time in or near Genoa. His impressions of this visit, *Pictures from Italy* (1846), were illustrated with four drawings by Samuel Palmer.

In his lifetime Palmer's reputation, such as it was, derived chiefly from his 'charming water-colour drawings'. In these innocuous words Frederick Kitton reflects the taste of the times, which was less for those mystical and contemplative aspects of Palmer's work that arouse interest today than for his romantic vision of the English countryside. To those aspects of his work Dickens would almost certainly have been opposed, as he was to the vision of the Pre-Raphaelites. What appealed to him about Palmer's drawings was, again to quote from Kitton, that they were 'faithful representations of Nature'; which impeccable achievement was no doubt reinforced by the gratifying knowledge that 'they were adapted from sketches made on the spot'. The drawings, executed with great delicacy, are in pencil and show four faintly melancholy scenes – Pompeii, the Villa d'Este, the Colosseum at Rome, and a vineyard. The price for the four was twenty guineas: a

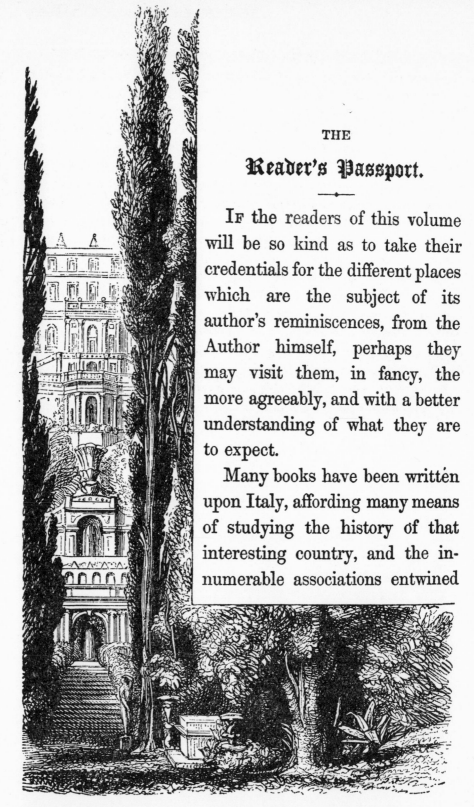

THE
Reader's Passport.

IF the readers of this volume will be so kind as to take their credentials for the different places which are the subject of its author's reminiscences, from the Author himself, perhaps they may visit them, in fancy, the more agreeably, and with a better understanding of what they are to expect.

Many books have been written upon Italy, affording many means of studying the history of that interesting country, and the innumerable associations entwined

Above 'The Villa d'Este at Tivoli', and *opposite* 'The Street of the Tombs, Pompeii', by Samuel Palmer, illustrations to *Pictures from Italy*.

modest sum that can hardly have compensated Palmer for the intense anxiety that he endured over the engraver's efforts to transfer his feathery lines and subtle gradations of tone onto the wood-block. His anxiety was needlessly acute: in their own way his drawings are among the best of Dickensian illustrations.

After *Pictures from Italy* came *Dombey and Son*, then *David Copperfield*, and in March 1852 *Bleak House* began to appear in monthly parts. All three were illustrated by Phiz. In the meantime, *A Child's History of England* (3 vols., 1852–3–4) had begun as a serial in *Household Words*. This was the realization of an idea that Dickens had had in mind for nearly ten years, prompted by the innocent hope that it might act as a warning to his eldest son against the perils of High Anglicanism and the mischief of Tory politics. Even Forster had to admit that it 'cannot be said to have quite hit the mark'. Each of the three volumes contained a tediously elaborate frontispiece by F. W. Topham, who, like Stanfield, Maclise and Stone, was a friend of Dickens – the most probable explanation of Dickens's acceptance, apparently without criticism, of drawings so laboured and undistinguished.

Throughout his life his friendships were of the utmost importance to Dickens. The reassurance demanded by his vanity, the stability required by his emotional temperament, and the need for others to participate in his gregarious way of life, made him crave friendship as avidly as the anchorite craves solitude. But for the friendship that he gave so generously there was usually a price to be paid, which was that of unqualified loyalty. There seems to be no doubt that it was largely because he believed Phiz had failed him in this that in 1859 they parted company.

It so happened that the climax came at a time when Dickens was already overwrought for other reasons; his separation from his wife a year earlier, with all the unpleasant publicity that followed it, for which his own injudicious actions were alone responsible, had left his heart, as he confessed to his friend Edmund Yates, 'jagged and rent and out of shape'.

He was still smarting from this self-inflicted injury when, a year later, *All the Year Round* made its appearance under the aegis of Chapman and Hall and with himself as editor. Its publication followed – in fact, for a few weeks overlapped – the final issues of *Household Words*, which he had been editing for the publishers, Bradbury and Evans. A quarrel had sprung up between them, however, because they had refused, or so Dickens believed, to allow the publication in *Punch* of a personal statement about his domestic situation. In a misguided effort at defiance, Bradbury and Evans decided to issue a new periodical of their own, called *Once a Week*. According to the biography of Dickens by Hesketh Pearson,[9] Phiz agreed to accept a position on the staff. Although Professor Edgar Johnson's biography,[10] the most intimate and comprehensive account of Dickens's life and career that we are likely to see, makes no mention of this, and though, even for someone as unworldly as Phiz, it might have seemed a strange thing to do, there also seems to be a strong possibility of its being true. Although in a letter from Phiz to an acquaintance it is suggested that their relations were not quite as friendly as usual, there is no indication that they were at breaking point, nor has anything come to light that would suggest any other reason for Dickens's sudden abandonment of Phiz after an amicable and outstandingly successful association lasting for twenty-three years. It could hardly have been that Dickens objected to Phiz illustrating novels by other authors. He had already illustrated a number by Charles Lever, as well as by Dickens's friends, Harrison Ainsworth and Bulwer Lytton. If it were this that Dickens objected to, it is inconceivable that he would have nourished such a grievance in secret. The world would soon have known about it. Certainly Phiz had no inkling of the fact that he was going to be dropped and one can sympathize with his *cri de coeur* in a letter to a friend: 'Confound all authors and publishers, say I. There is no pleasing one or t'other. I wish I had never had anything to do with the lot.'

Dickens, in dismissing Phiz, did himself a considerable disservice. His illustrators thereafter were for the most part a mediocre and uninspired lot whose work reflects little of the quality of Dickens's imagination. That he accepted such work apparently without remonstrance or criticism does, however, reflect something of his innate philistinism. Although the natural liveliness of his intellect runs through almost everything he wrote, Dickens had little intellectual curiosity, in the sense of an interest in abstract ideas or philosophical concepts, and his taste was decidedly commonplace. In this he typified ironically the bourgeoisie that he often ridiculed, but fortunately his opinions, unlike theirs, were not inflexible. His reaction, for instance, to Impressionist painting, which he saw for the first time in Paris in 1855, at an exhibition that included works by Corot, Manet, Courbet and Degas, was to think 'how timid and conventional seemed his own friends, Egg, Ward, Frith and Stanfield' by comparison. Yet only a few years earlier he had denounced Millais's picture in the Royal Academy, 'Christ in the House of his Parents', in a criticism as venomous as it was ill-founded:

You will have the goodness to discharge from your minds all Post-Raphael ideas, all religious aspirations, all elevating thoughts; . . . and to prepare yourselves, as befits such a subject – Pre-Raphaelly considered – for the lowest depths of what is mean, odious, repulsive and revolting.

You behold the interior of a carpenter's shop. In the foreground of that carpenter's shop is a hideous, wry-necked, blubbering, red-headed boy, in a bed-gown; who appears to have received a poke in the hand, from the stick of another boy with whom he has been playing in an adjacent gutter, and to be holding it up for the contemplation of a kneeling woman, so horrible in her ugliness, that she would stand out from the rest of the company as a Monster, in the lowest gin-shop in England. Two almost naked carpenters, master and journeyman, worthy companions of this agreeable female, are working at their trade; a boy, with some small flavour of humanity in him, is entering with a vessel of water . . . Wherever it is possible to express ugliness of feature, limb or attitude, you have it expressed.

To the credit of accuser and accused, this diatribe was later forgiven and forgotten in a friendship that lasted until Dickens died.

The literalism that was part of the Pre-Raphaelite creed which so displeased Dickens, did not, strangely enough, displease him in illustrations for his own works. Nothing could have been more literal – or more stiff and uninspired – than the work of Phiz's successor, Marcus Stone, the son of Dickens's old friend Frank Stone, and the illustrator of *Our Mutual Friend* (1865), one of the three novels that were to bring Dickens's career to an end. Later, with Dickens's approval, Stone was chosen to re-illustrate *Little Dorrit* and *A Tale of Two Cities* in their cheap editions, as well as other works in the Library Edition (1862), for which he was also to illustrate *Great Expectations*, unillustrated on its first publication a year earlier. The defence of youth as an excuse for Stone's inadequacy would be easier to sustain – he was twenty-four when he illustrated *Our Mutual Friend* – were it not that the talents of Millais, Holman Hunt, Richard Doyle, Keene and others were considerably more precocious than his own. The fact is that whatever other talents he may have developed – later in life he achieved some degree of fame and fortune as a painter of maudlin pot-boilers with a Regency flavour – as an illustrator he was no better than a hack.

Preliminary drawing by Luke Fildes from *Edwin Drood*, together with the final version (opposite).

Last in the long line of Dickens's illustrators was another young man, Luke Fildes, then aged twenty-five, whose work was introduced to Dickens by Millais. Dickens was impressed by it, and, when they met, by Fildes's insistence that he was not a comic artist. For the story Dickens had in mind this was an advantage. It was *The Mystery of Edwin Drood* (1870). Though Fildes, like Stone, was to make his name as an Academic painter, it was as the illustrator of Dickens's last novel that he first became known. His illustrations, however, partly owing to technical difficulties in their reproduction, do less than justice to the assurance and sensibility of his preliminary drawings, which are as near to the sombre mood of the novel as the drawings of Phiz to the jubilant spirit of *Pickwick*.

The works of Dickens exercise a perpetual fascination for artists and also offer them a perpetual challenge. The reader who makes his first discovery of *Pickwick, Nickleby, Chuzzlewit* or *Copperfield* in an edition with Phiz's illustrations is bound to feel on re-reading the same stories illustrated by other artists that something in their work is missing; something intangible perhaps, but which provokes a sense of imperfection. Dickens may have been exacting in the demands he made upon his artists, and upon Phiz especially, and his acute and unremitting interest in their efforts must sometimes have been exasperating, particularly when time was short. But that there developed between himself and Phiz an almost perfect understanding is shown by the continued popularity of Phiz's illustrations as against those of the innumerable artists who have since tried their hands at illustrating Dickens.

Nearest in feeling, perhaps because of also being nearest in time, was Fred Barnard, whose drawings appeared in the *Household Edition* (1871–9), to which he contributed nearly 450 illustrations. Although in technique there is little affinity between Barnard's work and that of Phiz, they share a precise appreciation of the nuances of Dickens's humour and a sensibility no less acute to his changes of mood and atmosphere.

In almost everything that Dickens wrote there are detailed descriptions of people, places and events that leave the artist with little excuse for factual error. But though it may not be difficult to suggest with some degree of accuracy the shape of a lamp-post or a soup tureen, the cut of a coat, or the resemblance of an umbrella to something only Dickens would have thought of, the artist is nowadays faced with one insuperable obstacle – that of re-creating a vision of the nineteenth century from the perspective of the twentieth. The historian making the same attempt can reinforce his impressions with analogy, metaphor, comparison, correspondence, statistics and the whole apparatus of scholarship. The artist has no such aids. He stands alone, armed only with a set of facts. Nevertheless, some interesting attempts to re-illustrate Dickens have been made in the past fifty years or so by artists as different as Arthur Rackham, Barnett Freedman, Frank Reynolds and Edward Ardizzone, to name only a few of those who have accepted the challenge of re-creating Micawber, Miss Havisham, Sergeant Buzfuz and the rest. But under the inescapable influence of time, reflected in profound differences in style and technique and by up-to-date methods of reproduction, they remain as firmly lodged in their own era as Cruikshank, Phiz and Doyle in theirs.

Of these three, the best-remembered, although, ironically, in some ways the least accomplished, is undoubtedly Phiz. His were the prototypes of all

Illustration by Arthur
Rackham from
A Christmas Carol.

but a few of Dickens's most famous characters. They are familiar still and
have had their influence on all Dickens's subsequent illustrators. But if in
this respect the art of Phiz is unique, so was the source and abundance of
his opportunities. And so we come full circle: no author ever gave greater
inspiration to an illustrator than Dickens, and for that inspiration, generations of readers will continue to be profoundly grateful.

Dickens in America

Dickens's first visit to America in 1842 was the result of the enormous popularity of his works there [6]. As the monthly issues of the novels arrived by ship, excitement mounted, and 'Is Little Nell dead?' was a question shouted from the quayside when the next instalment of the 'Old Curiosity Shop' was awaited [14]. The voyage across the Atlantic [2 and 3] was not without its hazards, for at one moment shipwreck was feared; but when Dickens arrived at Boston, his reception was like that of a monarch. A striking likeness was made of him by the sculptor Henry Dexter [1], and a series of receptions, balls and visits to celebrities arranged [7, 8, 9, 10 and 11]. Although his welcome could not have been more warmhearted, and he made many friends within a short time, he found certain aspects of American life displeasing, not least slavery [5 and 15], and he was vigorous in his protests against the failure of American publishers to observe the international copyright convention. As always when he was abroad, he longed for home, and especially he missed the company of his young children [4]. His critical views of America were later expressed in 'American Notes' and in 'Martin Chuzzlewit'; but these outspoken works did little to affect the sale of his novels, and his reputation increased until he was persuaded once more to cross the Atlantic for the purpose of giving a series of Readings [17 and 18]. Although already an ailing man, he showed all his old enthusiasm and irrepressible energy, entering into the spirit of such frolics as the great 'walking match' [13]. Above all, he reaffirmed his great affection and admiration for the American people in terms which removed for ever any prejudice or rancour which his first visit may have occasioned. He remarked on the great social changes he had seen, and he confessed that he was not 'so arrogant as to suppose that there have been no changes in me'; and although he declared that he had no plans to write another book on America, he promised that he would record his appreciation of the renewed hospitality he had received by printing a special appendix to his two books relating to that country, emphasizing that 'this I will do and cause to have done, not in mere love and thankfulness, but because I regard it as an act of plain justice and honour'. In short, Dickens was one of Britain's greatest ambassadors to the United States, and in his farewell speech in New York he declared that 'if I know anything of my countrymen . . . the English heart is stirred by the fluttering of those Stars and Stripes as it is stirred by no other flag that flies except its own.'

1 A bust of Dickens made soon after his arrival in Ameri
by Henry Dexter, 1842.

1

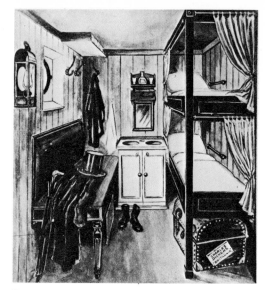

2 A sketch of Dickens on board the *Britannia*, 1842.

3 The state-room occupied by Dickens and his wife on the *Britannia*.

4 Maclise's picture of Dickens's children, Charley, Mamie, Katey, and Wally, which the novelist took with him to America. Grip the raven is seen on the right.

5 An American theme illustrated in
Martin Chuzzlewit.
6 The cover of the 1842 American
edition of *Barnaby Rudge*.
7 The programme of a skit by the
American comedian Joe Field, performed
at the Tremont Theatre, Boston, 1842.

5

6

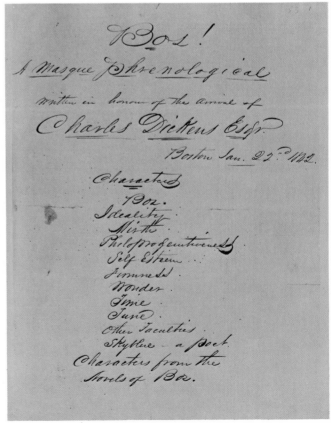

7

☛ *overleaf*
8, 9, 10, and **11** Press notices, greetings,
and illustrations connected with
Dickens's first visit to America, and
impressions of 'The Great Boz Ball'.

THE EXTRA BOZ HERALD.

NEW YORK, TUESDAY MORNING, FEBRUARY 15, 1842.

PORTRAIT OF DICKENS.

Boz.

22. Old Weller putting Stiggins's head in the Horse Trough

19. Quilp Fighting the Stuffed Figure

20. Nicholas Teaching French to the Kenwigs.

21. Bumble and Mrs Corney Taking Tea

Mrs. Leo Hunter's Dress Déjeuné

The Ball

The Middle-aged Lady in the Double-bedded Room.

Mrs. Bardell faints in Mr. Pickwick's arms.

Oliver Twist at Mr. Maylie's Door.

Mrs. Bardell Encounters Mr. Pickwick in the Prison.

Little Nell and her Grandfather, the Military Gentleman and Mrs. Stton's Unexpected Appearance.

Little Nell Leading her Grandfather

The Red-nosed Man Discometh.

Mr and Mrs Mantilini in Ralph Nickleby's Office

The Stranger Watching Barnaby in the Cottage.

Postillion's Quadrille

Tableau Vivant

The Stranger Scrutinizing Barnaby's Features in the Widow's Cottage.

March.

Tableau Vivant

The Pickwick Club.

Contra Dance.

Tableau Vivant

Washington Irving in England and Charles Dickens in America.

9

The Great Boz Ball.

AIR—*The Old School House.*

The great Boz ball—the great Boz ball,
Comes off on Monday night ;—
The high, the low, the short and tall,
Are eager with delight.
With rosettes pendant from their coats,
And cock'd hats under arm,
The managers with tuneful throats,
Will bear away the "palm :"
In silken vests and satin tights,
And buckles on their knees.
They'll pirouette about the lights
Like glow-worms 'mongst the trees.
The horses, heads t'wards Chatham Square,
Their tails right down Broadway—
The Locofocos must not stare
Nor round the platform stay :
No bankrupts there—all good cash men,
Who represent New York
In finance and in fashion, when
They've wherewithal to fork.
There's Major Generals, Brigadiers,
Lieutenant Colonels, and
Sergeants, Corporals, Grenadiers
Of the true Spartan Band—
The Mayors of Brooklyn and New York,
Of Jersey City, too—
There's Downing to relieve the cork,
And serve the oyster stew.
Oh ! Boz, if e'er you wish to draw
A character complete,
Discuss an oyster, boil'd or raw,
At number Nine, Broad street.)
There's Dodsworth's Band—two hundred strong—
So shrill, it makes one quake—
"The Fire," so saith some idle tongue,
Has got the stomach-ache.
And there's the corps of editors
From Wall street, and from Ann—
The latter have no creditors,
Cash system, to a man.
Oh ! what a glorious sight 'twill be,
To see the great Boz cut
A pigeon-wing— then, forward, three—
But mum—my mouth is shut—
The great Boz ball—the great Boz ball,
Comes off on Monday night ;
The high, the low, the short and tall,
Are eager with delight.

PHIZ.

10

View of the Interior of the Park Theatre on the night of the Great BOZ BALL; with the Elizabethan Chamber, and the Tableax from Boz's Works.

11

12 Broadway as it looked at the time of Dickens's second visit.
13 Dickens as umpire, and self-styled 'Gad's Hill Gasper', Boston 1867.
14 Little Nell looking at her creator: a statue in Frank Park, Philadelphia.
15 An American cartoon with ironical letterpress recalling a well-known expression from *Martin Chuzzlewit*.
16 1876 edition of the American Reading version of the famous Christmas Story.
17 and **18** Tickets of admittance to two of the Readings, during his second American visit.

12

DICKENS AS UMPIRE IN A WALKING MATCH IN AMERICA.

From a new drawing by Ralph Cleaver, illustrating the scene described in Dickens's correspondence.

13

14

"A MAN AND A BROTHER."

Uncle Sam.—"WAL, CHARLEY, I GUESS YOU'RE WELCOME; LET ME INTRODUCE TO YOU OUR NEW BROTHER FROM DOWN SOUTH—'THE MOST REMARKABLE MAN IN THE COUNTRY.'"

15

CHARLES DICKENS'S

DRAMATIC READINGS

AS READ IN AMERICA.

DOCTOR MARIGOLD.

BOSTON
LEE & SHEPARD, Publishers.
1876.

16

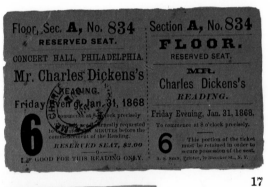

17

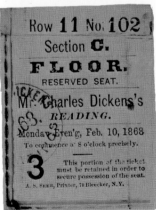

18

CHARLES DICKENS.

Entered according to Act of Congress, in the year 1867, by J. GURNEY & SON, in the Clerk's Office of the District Court of the United States, for the Southern District of New York.

J. Gurney & Son   707 Broadway. N.Y.

Dickens's Reputation: a Reassessment

E W F Tomlin

With the novels of Dickens, a new kind of audience was brought into being, at once varied and far-flung, taking in both the cultivated and the underprivileged. Dickens's reputation, then as now, differs in *kind* from that of other writers. Indeed, no writer of the age, not even Scott, was able to sustain a comparable effort of entertainment, commanding a public so huge that, as Forster remarked, it went beyond that normally reached by the printed word. The tide of Dickens's success surged into every corner of society; and on its recession (though this was never complete), it left a host of characters high and dry who became in due course known to thousands who might be unfamiliar with the novels in which they appeared. Today, many more know of Mr Pickwick and Mrs Gamp than have read through *Pickwick Papers* and *Martin Chuzzlewit*. Hence a relationship between Dickens and his public unlike that of any other writer: a relationship which, established when he was in his middle twenties, grew in intimacy for more than thirty years. Nor was this bond forged solely through the novels. In *Household Words* and its successor *All the Year Round*, which maintained a steady circulation of 100,000 and must have enjoyed a readership thrice that number, Dickens, as master in his own house,[1] could communicate his ideas on a great variety of subjects, from Poor Law Reform to the Noble Savage, from blasphemous public speech to the habits of Mormons, but always with that 'brightness' of approach which made his readers look upon him as a personal friend, as well as a champion of public causes.

What was the secret of this prodigious success? Although the appearance of *Pickwick Papers* proved a unique literary event, there might well have been no *Pickwick* if *Sketches by Boz* had not revealed a talent both striking and original. Forster described the *Sketches* as 'a book that might have stood its ground, even if it had stood alone'; and he pointed out that the *Sketches* were 'more talked about than the first two or three numbers of Pickwick'.[2] Dickens had become a voice of his time; for there was all the difference between 'the world of Boz and the worlds of the "silver-fork" novels, of the Annuals, of romantic-historical thrillers and "political-economy" tales, and of the less sharp but still distinctive difference from the comic worlds of Hood and Hook . . .'.[3] In the words of the *Court Journal*, Boz was a 'kind of Boswell to society'. His *vignettes* of 'every-day life and every-day people' (the sub-title of the book) excited by their astonishing fidelity of observation and lively humour, together with an ability to come to terms with the grim and even the macabre. One of the most enthusiastic reviews of the *Sketches* was from the pen of George Hogarth, Dickens's future father-in-law, in the *Morning Chronicle*, on which Dickens himself was working as a reporter. The *Satirist*, in an equally

MR. PICKWICK'S
COLLECTION OF SONGS.

YATES, as "MR. PICKWICK."

CONTENTS.

May the young Queen be happy.
My Sailor's Heart.
She wore a wreath of Roses.
The Sailor Boy.
Life at White Conduit Gardens.
Mark'd you her eye?
Devil among the Lawyers.

He who can't my meaning spy,
Oh, crikey! Oh, good gracious.
Wine! wine! my boys!
Fat Sarah Gray.
Banks of the sweet Prinroses.
Paddy Blake and the Echo.
The Parish Beadle.

Smeeton, Printer, 74, Tooley-street.

An example of *Pickwick Papers* being used to promote a collection of songs (1840), with an illustration of the actor Frederick Yates playing the part of Pickwick in a contemporary dramatized version.

favourable notice, was the first to use the word 'inimitable' of Boz's work.

Nevertheless, it is with *Pickwick Papers*, or rather at a stage in the serial publication of that work, that we first become aware of a new kind of literature, giving rise to a 'Dickens industry' which still flourishes. During the decade following Dickens's death, more than four million copies of his works were sold in his own country, and by 1891 sales were running at a steady 330,000 copies a year. With the lapsing of copyrights, the number sold throughout the world is beyond computation. In the Everyman Library, Dickens is still the best-seller, with *David Copperfield* leading. (Three new paperback editions of this novel have just appeared, Penguin, Signet and Pan.) Sales of the novels in Europe and the Soviet Union are enormous. In the latter country, the total between 1945 and 1957 had reached 7,500,000. A new collected translation of the Works began to appear in 1957, the sales of which are expected to reach 18,000,000 copies.[4] Moreover, at home the 'Works of Dickens' are still the most popular among book prizes or gifts in schemes of sales promotion.

In surveying Dickens's reputation, we must distinguish between the

(below left) Title-page of a German edition of *Pickwick Papers*, 1879; (right) page from a Japanese translation of *A Christmas Carol*, 1902, with footnotes explaining the literal translation in the margin.

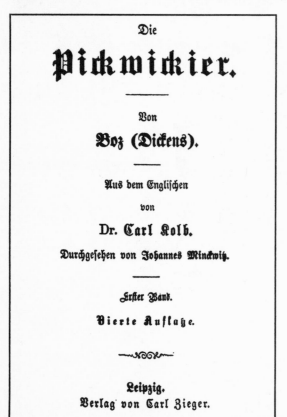

Die
Pickwickier.

Von

Boz (Dickens).

Aus dem Englischen
von
Dr. Carl Kolb.
Durchgesehen von Johannes Minckwitz.

Erster Band.
Vierte Auflage.

Leipzig.
Verlag von Carl Zieger.

〔194〕。四一—29 Same'tap＝same liquor＝同じ飲物、酒場。四一—らアャヒか，町下ちら〜酒はほと之か諸標宅物化リしか。（1
95〕。四二一—っAlways a delicate creature, 即ちスクルージを迎ひにきたる妖、幽靈が此の女をつれてゆったがが氣象はエラかったと言ふなり〔196〕。四二—7 God for-bid！＝May God forbid from gainsay.（イナヤ、トンでもコトトャ）〔197〕。四三—12. Scrooge seemed uneasy: 流石のスクルージも石く言はれてキマリが悪かつたものと見ゆ。〔198〕。

のと同じ〔195〕注管のゾハから御辞退申したいを答へた。借て斯固陋爺

さんの革盤も此の時馬車の上よくゝりつけられたので二人の子供は大

喜びで校長に暇乞して、馬車に入つて庭園の周りの徑を暢々として驅り

下ろした――急駛する車輪は常緑木の黑ずんだ葉から眞白な六出華

を水烟のやうに散らして突進した。

【196】一吹の風にも萎びさうな何時も物柔らかな女であつた。が、氣象

は凛々としてゐた』と幽靈が言ふ。

『さやうでござりました！』を抑へつけて言つて、『御尤な仰せ、何を

して〔197〕背戻ませうで、決してゝ。』

『繰づいて亡くなつたのだ。小供が有つたを思ふが。』

『一人』

『さう、れ前の甥だ！』

斯固陋爺は〔198〕何となく氣が濟まぬやうに見にたが、手短かに『左や

六十

(opposite, top left) Title-page of the first Italian translation of *Little Dorrit*, 1879; (top right) title-page of a Russian book on the Moscow Arts Theatre production of *The Cricket on the Hearth*, 1918; (bottom left) page from a Marathi translation of *David Copperfield*, 1955, with an illustration based on the original one by Phiz; (bottom right) title-page of a Persian translation, 1931, of *A Child's Dream of a Star*, one of Dickens's stories from *Household Words*.

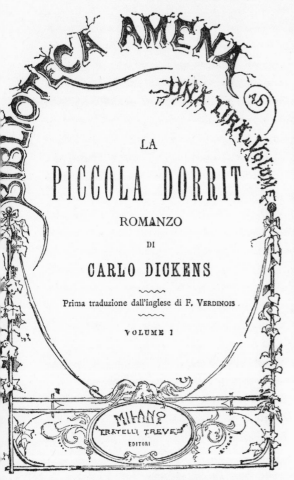

'हूं पिऊन तो माणूस तडफडून मेला.'

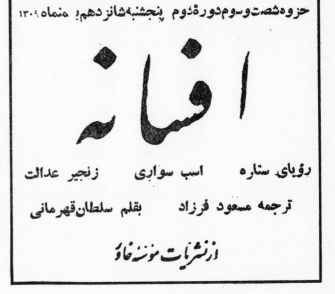

professional attitude to his work and his popular acclaim. Serious criticism of Dickens is commonly supposed to be of fairly recent development. Writing twenty years ago, Jack Lindsay declared that 'criticism of Dickens has so far been very largely at the level which Shakespearian criticism clung to before 1800',[5] and John Butt and Kathleen Tillotson echoed this in maintaining that 'Dickens studies have hardly passed beyond the early nineteenth century phase of Shakespeare studies; while the study of his text seems arrested in the early eighteenth century'.[6] Finally, Humphry House, in *The Dickens World*,[7] pointed out that Dickens studies had hitherto been biographical and social rather than literary.

If, however, we examine the record, we see that Dickens's pre-eminence, his radical difference from other novelists, were recognized from the start; and this meant that his novels, being more popular at more levels than any others, faced the professional critics with something for which they were unprepared. The history of Dickens criticism is the history of the intellectual response to his abiding popularity: a response now exultant, now grudging, now shot through with envy, but rarely purely negative. If Dickens has become an increasing pre-occupation of the critics, this is because his long hold upon the public has seemed to demand a special explanation; and what is remarkable is that the most sophisticated appraisals of our time, in Britain and in America and on the Continent, serve merely to confirm the general consensus of the reading public of 1836–7. If spiritually we are all Semites, literarily we are all (or nearly all) Dickensians, even if for different and sometimes conflicting reasons.

And so to return to *Pickwick*. The BBC Brains' Trust was once asked to name the world's two greatest novels. There was swift unanimity: *War and Peace* was one, *Pickwick* was the other. Yet *Pickwick* is not really a novel at all: it is a work of fiction which somehow beat the novel at its own game, or for a time took its place. *Pickwick* must have met the needs and tastes of readers in a special way, and evidently it still does so, because the *comedy* of Dickens is that which dominates modern humour. The 'new' humour might be said to take its rise from the point in *Pickwick* where, after a somewhat uncertain beginning (despite the brilliant parody of Parliamentary debate), the issue between Mr Blotton and Mr Pickwick is resolved by the former's avowal that he had used the word 'humbug' in its 'Pickwickian sense'. It is surprising how many commentators believe that the term 'Pickwickian sense' was a comment *on* Dickens rather than an expression originating in the first chapter of *Pickwick*.[8] Why Dickens's comedy exercises this domination is to explain the basis of his reputation.

In embarking upon *Pickwick*, however, the young author was saddled with a formidable task. 'The work will be no joke', he wrote with unconscious irony to his fiancée on 24 February 1836. The original proposal was, as we know, that he should write pieces about a series of sporting prints by Seymour; and although Dickens insisted upon being given a free hand, the early numbers fell surprisingly flat. Press notices were on the whole tepid; e.g. the *Atlas* described *Pickwick* as 'a strange publication' of which the reviewer had in vain endeavoured 'to discover the purpose', and as 'excessively dull'.[9] Furthermore, the suicide of the artist, which occurred a few days after Dickens had returned from his honeymoon, seemed to doom the project to failure. Then, with the introduction in the fourth number of a character with more vitality than the three 'disciples' of Mr Pickwick put together, the public fancy was stirred and finally captivated; but as G. H. Ford has pointed out,[10] the astonishing leap in sales, from 400 monthly to 40,000, was due not simply to the appearance of Sam Weller but to the publication in William Jerdan's *Literary Gazette* of extracts from Sam's famous monologues. The first number of *Pickwick* was published on 31 March. The extracts were published in the *Gazette* on 9 July and 13 August. Ford omits to mention, however, that the first extract of all, namely the story of 'The Cabman's Horse', was printed in *The Times* on 7 April, and that a passage, together with a not unfavourable notice, was published in the *Gazette* on 9 April. An extract was also published the same day in *Fraser's Literary Chronicle*. The following week the *Spectator* contained a reasonably good review. Even so, the early sales were most disappointing.[11]

The *Literary Gazette*'s 'intervention' remained crucial. Not merely did that review command a wide readership, but Jerdan personally urged Dickens to develop Sam's character 'to the utmost', in his review-extract of Part v on 13 August.[12] It was this enthusiastic notice, from a highly respected journal, which helped to set everybody talking about *Pickwick*; first, because so much attention was thereby drawn to it, and secondly, because it was seen to contain something for everybody. A cursory glance at the *Pickwick Advertiser*, a supplement stitched into the later numbers, shows for what varied tastes the book was catering. As Mary Russell Mitford wrote:[13] 'All the boys and girls talk his fun – the boys in the streets; and yet they who are of the highest taste like it most.'

At any moment in a country's history, 'everybody' means always a section of the people, just as 'Society' means a small privileged social group. In 1836, four years after the Reform Bill, 'everybody' meant primarily the middle classes, where the new political centre of gravity lay. Published as a book in 1837, the year Victoria became Queen, *Pickwick* 'coincided exactly with a shift of taste traced by literary historians to the same convenient date'.[14] The ethos of the Victorian middle classes, with its strict conventions and reticences, has come in for much obloquy; and Dickens was for long ridiculed for his general acquiescence in the spirit of the age, as if this were a serious blemish on his artistic integrity. A few years ago a broadcaster launched a tirade against Dickens for 'not knowing', in effect, that Nancy was a prostitute, and Edmund Leach has framed a more general indictment.[15] In point of fact, apart from his having created the character, Dickens knew well what he was about, as is clear from his avowal in the preface to *Pickwick* that he had written nothing calculated to bring a blush to the cheek of the most innocent person. Such an avowal implied not merely that he and his readers well knew what was likely to colour that cheek, but that the cheek was unusually sensitive to register embarrassment. When reticence is deliberate, as was here the case, there is a kind of permanent *presence* of the matter suppressed: and if there is any justification for reticence, at least in published work, it is simply that powerful effects can be obtained by an occasional rupture of the protective covering. In abandoning decorum, the writer may be depriving himself of a powerful engine of wit and satire, since increasing explicitness brings into operation the law of diminishing returns. A major artist, as opposed to one less endowed, always observes a measure of conformity in order to sharpen and render more effective his attacks on particular abuses. A writer like Jean Genet just avoids appearing totally repellent because of the aura of morality which surrounds his work, whereas, to descend several steps in the literary scale, the upper-class-snobbery of an Ian Fleming is unredeemed by an aura of something like nihilism. In short, Dickens's conformism in the realm of sexual morality may have made more devastating his attacks upon evils in other spheres. Satire launched from any but a moral redoubt descends to mere vilification.[16]

In accepting Victorian convention, Dickens was able to bring within the sphere of 'the respectable' – while maintaining his hold upon a public aspiring to gentility – subjects which had never been treated, at that level, before. The most 'living' characters in *Oliver Twist* are thieves, confidence-tricksters and whores, just as the best remembered scenes are those laid in sordid places. Dickens's attitude to his rogues and harlots differed markedly from that displayed by Fielding and Smollett; and the difference is significant. In Fielding especially, there is an impassable gulf between the respectable and the disreputable. Sophia in *Tom Jones* is set apart, inviolate; the chastity of her less fortunate sisters is considered fair game. In *Jonathan Wild*, satire, though biting, does not extend to the condemnation of a whole raffish way of life. This is accepted. Nor does Smollett, Dickens's favourite novelist, appear to deplore the fact that his rogues and scoundrels behave as they do. Dickens, at least in his early works, adopts a different attitude. He condemns the way of life, root and branch. He wants to see it destroyed. He seeks, though vaguely, the return of another and older order. He personally knew too much about poverty, squalor, and knavery to sentimentalize over them. 'I know,' he wrote in the autobiographical sketch for Forster in 1847, 'that I have lounged about the streets, insufficiently and unsatisfactorily fed. I know that, but for the mercy of God, I might easily have been, for any care that was taken of me, a little robber or a little vagabond.' Unlike Fielding, he does *not* think Agnes inviolable, and Little Emily, or the Marchioness for that matter, fair game. In some respects, Dostoevsky sentimentalized Sonia, beautiful character though she be, more than Dickens sentimentalized Nancy. We are not expected to believe that Nancy was a saint.

Those who reproach Dickens for slurring over the real profession of Nancy forget that in that 'family' book, *David Copperfield*, he introduces a character, Martha Endell, who is plainly a prostitute, if a reluctant one, and whose part in the story would be unintelligible if she were otherwise depicted. In the Notebook, so rarely referred to outside Forster,[17] there is evidence to suggest that Dickens even contemplated writing the story of a prostitute who is 'always tempting other women down'. True, he never wrote it, but neither did he plan to die at the height of his powers at the age of fifty-eight.[18]

In this connection, Taine's criticism of Dickens, perhaps the first substantial estimate to be made by a foreign writer, is of great interest. He begins by attributing Dickens's immense success to an ability to capture the interest of people habituated to an even round of life, so that their *vie quotidienne* becomes infused with a kind of fantastic incandescence. Dickens would hardly have objected to that judgement, at least in respect of certain of his works. In the 1853 preface to *Bleak House*, he declares that it has been his intention to dwell upon 'the romantic side of familiar things'.[19] But then Taine goes on to deliver an onslaught which critics have from time to time renewed. Dickens, he says, introduces too much 'morality and religion' into his work to attain to pure art. Love, to him, must always be subordinate to marriage. Of Steerforth's seduction we learn the remorse and misery but nothing of the passion.[20] We are shown vice in its sordidness without the 'psychological' truth which can lend it attraction. Stressing that the demand for 'morality and religion' may prove no more than a lip-service exercise, Taine suggests that this desire to appear moral, coupled with what he calls 'the trading spirit', issues in the typical English failing, hypocrisy. He admits that such hypocrisy becomes an easy target for Dickens's satire; but he argues that the national character which falls victim to it imposes on even so independent a writer as Dickens a restraint which, in the case of Balzac, was not operative. Vice made Dickens angry, but the very sincerity of his indignation prevented the artist in him from growing up. In Taine's view, the major artist is never angry, never given to moralizing; he presents virtue and vice with dispassionate candour, and his concern with vice must include how it has come to exercise its hold.

Naturally, Taine's strictures could apply equally well to some of Dickens's contemporaries. Thackeray chafed under the constraints of his time, though it is a moot point whether *Vanity Fair* would have proved superior had Becky Sharp been painted in her true colours, just as some of Zola's novels, *Germinal* for instance, may fall short of greatness because of the clinical realism in which the author indulges. An interesting 'test case' in this respect is Robert Graves's debowdlerization of the favourite among Dickens's novels, and his own favourite, in *The Real David Copperfield* (1933). This extraordinary *tour de force* is an attempt to recast the novel in the form it should or would have taken if Dickens had been released from the prevailing sexual convention. Yet if Graves is under the impression that the introduction of bedroom scenes and the re-routing of the plot improve *Copperfield* as a work of *art*, then he has surely failed to make his case.[21] Does it follow, to return to the other favourite, that Mr Pickwick's adventure in the lady's bedroom would have been more entertaining if the lady, instead of simply taking her hair down, had removed everything else and (what we may suppose Mr Graves, if he were writing the 'Real Pickwick Papers', to have insisted upon) popped into bed with that venerable gentleman? In general, then, we may be justified in concluding that Dickens's popularity was grounded partly upon his deliberate acceptance of prevailing moral conventions, though he was on one occasion stung into an admission much like that of Thackeray, concerning the very morality which Taine had described as such an incubus.[22] For a writer whose main attention is on subjects other than sex in the raw[23] would clearly, in those days, have exerted a much wider appeal than the more 'sophisticated' writer on the one hand and the avowed pornographer on the other. In addition to his main body of readers, he would command the interest of the pre-adolescent and of the old. If the same does not hold today, it is not because these two social groups have ceased to be important parts of the reading public, but because the young are made sexually conscious at an earlier age, and the jaded palates of the old are partly ministered to by the sensationalism of violence. And it may be that Dickens's continuing popularity, among large

The Middle-aged Lady in the Double-bedded Room.

An illustration from an American newspaper *The Extra Boz Herald*, 1842, based on the original Phiz illustration to *Pickwick Papers*.

sections, is due precisely to the reasons for which Robert Graves condemned him, namely that he affords a welcome relief from the Real David Copperfields and Real Nymphet Nancies, Marthas and Alices with whom we have to do on the screen, big and small, and in the post-*Chatterley* novel.

Thus, although the modern criticism of Dickens, beginning perhaps with Edmund Wilson's fine study, 'Dickens: the Two Scrooges',[24] has sought strenuously to replace the image of the Family Novelist by one more sophisticated, Dickens saw himself, at least during the first part of his career, in precisely this benevolent role. Indeed, he gloried in it. Time and again his attitude is brought out in his letters to Forster. After writing the most famous of his Christmas books, he was in the habit of referring to his point of view, especially in relation to the periodical *Household Words*, as 'Carol philosophy'. The very title of that periodical indicated the kind of influence he wished to exert; and so accustomed was he to being a household word himself that Forster had some difficulty in convincing him, when he proposed in 1858 to adjust the title to *Household Harmony*, that, in view of the publicity attending his domestic rift, such a change would be unfortunate. This overtly moralistic approach was fully compatible with high ideals concerning the function of the novel, which he wished to raise in the general estimation. Indeed, he believed himself to be sustaining the novel's integrity 'through a kind of popular dark age'. Such organizations as the Guild of Literature and Art, which he founded, were intended to further this aim; and he lost no opportunity of condemning as a 'national disgrace' that branch of fiction, led by G. W. Reynolds, which traded in what was then considered salacity. Moreover, Forster, though he did not always see eye to eye with Dickens, especially in later life, probably reflected his friend's own views when pronouncing upon the merits of the novels. In these pronouncements, moral intent and teaching took precedent over literary merit. This may strike us as old-fashioned, until we realize that, among some of our critics, literature itself is set up as the repository of 'civilized values', the ethical being absorbed into the literary. Of *Oliver Twist* Forster remarked that 'the purpose was not solely to amuse', for 'with only the light arms of humour and laughter and the gentle ones of pathos and sadness, he carried cleansing and reform into those Augean stables' (i.e. 'the prisons and the parish practices of his country'). And although he described Dickens as 'this least didactic of writers', rarely given to 'sermonizing', he remarks of *The Old Curiosity Shop* that its 'grasp of reality' included 'the discernment of good under the least attractive forms, and of evil under its most captivating disguises . . .', even adding that 'many an oversuspicious person will find advantage in remembering what a too liberal application of Foxey's principle of suspecting everybody brought Mr Brass to; and many an overhasty judgement of poor human nature will unconsciously be checked, when it is remembered that Mr Nubbles *did* come back to work out that shilling'. And he sums all this up by saying that 'I am not acquainted with any story in the language more adapted to strengthen in the heart what most needs help and encouragement, to sustain kindly and innocent impulses, to awaken everywhere the sleeping sense of good.' Then he adds, almost as an afterthought: 'Its effect as a mere piece of art, too, considering the circumstances in which I have shown it to be written, I think noteworthy.' Again, he finds in *Barnaby Rudge* 'much manly upright thinking'. In the *Christmas Carol*, as might be expected, he discerns an appeal to 'the selfish man to rid himself of selfishness; the just man to make himself generous; and the good-natured man to enlarge the sphere of his good nature. Its cheering voice of faith and hope . . .' etc., etc. Of *David Copperfield*, which he considered the most successful among the novels for 'unity of drift and purpose', he remarked that 'by the course of events we learn the value of self-denial and patience, quiet endurance of unavoidable ills, strenuous efforts against ills remediable: and everything in the fortunes of the actors warns us, to strengthen our generous emotions and to guard the purities of home.' In *Little Dorrit* again, he discerns the author's 'clear design, worthy of him in a special degree, of contrasting, both in private and in public life, and in poverty equally as in wealth, duty done and duty not done.'

This selection of comments is open to the stricture that Forster was primarily a biographer and not a literary critic. But apart from the fact that he devoted several chapters to 'Dickens as a novelist', beginning with an attack upon Taine, his judgements are of interest as revealing what, in offering them, he believed to be critically apposite. Although it may be denied that a novelist has a right to instruct his readers in moral virtue, many readers not merely believed themselves to be instructed but assumed that instruction, under the pleasing guise of entertainment, was part of a novelist's job. When in 1847, with *Dombey* on his hands, Dickens felt he might be unable to complete *The Haunted Man* in time, he expressed regret at having to 'leave any gap at Christmas firesides which I ought to fill'. The Christmas books and stories were intended to be 'seasonal'; they extended not merely the compliments but the message of the season. And if it is maintained that they lack art, some other term will have to be invented to describe the lasting appeal exerted by *A Christmas Carol* and by the Mrs Lirriper stories, if by none of the others. (The number in which Mrs Lirriper first appeared sold 220,000 copies in six weeks). Certainly, Dickens wrote *Chuzzlewit* to expose the evils of selfishness, as he wrote *Dombey* to expose the evils of pride. Forster points out that Sara Coleridge was anxious that her children should enjoy as much 'the very marked and available morals' of *Chuzzlewit* as the 'fun'. And in writing *The Chimes* Dickens declared to Forster (1844) that he had 'a notion of making a great blow for the poor', so that the book might have 'a grip upon the very throat of the time'. No man took more seriously 'the eternal duties of the arts to the public'.[25] In short, criticism cannot turn its face against what a writer professes to be doing, however valid its elucidation of what he may otherwise have achieved.[26]

The tendency of the successful writer, and perhaps even more the successful publisher, though not always of the critic,[27] is to believe that the recipe can be repeated. The remarkable fact about Dickens is that he repeated the success of *Pickwick Papers* not merely after but during the writing of that work; and in a sense he performed this feat twice over. The first instalment of *Oliver Twist* appeared in February 1837 (*Pickwick* came to an end in November): and before *Oliver Twist* itself was half-finished, *Nicholas Nickleby* was begun. The latter was brought to a close in September 1839, and its reception proved, as Arthur Waugh wrote,[28] that 'success was no wayward or ephemeral achievement, and that its author had qualities which were likely to endure. . . . Henceforth he was no longer a newcomer, challenging recognition, but a familiar and expected favourite.' Two months before completing *Nickleby*, however, Dickens had conceived the idea of a different kind of publication altogether. This was to take the form of a weekly periodical of which he was to write the entirety. The aim was to resume the *Sketches* which had first brought him to public attention, and to detach some characters from *Pickwick Papers* with a view to exploiting their success. Beginning in April 1840, the experiment which launched *Master Humphrey's Clock* was short-lived. Although the sales of the first numbers reached 70,000 copies, this figure was not maintained; and Dickens, realizing that the public wanted another of his serials, decided to turn a short tale or 'little child-story', as he called it, into a long one. This was *The Old Curiosity Shop*. Even then, the response was not immediate. The characters from *Pickwick* and some of the familiar 'tales' occupied three issues between the first and second chapters of the novel. It was only the introduction of Dick Swiveller, like that of Sam Weller at a similar moment, which initiated the great success which Little Nell consolidated.[29]

Whereas *Pickwick Papers* had provided a new comedy, *The Old Curiosity*

Shop provided a new pathos. To this extent the one work complemented the other. (Steven Marcus has pointed out another complementarity. *Oliver Twist* was 'in the writing three months before *Pickwick Papers*, with Pickwick's entrance into the Fleet, undertook the kind of social satire with which *Oliver Twist* is launched. Dickens is that unique instance – a novelist whose first book may be said to have been influenced by his second.'[30]) The reason why *The Old Curiosity Shop* has worn less well than *Pickwick Papers* has been much debated. Is it that the sources of mirth are relatively constant, whereas those of pathos seem to vary? Certainly the practice of shedding tears, as a social convention, changes from generation to generation, at one moment being respectable and at another a source of acute embarrassment. This is a point to which we shall return.

In its time, *The Old Curiosity Shop* struck home as surely as did *Pickwick;* but Little Nell enthusiasts, such as Francis Jeffrey, Macready, Thomas Hood, and even Edgar Allan Poe, not to mention the anonymous millions who wept copiously over her slow decline and death, have no equivalent today, nor can we imagine a generation arising which will again take her to its heart, unless our culture should undergo total transformation.[31] It is the *Pickwick* tradition which has survived, and this has a direct bearing upon the maintenance of Dickens's popularity.

It is curious, therefore, that some of the earliest and most weighty criticism of Dickens should have been directed as much against the humour, or its mechanism, as against the pathos. There were on occasion bitter condemnations in the manner of the old *Edinburgh Review*, tilting desperately at the prevailing adulation. An example is Sir James Fitzjames Stephen's onslaught in the *Saturday Review* (1859) on *A Tale of Two Cities*.[32] But the first considered and comprehensive attack upon Dickens as a novelist, apart from that of Taine, was an article by G. H. Lewes, published in the *Fortnightly Review* in February 1872, which Forster took pains to rebut. Like Taine, Lewes concedes almost everything to Dickens short of supreme greatness. If he damns, it is with high praise. He does not engage in literary criticism proper. As a former friend of Dickens, and as a critic no less interested in the sciences than in the arts, he seeks to probe Dickens's psychology. Recalling a remark of Dickens that he could distinctly 'hear' everything his characters said before he wrote it down, Lewes concludes that the novelist was subject to recurrent hallucinations, and that his imaginative gifts were, in part at least, due to an abnormal mental condition. In other words, he believed that Dickens, like Hamlet, was 'a little mad'. When he voiced this opinion, such assertions were considered rather more daring than they would be today.[33] One can understand

Forster's indignation, and why his attack on Lewes is the most stinging
in his otherwise charitable biography. Although much light fun has been
made of Forster, he was a faithful and selfless friend of more than one man
of genius. Apart from that, he was a capable lawyer and man of business,
and incidentally he was a Commissioner in Lunacy; and this may have fed
his animus against Lewes, whose researches into the abnormal may have
seemed to him in this instance wide of the mark.[34] Nevertheless, Lewes's
attack, whatever its psychological foundation, is one of the first to accuse
Dickens of excessive caricature and exaggeration. We find the criticism
foreshadowed in so early an assessment as David Masson's discussion of
Dickens and Thackeray in his *British Novelists and their Styles* (1859), one
of the earliest and best examples of criticism in the modern sense; we find
it repeated in Gissing, though Gissing worshipped Dickens this side
idolatry; and in many a lesser critic. And it is one of the reasons why people
commonly object to Dickens, complaining that his humour, like his pathos,
is too far-fetched.

Dickens was not unaware of the temptations to which his exuberant
imagination could lead him. Writing to Lord Lytton, he confessed that it
was his 'infirmity to fancy or perceive relations in things which are not
apparent generally', and that he had 'such an inexpressible enjoyment' of
what he saw 'in a droll light' that he was tempted 'to pet it like a spoilt
child'. Forster rightly argued that such spoiling of the child led on occasion
to the grotesque. Undoubtedly, it did so; but the *genre* has since returned to
favour. For an interesting study of the grotesque in Dickens, we may go to
Dickens and Kafka (1963) by Mark Spilka. On the other hand, William
Ross, editor of *Discussions of Charles Dickens*,[35] warns that 'the recent
tendency to make Dickens over into our own twentieth century neurotic
image has gone too far'.

The defence of Dickens against excessive caricature and exaggeration
began as early as *The Old Curiosity Shop*. A writer who had some experience
in the matter, Poe, observed, in writing of that novel in 1841, that 'no
critical principle is more firmly based in reason than that a certain amount
of exaggeration is essential to the proper depiction of truth itself'; and he
went on to remark that 'we do not paint an object to be true, but to appear
true to the beholder'. Writing eighty years later, with the whole of
Dickens's work open to inspection, George Santayana, for whom Dickens
was 'the perfect comedian', remarked that 'when people say that Dickens
exaggerates, it seems to me that they have no eyes and no ears. They probably have only *notions* of what things and people are; they accept them
conventionally, at their diplomatic value.'[36] The character most often cited

by the hostile critics is Mr Micawber, who can be relied upon, whenever he enters the story, to say approximately the same things. An even more striking example perhaps is Mrs Gamp; and it is noteworthy that when she is roundly castigated at the end of the novel by Old Chuzzlewit, her reaction is such that, almost as if the machinery of her character were set going at an abnormal speed, her entire repertoire comes tumbling out phrase by phrase. Yet it is clear that in these and other characters, Dickens deliberately contrived such repetition. Mr Micawber was not conjured out of the air: Dickens had in mind his father. Nor, for that matter, was Mrs Gamp; Dickens modelled her on a real personage. Next, it may be asked what human norm the critics have in mind by which they measure these so-called distortions of nature. Alain, Orwell and Morse all defend Dickens against the charge of exaggeration, though not for the same reason as Santayana. They hold that Dickens's characters inhabit a kind of eternity which lends them the appearance of monstrosities. But Dickens's most grotesque characters are not all exaggerations. Of what are Quilp and Silas Wegg the caricatures? John Holloway makes the point that 'caricature . . . registers the distortion, the contortion, of man by society'.[37] Santayana, whose essay is surely one of the most percipient studies of Dickens, pursues the subject as follows:

The world is a perpetual caricature of itself; at every moment it is the mockery and the contradiction of what it is pretending to be. But as it nevertheless tends all the time to be something different and highly dignified, at the next moment it corrects and checks and tries to cover up the absurd thing it was; so that a conventional world, a world of masks, is superimposed on the reality, and passes in every sphere of human interest for the reality itself.

Accordingly, Santayana concludes that 'humour is the perception of this illusion, the fact allowed to pierce here and there through the convention, whilst the convention continues to be maintained, as if we had not observed its absurdity.'

The nature and function of humour, and of Dickens's humour in particular, have hardly been better defined, though Chesterton comes near to it in the brilliant book he published in 1906, when Dickens's reputation among the critics was in one of its troughs. What Santayana fails to explain, here or elsewhere, is *why* the world should be 'a contradiction of what it is pretending to be'. Such a view is intelligible only if we presuppose a measure of imperfection in human nature itself. Humour would have no place in a perfect world. When the miracle and mystery plays wished to introduce a comic element, in response to a popular craving, they were obliged to bring in a character who had been turned out of

heaven, namely Satan. Master of humour though he was, Dickens held no
strong theological beliefs inclining him to the view that mankind had
suffered a Fall. His attitude to Christianity and to the Christian festivals
bears little relation, as Edgar Johnson has pointed out, to Christian dogma
or the niceties of theology;[38] and although Forster stressed the thoughtful
side of Dickens's nature, he also makes the illuminating observation that
'there was for him no "city of the mind" against outward ills, for inner
consolation or shelter. It was in and from the actual he still stretched
forward to find freedom and satisfaction of an ideal':[39] a point echoed, in
more critical tones, by others. *The Life of Our Lord*, written in 1849 but
not published until 1934, was intended, like *A Child's History of England*, for
the edification of his family. Although perhaps a rather better work than
critics have held, it is infused with an undogmatic, almost Tolstoyan out-
look, such as Dickens preserved throughout life, and in terms of which he
wrote an illuminating passage at the close of his will.[40] But a man's avowed
beliefs need not be those which crystallize out from his works. Rex Warner
has argued,[41] in contrast to some other critics, that Dickens did not
sentimentalize human nature. At the same time, he differed from many
other reformers in his *disbelief in institutions*.[42] It would perhaps be near
the truth to say that, since he had spent early in life *une saison en enfer*,
which left its mark permanently upon him, he had an intuitive understanding of the inherent tragedy of existence, and that his humour was a
native endowment enabling him to face his hidden anguish and disillusion.
T. S. Eliot has remarked that the reality of Dickens's characters seems
to descend upon them 'by a kind of inspiration or grace';[43] but this would
be true only of the great comic creations, Micawber, Pecksniff, Mantalini,
Gamp. Whatever else humour may be, it is a form of *release*.

To return to the pathos, it is worth enquiring at what point and for what
reason this ceased to reduce audiences and readers to tears, and came to be
regarded as insufferably mawkish, and what effect this change has had on
Dickens's fame. For many years the story of Little Nell provided readers
on both sides of the Atlantic, and in Europe too, with as much a 'release'
as the humour.[44] The statue in Philadelphia of Nell gazing up at her creator
is sufficient proof of this marked effect; nor is that piece of sculpture lacking
in a certain quiet beauty. Although the sociologist should here properly
intervene, no survey of Dickens's reputation can evade this problem. We
have to do with a change of convention, and perhaps with a deeper social
change. Until the end of the Edwardian period, if we are to rely upon such
an interesting social chronicle as E. F. Benson's *As We Were* (1930), it was

customary for a certain amount of decorous weeping to take place at gatherings where a pathetic song or recitation was given. Perhaps the First World War, with its enormous casualty lists, put a stop to this polite convention, by providing enough real rather than imaginary reasons for tears, just as the Second World War killed the French Grand Guignol, which had lost its excitement for a public familiar with the 'conventions' of Buchenwald and Auschwitz. The nineteenth- and early twentieth-century indulgence in vicarious grief and sentiment would seem to have implied an excess of feeling seeking outlet; and this may have been due partly to what Beatrice Webb, a woman of powerful emotions herself, called 'a social consciousness of sin'. It is the waif-Marchioness and the stray-Nell, and not the privileged Rose Maylie, Agnes Wickfield, Esther Summerson, Bella Wilfer or Edith Dombey, who are supposed to wring our hearts; and the same would apply to the tragic male characters, the despairing Fleet prisoner in *Pickwick*, Trotty Veck, Smike, and Jo. In other words, the pity was expended for the helpless and innocent outcasts: those for whose blood, toil and sweat an acquisitive society had nothing to offer but its tears. The innocence is important: we pity Oliver more than the Artful Dodger. The privilege is important: we smile at Dora, but she does not arouse our anguish like Little Nell. The virtual disappearance in the West, if not of poverty then of pauperism, as a permanent and seemingly irremediable social condition, and therefore as a constant reproach to persons of feeling, has rendered the sentimental portrayal of 'professional' social outcasts not merely insupportable but a trifle absurd. Aldous Huxley's tirade against such characters as Little Nell in his essay *Vulgarity in Literature* (1930), and many a similar attack,[45] are due to the sense of being emotionally blackmailed.

No doubt the pre-emancipated woman, precisely because of her restricted and hedged-about life, became the object of sentimental solicitude for a somewhat similar reason. Her 'innocence' was heightened to the point where she became Patmore's 'angel in the house', of whom Agnes and Florence are the fictional prototypes, and thus the guardian of morals. This is not a fanciful speculation. In 1847 was published the first *Ladies Newspaper*. According to the advertisements, the aim of the proprietors was 'not only to exclude all that is objectionable, but to be lavish of information on the useful and the elegant; and in an interesting and unswerving spirit to advocate those high truths, Religious and Moral, of which WOMAN, *unfettered by ambition and comparatively free from the turmoils of the world*, has ever been the faithful Guardian.'[46]

The modern revulsion against Little Nell, as also against such excursions into the pathetic as *A Child's Dream of a Star*, which Dickens wrote for

Household Words (April 1850) to lend an early number some tenderness, has overshadowed some of his more successful essays in pathos; for Dickens's continued popularity is surely due partly to the fact that he can delineate a pathetic scene with mastery when he is not probing obsessively for the tender spot, or exploiting a 'reserved' subject. Nicholas Nickleby is in tears within a few lines of being introduced to the reader, and tears flow so freely throughout the novel as would have left their real counterparts dehydrated. The amount of weeping done by characters in *Copperfield* from the time of Mrs Strong's confession onwards is prodigious. Nearly all the characters are in tears for some of the time, including Betsey Trotwood and even Mr Micawber. Among the major characters, only Uriah Heep remains dry-eyed, but this is because he has other and no less violent emotions to occupy him. (This may have something to do with the inferiority of the second part of the novel to the first.) And the reader was clearly supposed to be set off himself by this parade of grief. Today, such a reaction would appear ludicrous and forced, as do certain of the episodes themselves, especially when the characters switch, under emotion, to a peculiarly insipid rhetoric. Annie Strong's unburdening is a case in point. It is not so much a woman as an abstract 'virtue' declaiming; and as she has nothing really to unburden herself about, the effect is particularly vapid. Many of Little Nell's speeches are delivered in the same vein. If she had but once engaged in *badinage* with Codlin and Short, we should have recognized her humanity. Nevertheless, when Dickens ceases to probe, to exploit, and above all when he can bring a touch of humour and even farce into a situation otherwise distressing, he can achieve masterpieces of true pathos. Traddles's fiancée Sophy is surely a more vivid character than Agnes – even though we hear about her so fitfully – because she is first brought to life in the context of her preposterous family.

Detail from an illustration by Phiz from *Nicholas Nickleby*, showing Madeline fainting and one of her companions in tears.

Unfortunately, when Dickens achieved what might well be considered the perfect pathetic conclusion to a story, namely the first version of the end to *Great Expectations*, he was persuaded, against his better judgement, and incidentally that of Forster (it was at Bulwer Lytton's prompting), to turn it into a happy ending. The original is consistent with the story and perfectly muted, without a touch of the old rhetoric. Pip chances to meet Estella in London, and notices the sombre change in her. 'I was glad afterwards to have had the interview; for in her face and in her voice, and in her touch, she gave me the assurance that suffering had been stronger than Miss Havisham's teaching, and had given her a heart to understand what my heart used to be.'

It is perfect – and was discarded.[47]

That audiences in Dickens's lifetime responded with equal relish to the pathos and to the humour we know not merely from his sales but from the response to the Readings. Indeed, in composing the serial parts of his novels, he endeavoured to maintain a balance of the two qualities. What he never did, and for this he has been reproached, was to exert any purely intellectual appeal. It is remarkable that among his characters there is not a single credible 'intellectual', nor even, as George Orwell says, any character with any 'mental life'.[48] Santayana remarks 'how insensible Dickens was to the greater themes of the human imagination – religion, science, politics, art.' And A. O. J. Cockshut[49] speaks of 'the meagreness of his intellectual comment on what he had seen' by contrast with his 'incomparable power' of imaginative observation. On the contrary, Mrs Wititterly in *Nicholas Nickleby*, with her intellectual pretensions and her 'soul'; the clever 'transcendentalist' American ladies in *Martin Chuzzlewit;* and the Hon. Mrs Skewton in *Dombey* with her harping on 'nature' and 'heart', are devastatingly satirized; and dear old Dr Strong's most sympathetic companion is after all not David Copperfield but Mr Dick. Even so, the absence of intellectual pretensions, though it may not have furthered his reputation among the few, did not detract from it among the many. There is also the interesting point made by John Bayley, writing of *Oliver Twist* in *Dickens and the Twentieth Century*,[50] that 'no novelist has profited more richly than Dickens from not examining what went on in his own mind. His genius avoids itself like a sleep-walker avoiding an open window.' What Henry James did for the novel, and Paul Valéry for poetry, seem to be incompatible with such popularity as Dickens enjoyed. The anonymous folk who came to leave flowers on his grave in 1870 felt that he was one of them, in which assumption they were more correct than they knew. 'To say that he was not a gentleman,' wrote Forster, 'would be as true as to say that he was not a writer; but if anyone should assert his occasional preference for what was even beneath his level over that which was above it, this would be difficult of disproof.'[51] In other words, Dickens, as much in his personal life as in his books, identified himself with the underprivileged; and this was to unite him with the mass of people in a way which post-1870 generations – and he died in an important year, that of the Education Act of another Forster – may find difficult to grasp.

The absence of intellectual interest was shown up more clearly when a competitor appeared on the scene. George Eliot, whose first book was published in 1857, provided not merely abundant moralizing but a great deal for the reader to think about. By the time of *Middlemarch* (1872), she had undoubtedly captured some of Dickens's public, and she was making increasing appeal to the growing number of the 'educated'. In her hands, the novel became a force for enlightenment more openly and on a higher level than Dickens had sought to make it. Not that George Eliot's capacity for entertainment should be underestimated. She had a marked comic gift; high-souled female guardians of morals were not necessarily among her best characters. Her great influence is indicated by her sales, and the immense sums she earned for her later books. Furthermore, she introduced a new class of character into the novel, namely the traders and labourers of the Midlands, for whom she became as gifted a spokesman as Dickens had been for the Londoner. Dickens knew his England well, as Walter Dexter demonstrated in a series of studies;[52] but although Dickens was a tourist in Scotland, Yorkshire, and the West Country, and although he lived for long periods abroad, he was above all a Londoner. When he first purchased Gad's Hill, he had no intention of living there permanently, the pull of London remained so strong. Ivor Brown has pointed out in his chapter on 'Dickens as Social Reformer' how different London was, and how different Dickens found it to be, from the industrial North. During his Yorkshire journey in quest of material for *Nickleby*, he described how he travelled, with Hablôt K. Browne, through such 'miles of cinder-paths, and blazing furnaces, and roaring steam-engines, and such a mass of dirt, gloom and misery, as I never before witnessed.' It is perhaps his permanent hankering for an even *earlier* London (several of his novels, e.g. *Pickwick*, *Nickleby*, *The Old Curiosity Shop*, and *Little Dorrit* are back-dated) which has appealed to later generations, for whom not merely the City but now Highgate, Islington and Canonbury possess a charm faintly recalling the pre-railway era. During the Festival of Britain in 1952, no visitor could fail to have been struck by the numerous places associated with Dickens, who, with Shakespeare, monopolized the South Bank. 'The streets of London', as Christopher Hibbert has said in his chapter, 'were the heart and the inspiration of the Dickens world.' It may also be recalled that the original content of *Master Humphrey's Clock* was to be, in Magog's words, 'legends of London and her sturdy citizens from the old simple times' – another evocation of that more ancient and natural order for which Dickens preserved a nostalgia.

George Eliot was followed by talents as original as Meredith, James, Hardy, and Conrad. These authors were by some considered superior to Dickens, especially in so far as they gave their readers a sense of superiority. It was no doubt for this reason, apart from the normal swing of the pendulum, that not long after Dickens's death the *critical* estimate of his work began, if only momentarily, to plummet. As a writer in the *London*

Quarterly Review observed in 1871: 'Though Dickens's works are still by far the most popular of his age, we have never met a single man of high cultivation who regarded Dickens in the light of an artist at all, or looked upon his books as greatly worthy the attention of persons capable of appreciating better things.'[53] Among the intelligentsia such a judgement was not untypical, nor, as Professor Ford adds, was it uncommon during the sixty years to follow. Fellow novelists such as Thackeray and Trollope could be condescending enough, the latter particularly about Dickens's style; and Henry James held the view that from *Bleak House* onwards Dickens had been forcing himself, and that *Our Mutual Friend* was 'dug out with a spade and pickaxe'. Leslie Stephen said that Dickens's appeal was chiefly to the semi-literate,[54] and Leslie Stephen's daughter, Virginia Woolf, compared Dickens unfavourably with George Eliot, a writer, as she said, for 'grown ups'.[55] Robert Graves[56] assumed, against all evidence, that Dickens was no longer read except by 'the great backward public of the depressed provinces and semi-residential suburbs', but admitted, in terms similar to those used by the intellectuals who defended *Fanny Hill*, that 'he supplies plentiful and interesting detail about houses, cottages, inns, schools, offices, shops, prisons, streets, water-fronts,' etc. etc., holding this to be 'perhaps the strongest incentive to reading him in the original'! Nor are such aspersions as we have cited uncommon today, despite the great 'Dickens boom' of which J. Hillis Miller has spoken. By contrast, A. E. Dyson, in his admirable introduction to the symposium *Dickens* (1968), points out that 'no one pretends any longer that he is unread, or that his readers are too lower middle class to count'. It was the aim of Monroe Engel's *Maturity of Charles Dickens* (1959) to 'insist that Dickens can and should be read with pleasure and no restriction of intelligence by post-Jamesian adults'.

Yet if the critical estimate of Dickens reached its lowest point in the early years of this century, it may seem a paradox that in 1902 the Dickens Fellowship should have been founded. This was not a desperate move to salvage Dickens's works from popular neglect. There was no popular neglect. To quote Professor Ford again: 'the qualities which have sustained Dickens's fame among less critical readers have included those already discussed as making the strongest appeal to the general Victorian public'.[57] But the interesting fact is that Dickens now enjoys a reputation among *critics*, as an accomplished and conscious artist, far higher than ever before. The *Guide to Doctoral Dissertations in Victorian Literature, 1886–1958*, contains details of fifty Ph.D. theses on Dickens before 1950, but thirty-two theses between 1950 and 1958 – that is, over half as many as in the ninety-four years prior to 1950.[58] Moreover, in the *Bibliographies of Studies in Victorian Literature for the Ten Years 1955–1964*, edited by Robert C. Slack, Volume 3,[59] there are listed more than twice as many articles on Dickens as on any other Victorian writer.

Far from the Ellen Ternan revelations causing the popular disenchantment that might have been expected, they may actually have helped to sustain the renewed interest in Dickens. On the four hundredth anniversary of Shakespeare's presumed birthday in 1964, the *Daily Mirror*, anxious to make its special or specialist contribution to the general celebrations, carried the headline: '400 Years To-day, and Now the Shocking Truth about William Shakespeare'. In fact, the truth, shocking or not, had been known to most people, including presumably some readers of the *Daily Mirror*, for some time. The 'shocking truth' about Dickens had been known at least since Thomas Wright's revelations, published originally in the *Daily Express* in 1934, and confirmed in *Dickens and Daughter* (1939) by Gladys Storey, in Ada Nisbet's *Dickens and Ellen Ternan* (1952: revised in 1953), and in Edgar Johnson's biography. There is no evidence that 'the truth' has injured his reputation.[60] And just as these biographical revelations, however interpreted, have shown Dickens to be a more complicated, possibly a somewhat less attractive, yet doubtless a more remarkable man than was thought, so his work is now seen to exhibit qualities, and to possess dimensions, of which the critics of yesterday seemed unaware. In short, the deep and enduring appeal of Dickens is perhaps better understood now that his 'special relationship' with his readers has given place to one less personal. While the novels were being serialized, usually for a stretch of nineteen or twenty months, he was engaged in a dialogue in which the public, apart from direct contact by letter (which was not infrequent[61]), were able to participate by their patronage. This patronage could be withheld or extended as inclination dictated. On the other hand, serial publication often necessitated cutting, especially at the last moment, and the comic episodes were those most frequently sacrificed.[62] There was even a moment, after *Chuzzlewit*, when Dickens contemplated abandoning the serial form altogether. It is now possible to have the novels as Dickens originally wrote them; and this is the aim of the Oxford Dickens, as well as the Signet Classics and Pan Books editions.[63]

The new criticism of Dickens has gone hand in hand with systematic Dickens studies, both textual and sociological. These latter date from before the war, and include the Nonesuch Dickens,[64] the separate publication of Dickens's letters to his wife, *Mr and Mrs Charles Dickens*,[65] the biographies of Wright (1935), Pope-Hennessy (1945), Pearson (1949), Lindsay (1950), Symons (1951), Johnson (1953) and Hibbert (1967). Of these the most comprehensive is that of Edgar Johnson, without question the greatest biography of Dickens since Forster, and unlikely to be superseded for several generations; with which we may group in particular the Clarendon Edition of the novels and the Pilgrim Edition of the letters.[66]

Having claimed that never has Dickens enjoyed so high a critical reputation as today, we may venture further: we may affirm that some of the best contemporary criticism has been Dickens criticism. It is curious that Paul Elmer More should have declared that Dickens 'will not bear analysis'.[67] Even although he would appear to place Dickens apart from the writers of his Great Tradition, F. R. Leavis is without doubt among the distinguished Dickens critics; nor is his approval confined to *Hard Times*, as is sometimes supposed. In the *Spectator* for January 1963, he went so far as to say: 'I would without hesitation surrender the whole *oeuvre* of Flaubert for *Dombey and Son* or *Little Dorrit.*'[68] And we may agree with Marcus that Leavis's analysis of Dickens's *style* is the best that has so far been made.[69] Works such as Marcus's own *From Pickwick to Dombey* (1965), which is to be followed by a companion volume, J. Hillis Miller's *Charles Dickens, the World of His Novels* (1958), A. O. J. Cockshut's *The Imagination of Charles Dickens* (1961), K. J. Fielding's *Charles Dickens, A Critical Introduction* (1958), the extremely interesting study by Mark Spilka *Dickens and Kafka* (1963), and Monroe Engel's *Maturity of Dickens* (1959), the symposia *Dickens and his Readers* (1955), *The Dickens Critics* (1961), and *Dickens and the Twentieth Century* (1962), not to mention the works of continental scholars such as Sylvère Monod's *Dickens Romancier* (1954), have underlined the unity of Dickens's work, his symbolism, and his poetic method. As K. J. Fielding has pointed out,[70] Dickens criticism has grown so subtle and complex that the wheel is beginning to come full circle, and 'by some sophisticated by-ways, after intensive study and careful thought, we have been brought back to a sensitive appreciation of what Dickens's novels ought to mean to a good reader'; and this links up with our earlier point that twentieth-century professional criticism and appreciation have confirmed in the main the consensus of the ordinary nineteenth-century reader.

In a recent article,[71] D. W. Brogan confessed that he preferred biographies of novelists (e.g. Thackeray) to the novels themselves. But naturally no one would search out details of the life of Thackeray but for the works that bear his name. The same principle applies to books which discuss Dickens's attitude to various social problems, though we must bear in mind that Dickens made a formidable reputation as a journalist, and that his talents in this sphere alone could have brought him to the forefront of public attention. A collection such as *The Uncommercial Traveller*, which contains many admirable pieces, is increasingly read and cited. Recent studies such as *Dickens on Education* (1959) by J. Manning, *Dickens and Crime* (1962) and *Dickens and Education* (1963), both by P. A. W. Collins, and *Love and Property in the Novels of Charles Dickens* (1968), by Ross H. Dabney, derive their interest and justification from their promotion of a deeper understanding of the novels. In the last of these works, the point is made that many of Dickens's love situations are, as so often in the Victorian era, bound up with property-situations, but that in more than one case the lovers are brought together in consequence of a loss, rather than a gain, of fortune. Little Dorrit and Arthur Clennam feel free to avow their love only

First page of *Dombey and Daughter* by Renton Nicholson, 1850, published a few years after *Dombey and Son* appeared in monthly parts (1846-8).

DOMBEY AND DAUGHTER.

CHAPTER I.

DIM LOCALITIES OF LONDON—DESCEND WITH ME —A QUEER NEIGHBOURHOOD AND THE INHA-BITANTS THEREOF DESCRIBED—ALL IN THE SHADES BELOW—PETER THE HERBALIST, SOOTH-SAYER, AND QUACK-DOCTOR INTRODUCED—HIS INDULGENCES VIVIFIED—A COLD NIGHT—AN EVENING CALL—MRS. FRIBBLE, THE OBJECT OF HER VISIT—THE DOCTOR'S RESOLVE, JOURNEY IN PURSUIT OF FAME, &c.

There are in London localities as little known to the majority of the denizens of the "great wen," as the icebergs of the northern seas, or the scorching sunfires of the distant tropics—less known, certainly, less known; for into the recesses of some dark metropolitan obscurities the mind is never led, even by books, by maps, or charts; while the penetrating lamp of discovery has been lighted by the enterprise of skilful hu-manity, over the latitude and longitude of lands and seas, of deserts and of rivers, far, far be-yond the trace of the camel's foot, or the voice of even barbarian mortality.

Descend with me, oh! fair and gentle reader, descend with me to the level of the Thames. I when they both suffer total financial ruin. The intricate plot of *Bleak House* is unravelled only when the Jarndyce suit, coming to an end, has swallowed up all the money. This is perhaps another clue to the popularity of Dickens, at least in his day. Being mostly poor, or with the ever-present threat of poverty hanging over their heads, his readers did not always respond to the 'success story' as conceived in conventional materialist terms: Lucky Jim belongs to the Welfare State, not to the state of *laissez-faire*. And it is remarkable how many of Dickens's heroes and heroines are not merely illegitimate but revealed as such in the *dénouement*. Oliver Twist is illegitimate, whereas his profligate half-brother Monks is not; Esther Summerson is illegitimate, and so is Arthur Clennam. Here again, Dickens's lesson was probably not lost upon a society in which birth counted for so much; for Dickens's audience had for the most part no pretensions save to a neat gentility at best, and the exaltation of the humble, the meek, and the despised was part of their own instinctive understanding of the Gospels, whatever the multiplicity of wealthy benefices might suggest.[72]

Finally, there are the numerous extensions and adjuncts to Dickens's reputation: the films to which his novels have shown themselves so readily adaptable, for reasons which Emlyn Williams has given in his chapter on 'Dickens and the Theatre': the musicals, particularly the extraordinarily successful *Oliver*, and more recently its film version.[73] The projection of Dickens on stage and screen would seem to have increasing potentialities, even though extreme liberties are taken with his work, as indeed they were in his lifetime.

As to that work, it is so vast and many-sided, and retains to this day such vitality, as to be able to sustain the shock of the most bitter detraction, and equally to survive praise which is insidious in its one-sidedness. We may be confident that whatever men may be reading in another century, they will be reading Dickens: for his influence has become a necessary ingredient in our civilized life, and his gift was capacious enough to have satirized *in advance* the humbug, pretentiousness and chicanery to which human nature is predisposed. For zest and gusto this endowment is without a parallel; no-one 'stops the show' like Dickens. It is because his art both 'antedates' the novel and may well survive it; it is because he is at heart a traditional teller of tales and the inventor of a mythology concerning people larger than life,[74] that his appeal remains perennial. His reputation both in his own country and abroad has long burst the narrow banks of 'literature' and become part of everyday existence; and that is why he so well merits the title, conferred on him by *The Times* at his death, of the Great Commoner of English Letters.

Dickensiana

The 'Dickens Industry' dates from the triumphant success of 'Pickwick', which swiftly made Boz a national figure. With their quirks, mannerisms, and unforgettable sayings, the Dickensian characters began to set a fashion which has never quite become outmoded. They were used to embellish every sort of advertisement as well as cigarette-cards [5], calendars [7], and song sheets [8]. Accessories of every variety played upon Dickensian themes [1], and such a master of his craft naturally lent his name, or rather had it borrowed, for advertisements for pens, ink and writing equipment [2 and 3]. Moreover, the titles of the books and pictures of their author were repeatedly used for sales promotion of all kinds of goods [4 and 6]. There were Pickwick hats and cigars, Weller corduroys, and Dolly Varden bonnets, while even today an umbrella is often called a 'gamp'.

No sooner had Dickens become the most popular novelist of the English-speaking world than there was a demand for translations of his works [9-15], and today there are few major languages in which they have not been rendered. The universality of his humour has made him popular in East as well as West; and neither changing social conditions nor ideological differences have lessened his appeal. Dickens has a particular attraction for the enormous reading public of the Soviet Union, where his sales have run into millions. (This has been partly responsible for the impression, widely shared, that contemporary Britain resembles the Britain of Dickens's day.) He has also a faithful public in India, where two of his sons were stationed, and even Japan, where despite cultural differences, the great type-characters, Pecksniff, Micawber, Mr Dombey, and the melodramatic plots, are appreciated on account of their compatability with the comic Noh and the Kabuki tradition. Only Shakespeare has outstripped Dickens in world influence, and in the way in which his characters have become part of everyday life.

☞

1 A Dickens bookma
'Learning by study must be won,
'Twas ne'er entailed from sire to son.'

1

Dickens

2

2 and **3** Dickens (with other celebrated writers) singing the praises of Draper's Ink and writing with one of 'C. Brandauer & Co's circular pointed pens'. He was a favourite subject for pen-and-ink advertisements.

4 'Anti-Bleak House': part of an advertisement for warm winter clothing by a City tailor, 1888.

5 A series of cigarette-cards showing characters from the novels.

6 An advertisement issued by New Seasons Tea, in which the well-known profile supplies the missing word.

3

ANTI-BLEAK HOUSE.

A BLEAK HOUSE that is indeed, where the north winds meet to howl an ignoble concert, and bitter blasts mourn like tortured spirits of rebels, who, though prisoners, are unsubdued; where the whirlwind and the hurricane vow their vengeance; and the walls and timbers creak resistance, and, like wounded gladiators, rise again boldly to defy the antagonist. Woe to the inhabitant of the Bleak House if he is not armed with the weapons of an OVERCOAT and a SUIT of FASHIONABLE and substantial Clothing, such as can only be obtained at E. MOSES & SON's Establishments, Aldgate and Minories, New Oxford-street, and Hart-street, London; or 36, Fargate, Sheffield, or 19, Bridge-street, Bradford, Yorkshire. Who would covet a Bleak House in the month of March, when the old winds take out a fresh license, and to celebrate their re-commencement in a roaring trade, toss over a few houses, and as if churches were not good enough, but must be punished by their harmless spires being blown down,—or tear up a tree or two to save the boys the trouble of stealing the fruit next autumn, then becoming more mischievous, they toss over an unprotected traveller, and after that blow him up in grand style. But the Anti-Bleak House, the establishment whose inventions can annihilate the effects of biting, pinching, screwing, and driving bleak winds, is E. MOSES & SON's; they are determined their garments shall be proof against bleak winds and heavy showers, against cold blasts and sweeping hurricanes: for this purpose they have invented garments which no wind can penetrate, which fit so exactly to the person of the wearer, that they render him secure as if he occupied an Anti-Bleak House, where the March winds having received due notice to quit, dare not remain for fear of having double rent to pay, by spending their fury without any recompense. E. MOSES AND SON are perfectly satisfied of the resistance their dress will offer to wind or water, being prepared specially for March, strong, but neat, fine, but substantial, warm, but light, comfortable, but fashionable, the designs of artists, whose fame is identified with the success of E. MOSES & SON for manufacturing the only elegant and Anti-Bleak garments in the kingdom, these are characterised by interminable variety, intrinsic excellence, superb quality, and unprecedented in the lowness of the charge—they are the quintessence of fashion, the emblems of true taste, the unrivalled embodiments of grace and neatness, and the approved essentials of gentility and durability.

4

6

☛ *overleaf*

7 A sentimentalized version of Paul and Florence Dombey painted by Jessie Willcox Smith for a Scribner's calendar, 1912.

8 The cover of a Victorian songsheet for 'Jullien's Chimes Quadrilles'.

Paul Dombey and Florence on the Beach at Brighton

His favourite spot was quite a lonely one, far away from most loungers; and with Florence sitting by his side at work, or reading to him, or talking to him, and the wind blowing on his face and the water coming up among the wheels of his bed, he wanted nothing more.

JULY						
Sun	Mon	Tue	Wed	Thur	Fri	Sat
	1	2	3	4	5	6
7	8	9	10	11	12	13
14	15	16	17	18	19	20
21	22	23	24	25	26	27
28	29	30	31	Su	Su	Su

AUGUST						
Sun	Mon	Tue	Wed	Thur	Fri	Sat
				1	2	3
4	5	6	7	8	9	10
11	12	13	14	15	16	17
18	19	20	21	22	23	24
25	26	27	28	29	30	31

SEPTEMBER						
Sun	Mon	Tue	Wed	Thur	Fri	Sat
1	2	3	4	5	6	7
8	9	10	11	12	13	14
15	16	17	18	19	20	21
22	23	24	25	26	27	28
29	30	Su	Su	Su	Su	Su

LONDON, PUBLISHED BY JULLIEN, 3, MADDOX ST. NEW BOND ST.

9

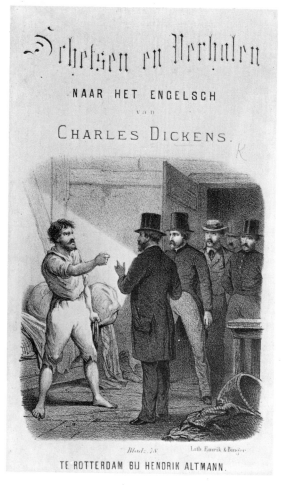

Schetsen en Verhalen

NAAR HET ENGELSCH
van
CHARLES DICKENS.

Bladz. 78.   Lith. Emrik & Binger

TE ROTTERDAM BIJ HENDRIK ALTMANN.

10

DICKENS:

NEHÉZ IDŐK

KARÁCSONYI ÉNEK

RÉVAI TESTVÉREK IROD. INT. R.T.

11

Charles Dickens
Kapetan Smjeli
ILUSTRIRAO
ROBERT STEWART SHERRIFFS

MLADOST
ZAGREB 1951

12

Lorsque le spectre fut à côté de la fenêtre, elle était grande ouverte (page 40)

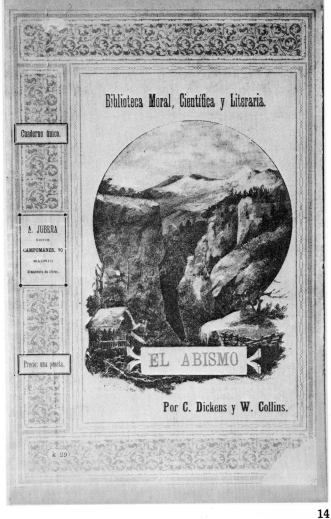

9–15 *Dickens in translation:*
9 Dutch (*Sketches and Stories*).
10 Hungarian (*Hard Times and Christmas Carol*).
11 Serbo-Croat (*Captain Boldheart*, from *Holiday Romance*).
12 Sinhalese (*David Copperfield*).
13 French (*A Christmas Carol*).
14 Spanish (*The Frozen Deep*).
15 Chinese (*David Copperfield*).

16

Notes

Preface

1 *Charles Dickens: His Tragedy and Triumph* (1953), p.46.
2 Ibid., p.x.
3 *The Imagination of Charles Dickens* (1961), p. 175.
4 Graham Greene, Introduction to *Oliver Twist* (1950), quoted in *The Dickens Critics* (1961), edited by George H. Ford and Lauriat Lane, Jr.
5 *The Critical Quarterly*, II (1960). See pp.101-08.
6 Introduction to *Little Dorrit* (1953), quoted in *The Dickens Critics*.

The Great Inimitable

1 Cf. his article on Dickens in the *Dictionary of National Biography*.
2 *Per Amica Silentia Lunae* (1917).

Dickens and his Illustrators

1 The chronology of Dickensian illustration is complicated by a number of factors, principally by changes made between the appearance of the novels in monthly parts, which was how most of them were first issued, and their publication in book form. It is to the latter that dates given here in brackets refer.
2 There seems to be little doubt that *More Hints on Etiquette* (1838), written under the pseudonym of Παιδάγωγος and with woodcuts by Cruikshank, is not, as is sometimes claimed, by Dickens.
3 *Charles Dickens* (1906).
4 *The Letters of Charles Dickens*, ed. Madeline House and Graham Storey, (1965.)
5 'Dickens and his Illustrators', The Nonesuch Dickens *Prospectus* (1937).
6 *The Letters of Charles Dickens*, ed. Madeline House and Graham Storey (1965).
7 *Ibid.*
8 *Ibid.*
9 *Dickens: His Character, Comedy and Career* (1949).
10 *Charles Dickens: His Tragedy and Triumph* (1953).

Dickens's Reputation: a Reassessment

1 'The statements and opinions of this Journal generally are, of course, to be received as the statements and opinions of its Conductor.' Note, *All the Year Round*, 26 December 1863. A volume of Dickens's uncollected writings in *Household Words*, edited by Professor Harry Stone, has just appeared.
2 Cf. also *Dickens at Work*, John Butt and Kathleen Tillotson (1957), p.35.
3 *Op. cit.*, p.37.
4 Cf. Boris Gilenson, 'Dickens in Russia' (*The Dickensian*, January 1961). The Soviet Government issued a stamp with Dickens's portrait to commemorate the 150th anniversary of his birth.
5 *Charles Dickens* (1950).
6 *Op. cit.*, p.8.
7 1941, p.11.
8 Dickens also used the expression in writing to his publisher on 25 February 1836.
9 Forster was incorrect in saying that *Pickwick* was not advertised. Notices appeared in the *Athenæum*, the *Observer*, *The Times*, *John Bull*, etc.
10 *Dickens and His Readers* (1965), pp.5–6.
11 Cf. *The Origin of Pickwick* (1936), by Walter Dexter and J. W. T. Ley, where all the known reviews are cited.
12 The only London paper other than the *Gazette* to review Part IV, *Bell's Life in London*, made no mention of Sam Weller, while of London papers, only the *Gazette* noticed Part V. Sales began to pick up with Part VI, and then there was a rush for back numbers.
13 In a letter written to an Irish friend on 30 June 1837.
14 Ford, *op.cit.*, p.12. Cf. also Steven Marcus, *From Pickwick to Dombey* (1965), p. 28. Writing later to Wills, his assistant editor on *Household Words*, Dickens cautioned him against being 'unnecessarily offensive to the middle classes' – but here the word 'unnecessarily' should be taken into account.
15 Cf. *A Runaway World?* (1968), p.54. To say that Dickens ignored the rampant prostitution in London streets is to ignore the Preface to the third edition of *Oliver Twist* and his collaboration with Baroness Burdett-Coutts in welfare schemes, particularly the

establishment in 1847 of her Home for Fallen Women. See also Note 18.

16 As Robert Morse has pointed out, 'Usually, to point and illustrate his main theme, Dickens selects some social or moral situation in need of reform, and attacks it with hot indignation': *Partisan Review*, XVI, 1949, quoted in *The Dickens Critics* (1966) by George H. Ford and Lauriat Lane, Jr., p.204.

17 Book IX, Chapter VII. It is now in the Berg Collection of the New York Public Library. In fact, Forster did not reproduce the contents in its entirety, and two other public references were made: cf. Felix Aylmer's article on 'John Forster and Dickens's Book of Memoranda' in *The Dickensian* (December 1954).

18 In *The Chimes*, Lilian, the niece of Will Fern, becomes a prostitute in Trotty Veck's dream, and Good Mrs Brown's daughter, Alice, in *Dombey* has clearly sunk into vice – as indeed must have Good Mrs Brown herself. It is not inappropriate that Florence Dombey, falling into the horrible old woman's clutches, should wonder what Bad Mrs Brown could possibly be like. Finally, in *Little Dorrit*, Chapter XIV, Dickens goes out of his way to refer to such women, stressing that they were not to be despised as individuals. J. Hillis Miller, in his *Charles Dickens, the World of His Novels* (1958), Chapter VII, gives an excellent account of this passage.

19 Cf. his remark in the first number of *Household Words* (March 1850) that he aims 'to show to all, that in all familiar things, even in those which are repellent on the surface, there is Romance enough, if we will find it out.' The quality was first recognized in *Sketches by Boz*.

20 Yet, writing in the *Annales de l'Université de Paris*, 1967, No.2, the great French authority on Dickens, Sylvère Monod, insists that with Steerforth, Dickens 'a enfin compris que le Mal est séduisant'.

21 Interestingly enough, by preserving Little Emily's 'honour' until her intimacy with David, and by making her apparently commit suicide for love, Graves is observing a convention even more romantic and melodramatic than

that of Dickens. Apart from this, his attempts at humour are feeble and his style flat.

22 Cf. the interesting letter to Forster dated 15 August 1856; but Monroe Engel, in *The Maturity of Dickens* (1959), p.9, points out that the remarks are equivocal.

23 Barbara Hardy, writing in the *London Review* (Autumn 1967), makes the ingenious suggestion that food and drink take the place in Dickens of the sexual element demanded by mature comedy.

24 *The Wound and the Bow* (1941).

25 Letter to Macready (14 January 1853).

26 Symptomatic of the change of taste is the recent edition of the novels edited by the author's great-grand-daughter, Doris Dickens, in which, with young readers in mind, most passages of 'heavy moralizing' are omitted.

27 Cf. Steven Marcus, *From Pickwick to Dombey* (1965), p.5.

28 Introduction to *Nicholas Nickleby* (1902), Biographical Edition.

29 The rehabilitation of Pickwick and the Wellers, though occasionally amusing, largely misfired; but a later attempt to revive a famous character, Mrs Gamp, was outstandingly good. In order to add to the returns of a benefit performance for Mrs Macready, Dickens wrote a sketch which remained unpublished because the proposed illustrators did not play their part. Edgar Johnson has reproduced the text in his and Eleanor Johnson's *Dickens Theatrical Reader* (1964), under the title of 'Mrs Gamp with the Strollers'.

30 *Op.cit.*, p.55.

31 It was Forster who persuaded Dickens to kill Little Nell, when the work was about half completed. He felt that such 'a gentle, pure little figure and form' should be lifted 'out of the commonplace of happy endings'. It may be remarked that Poe, one of Little Nell's most ardent champions, regarded her death as an artistic blemish, since it was 'excessively painful' and left 'a most distressing oppression of spirit upon the reader'. Pansy Packenham, in *The Dickensian* (January 1958), states that 'for the first time a common

domestic grief was given literary expression and found an echo in thousands of hearts'. But was it so common, and was it so 'domestic'?

32 Yet this novel has never waned in popularity. In Britain alone, sixty separate editions have been issued to date (cf. A. C. Dyson, *Dickens*, 'Modern Judgments', 1968, p. 9).

33 Yet in 1884 Henry James, in *French Poets and Novelists*, associated Dickens with Balzac in his 'force of hallucination'. In an article in the *Sewanee Review* (LVIII, 1950) Dorothy Van Ghent makes the same point with greater precision when she says that 'the point of view is hallucinated and often fearful, as the insecure and the ill-fed child's might be. It is not childish.' Gissing, in his *Charles Dickens: a Critical Study* (1898), stressed how Dickens was 'fond of characters hovering between eccentricity and madness'.

34 It is to be hoped that we may see before long a definitive life of Forster.

35 Boston (1962).

36 *Soliloquies in England* (1922).

37 Introduction to the Penguin *Little Dorrit* (1968).

38 *Charles Dickens: His Tragedy and Triumph* (1953), p. 484.

39 Book VIII, Chapter II.

40 N. C. Peyrouton, answering Edgar Johnson (*The Dickensian*, May 1963), stresses by contrast the orthodoxy of this little work.

41 'On Reading Dickens', *The Cult of Power* (1947).

42 His contempt for the House of Commons was expressed repeatedly in his letters. One of the 'books' in his false bookshelves was entitled 'Hansard's Guide to Refreshing Sleep'.

43 'Dickens and Wilkie Collins', *Selected Essays* (1932).

44 In Brett Hart's poem 'Dickens in Camp', it is Little Nell who is the favourite character.

45 If it is remarked à propos of our reference to the Grand Guignol and its deliberate horrors, that a new violence has now appeared, we can only seek for the emergence of a new kind of pathos; and this may perhaps be found among our Flower Children, with their

reply to any hostile accusation, 'We love you'. (cf. that interesting example of the new sentimentality, with its love-rock-a-bye-baby accompaniment, *Hair*).

46 *Vide The Dickens Advertiser*, by Bernard Darwin (1930) p. 99-101 (my italics).

47 Another unfortunate change, though made in deference to representations from the original, was the case of Miss Mowcher. Chapter XXII of *Copperfield* is surely one of Dickens's masterpieces of ruthless delineation. Chapter XXXII, written after being reproached, is an anti-climax, and the character becomes hardly more than a cog in the plot. It is only fair to add, à propos of the end of *Great Expectations*, that some modern critics believe Dickens to have been convinced of the *rightness* of Bulwer Lytton's view: e.g., Edward Wagenknecht in his speech at the Dickens Fellowship Conference Dinner, Boston, 9 June 1962, as reproduced in *The Dickensian* (September 1962).

48 *Inside the Whale* (1940). Despite his claims to be an advanced educationalist, Wackford Squeers is as contemptuous of metaphysics as a modern analytical philosopher. cf. *Nickleby*, chapter LVII.

49 *The Imagination of Charles Dickens* (1961), p. 65.

50 1962, edited by Gabriel Pearson and John Gross.

51 Forster, somewhat to our surprise, calls this 'among those defects of temperament for which his early trials and his early successes were accountable in perhaps equal measure'. Again, in saying that 'he would take as much pains to keep out of the houses of the great as others take to get into them,' he adds, 'Not always wisely, it may be admitted'. (Volume II, Book VIII, Chapter 2.)

52 E.g. *The England of Dickens* (1925), also *The London of Dickens* (1923), and *The Kent of Dickens* (1924).

53 Quoted in *Dickens and His Readers*, by George H. Ford (1965), p. 70.

54 In the *Dictionary of National Biography*.

55 *The Common Reader*. It has been pointed out that this in itself is an immature reaction.

56 In his Foreword to *The Real David Copperfield* (1933).

57 *Op. cit.*, p. 173.

58 J. Hillis Miller in *Dickens Criticism: Past, Present and Future Directions, A Symposium* (Dickens Reference Center, Lesley College, Cambridge, Mass.), (1962), p. 25.

59 University of Illinois Press (1967).

60 It may perhaps be as well to point out that a liaison with Ellen Ternan has never been satisfactorily proved, despite the use of infra-red photography and other modes of investigation. The very interesting book *Charles Dickens and His Family*, by W. H. Bowen, privately printed by Heffer and Sons Ltd (1956), assembles evidence to suggest that Ellen was never Dickens's mistress, stressing the investigations of Walter Dexter and J. W. T. Ley in contravention of Thomas Wright (Cf. *The Dickensian*, Vol. LII, Part 1, No. 317). Another book on similar lines is Edward Wagenknecht's *Dickens and the Scandalmongers* (1965).

61 An example is the delightful exchange with a young boy who had written to him about *Nickleby*. Dickens's reply was selected by George Saintsbury, not always regarded as a Dickens enthusiast, for inclusion in his *Letter Book* (1922).

62 Butt and Tillotson, *op. cit.*, p. 22.

63 On recent paperback editions, cf. Trevor Blount, 'Keeping up with the Dickens Industry' (*The Dickensian*, May 1968).

64 Edited by Arthur Waugh, Walter Dexter, T. Hatton and H. Walpole (23 Volumes, 1937–8). This includes the Nonesuch *Letters of Charles Dickens*, edited by Walter Dexter (1938).

65 Edited by Walter Dexter (1935). These are not included in the Nonesuch Edition.

66 The general editors of the Clarendon Edition are K. Tillotson and the late John Butt. The first volume (*Oliver Twist*) appeared in 1966. The Pilgrim Edition of the Letters is edited by M. House and G. Storey, and the first volume, covering 1830–9, appeared in 1965, with W. J. Carlton, P. Collins, K. J. Fielding, and K. Tillotson as associate editors. Twelve volumes are planned.

67 *Shelberne Essays:* Fifth Series (1908).

68 See also his essay on *Dombey and Son* in *The Sewanee Review*, LXX (1962).

69 *The Great Tradition* (1948), p. 249–74, and Marcus, *op. cit.*, p. 10.

70 In *The Dickensian* (January 1963), reviewing *Dickens and the Twentieth Century*.

71 The *Spectator*, 27 December 1968.

72 It was not for nothing that one of Dickens's friends, Edwin Pugh, wrote a book entitled *Charles Dickens, The Apostle of the People* (1909).

73 We are surprised not so much at the liberties taken with the novel by Lionel Bart and others as at the puerility of some of the lyrics. Incidentally, those who reproach Dickens for his prudery with regard to Nancy and her profession may feel that the balance has been amply redressed by that young lady's blandly enthusiastic song, 'It's a fine, fine life'.

74 Lionel Trilling speaks in his Introduction to *Little Dorrit* (1953), (*The Opposing Self*, 1955) of Dickens's 'great general images whose abstractness is their actuality'.

Acknowledgements

The author and publishers would like to thank the trustees and owners of the museums and collections listed below for granting permission for the photographs to be reproduced.

ILLUSTRATION SECTIONS
References are to plate numbers.

The Life of Dickens
(*between pages 33 and 40*)
1, 7, 9, 10, 11, 12, 16, 17, 18, 19, 20, 21, 22, 23, 24, 25, 27, 28, 29, 30, 32, Dickens Fellowship; 3, 4, 5, 6, 8, 31, Mander and Mitchenson Collection; 13, 14, 15, 26, Victoria and Albert Museum.

Dickens's London
(*between pages 64 and 72*)
4, Dickens Fellowship; 1, 2, 3, 5, 6, 7, 8, 9, 10, 11, 12, 13, 14, 15, 16, Guildhall Library.

The Man of Letters
(*between pages 101 and 108*)
2, 11, 12, British Museum; 1, 3, 4, 6, 8, 9, 10, 15, 17, Dickens Fellowship; 14, collection of Emlyn Williams; 13, Mander and Mitchenson Collection; 5, 7, 16, Victoria and Albert Museum.

Social Conditions
(*between pages 133 and 140*)
1, 5, 6, 8, 9, 11, 14, 15, 16, British Museum; 2, collection of Nicolas Bentley; 13, Mander and Mitchenson Collection; 4, 10, 17, 18, 19, Dickens Fellowship; 3, Guildhall Library; 20, Victoria and Albert Museum.

Dickens Characters
(*between pages 169 and 176*)
12, 13, 21, 22, 23, British Museum; 14, Columbia Pictures Corporation; 24, 25, 27, Dickens Fellowship 1, 2, 3, 4, 5, 6, 7, 8, 11, 15, 18, 26, Mander and Mitchenson Collection; 16, 17, 20 (by permission of Rank Films), 19 (by permission of Metro-

Picture research: Julia Hornak.

Goldwyn-Mayer), National Film Archive; 9, 10, Victoria and Albert Museum.

The Illustrators
(*between pages 197 and 204*)
5, Aberdeen Art Gallery; 6, 10, 23, British Museum; 1, 4, 9, 19, 22, Dickens Fellowship; 24, Mander and Mitchenson Collection; 16, 17, 18, 20, 21, collection of Nicolas Bentley; 2, 3, National Portrait Gallery; 7, 8, 11, 12, 13, 14, 15, 25, Victoria and Albert Museum.

Dickens in America
(*between pages 229 and 236*)
1, 3, 4, 6, 9, Dickens Fellowship; 17, 18, collection of Emlyn Williams; 2, 13, 14, 15, 16, 19, Mander and Mitchenson Collection; 12, University of Texas; 7, 8, 10, 11, Victoria and Albert Museum.

Dickensiana
(*between pages 265 and 272*)
4, 7, 9, 10, 11, 12, 13, 14, 15, 16, British Museum; 3, 5, 6, Dickens Fellowship; 1, 2, 8, Mander and Mitchenson Collection.

LINE-DRAWINGS
References are to page numbers.

18, 47, 97, 98, 146, 156, 161, 162, 227, 239, 240, 262, British Museum; 45, 185, Dickens Fellowship; 62, collection of Emlyn Williams; 15, 50, 54, 182, 187, 195, Mander and Mitchenson Collection; 122, 123, Marylebone Public Library; 111, National Portrait Gallery; 79, 80, 83, 85, 86, 90, 93, 99, 119, 151, 152, 153, 155, 164, 167, Guildhall Library; 157, Radio Times Hulton Picture Library; 50, 52, 61, 181, 220, 221, 247, Victoria and Albert Museum.

Index

Figures in square brackets denote pictures within the illustration sections, and are preceded by the italicized number of the page on which they appear. Other figures in italics refer to the page-numbers of the line-illustrations.

The works of Charles Dickens are indexed separately at the end, and journals and magazines are listed together under 'publications'.

Ainsworth, Harrison, 222
Ardizzone, Edward, *204* [**24**], 226

Bacon, Francis, 163
Barnard, Fred, *204* [**22**], 226
Barrow, Charles, 42
Barrow, John, 145
Bayley, John, 257
Bazalgette, Sir Joseph, 165
Beadnell, Maria (later Mrs Henry Winter), *39* [**24**], and CD, 32, 46
Benson, E. F., 254
Bentley, Richard, stormy relationship with CD, 48–9, 51; Forster writes to, 212
Berners Street White Woman, 125, 129; CD's account of, 113; and Miss Havisham, 114–15; CD fuses image of Martha Joachim and, 116, 118; and CD, 121
Blacking warehouse, Warren's Blacking Pots, *34*; CD at, 44, 45, 88; York buildings near, 121–2
Blessington, Marguerite, Countess of, *39* [**27**]; and CD, 32
Bradbury and Evans, become CD's publishers, 51; CD severs relations with, 57; CD's quarrel with, 222
Brogan, D. W., 261
Browne, Hablôt Knight ('Phiz'), 11; 'Little Dorrit leaving the Marshalsea', *136* [**7**]; preliminary sketches for *Dombey*, *170* [**9**]; and *Pickwick*, 196, 225; anonymous engraving of, *197* [**4**]; 'Mrs Bardell faints', *206* [**16**]; 'dark plates' for *Dombey and Son*, *202* [**17**], 211; 'Nicholas instructs Smike', *203* [**18**]; 'The Fat Boy', *203* [**20**]; an

illustrator of distinction, 206; his association with CD established, 208; compared with Cruikshank, 208–9; fruitful alliance between CD and, 209, 212, 226; Chapman and Hall choose, 209–10; his weakness as a draughtsman, 210; his talent, 211; improvement in his work over the years, 211–12; CD discusses illustrations with, 213–14; works under difficulties, 214, 215; ill, 214–15; wood engraving for *Master Humphrey's Clock*, 216–17; and CD, 218, 222, 258; importance of his illustrations, 226; the best remembered of CD's illustrators, 226–7; illustration from *Nicholas Nickleby*, *256*
Buckland, Arthur, *204* [**23**]
Burgess, John Bagnold, *161*
Buss, Frances Mary, 209
Buss, R. W., 209
Butt, John, 242

Carlyle, Thomas, *102* [**4**], *185;* on CD, 63; at reading of *The Chimes*, 184
Cattermole, George, his drawing of Little Nell's grandfather, *171* [**10**]; a drawing for *Nicholas Nickleby*, *198* [**6**]; and Phiz illustrate *Master Humphrey's Clock*, 216–17; CD delighted with, 217–18
Chaplin, Charles, 18–19
Chapman and Hall, commission a novel from CD, 47; CD severs connections with, 51; CD's publishers again, 57; and Phiz as CD's illustrator, 208; choose Seymour as illustrator, 209; Cruikshank and, 218; *All the Year Round*, 222

Chartists, and violence, 142, 143; their six demands, 145

Chatham, CD's childhood in, 43; Dickenses leave, 44, 74

Chesterton, G. K., and the reading man, 17; on CD's enjoyment of his characters, 24-5; Priestley's comment on, 26; on attitude of mind of reformers, 165; and CD's optimism, 166; on alliance between Phiz and CD, 209; and CD's humour, 253

Children, child mudlarks, 82; stupefied by gin, 84; about Covent Garden, 91; at 'private' theatres, 94; child prostitutes, 95; watercress girls, 98; chimney sweeps, 135 [5], 155-6; in cotton mill, 146; in coalmines, 156-7; and the Factory Acts, 158

Cholera, epidemics in London, 87, 164; sanitation and, 161; Jacob's Island and, 162; a 'great social agency', 164

Civil Service, CD attacks incompetence in, 148; Trollope exposes means of entry into, 148; competitive selection for, 149

Clare, Mary, 176 [26]

Clarke, Mrs Cowden, on CD's performance in The Lighthouse, 182; CD on pleasure of applause, 184

Cockshut, A. O. J., on Our Mutual Friend, 10; his criticism of CD, 257; and Dickens criticism, 261

Coleridge, Sara (Mrs Samuel Taylor Coleridge), 250

Collins, P. A. W., 262

Collins, William Wilkie, 102 [4], 111; The Lighthouse, 54, 182; amateur theatricals, 54, 55; The Woman in White, 110, 111; collaborates with CD, 123-4; tours Cumberland and Midlands with CD, 124, 125; influenced by CD's work, 130; The Frozen Deep performed for charity, 186; on CD's performance, 187

Convicts, transportation of, 119-20; a convict hulk, 119

Coutts, Angela Georgina Burdett, Baroness Burdett-Coutts, 32, 39 [28]

Criminal population, 84, 132

Cruikshank. George, 196, 226; illustrates Sketches by Boz, 47, 206-7; his claim, 168; 'Oliver introduced to the respectable Old Gentleman', 172 [12]; CD, 197 [1]; self-portrait, 197 [3]; Noah Claypole and Charlotte, 198 [7]; 'Fagin in the Condemned Cell', 200 [11] and [12]; 'The Burglary', 201 [13, 14 and 15]; an illustrator of distinction, 206; 'Public Dinners', 207; does not illustrate CD's later works, 207-8; relations with CD, 208, 212, 216; Phiz compared with, 208-9, 211; his talent, 209; mistakes in his illustrations, 216; suggests Leech, 218

Dabney, Ross H., 262

de la Rue, Mrs, 32

Dexter, Henry, 228, 229

Dexter, Walter, 258; on CD's London, 11-12

Dickens, Catherine ('Kate'; née Hogarth), 34 [11], 39 [25]; and CD, 32, 127; her marriage, 48 55, 124; birth of first son, 49; to America, 49; CD on, 56; legal separation, 56, 124

Dickens, Charles Culliford Boz, 230 [4 ; born, 49; growing up, 55; and his parents' separation, 56; in business, 58

Dickens, Charles Huffam, 15, 33 [1-6], 34 [8], 36 [15], 38 [20], 40 [31], 101 [1], 102 [4], 105 [8, 9 and 10], 107 [13], 195, 197 [1], 230 [2], 234 [13], 236 [19], 266 [2 and 3]; his popularity, 10, 19-20, 57, 59, 61; and Ellen Ternan, 10, 21. 56, 57, 124, 129-30, 260; change in critical estimate of, 16-17, 258-61; the Readings, 19, 57, 59-61, 168, 184, 186-91, 228; and America, 19-20, 49-50, 59, 180, 188, 228; relationship with his public, 20-1, 238, 248-50; and money, 21, 51, 59, 185, 187, 188; as a social reformer, 22-3, 50-3, 132, 142-66; and the theatre, 27-8, 46, 54, 55, 78, 93-4, 115, 124, 178-9, 180, 182; effect of his childhood on his work, 28-9, 45, 53; and Maria Beadnell, 32, 46; his background and childhood, 42-5, 74, 78-81, 88-9, 178; the blacking warehouse, 44, 45, 88, 121-2; as a young man, 45-6, 100, 145; marriage, 48, 49, 55, 56-7, 124, 222; in Italy, 51, 219; and his family, 58, 60; ill, 58-9, 60-3; death, 61-3; on London, 74-5, 84, 95-6; walks about London, 76, 77-8, 95, 98-9; on slum children, 91; and prisons, 91-2, 152-3; and public execution, 92, 153; and Wilkie Collins, 110, 123-4, 125, 130; attitude to violence, 142-3, 157, 166; on democracy, 147; and Cruikshank, 208, 212; and Phiz, 208, 209, 212, 213-14, 216, 218, 222, 226; and Cattermole, 217-18; and Leech, 218; his friendships, 221-2; conforms to prevailing moral convention, 244-6; attitude to Christianity, 254

Dickens, Edward Bulwer Lytton ('Plorn'), 55

Dickens, Elizabeth, 38 [18]; moves into Marshalsea, 44, 88; opens a school, 88

Dickens, Frances Elizabeth ('Fanny'), 178

Dickens, John 38 [17], 42; occupation and personality, 43; and his son, 43, 45, 148, 151-2; transferred to London, 44, 74; in debtor's prison, 44, 88, 149, 152; emerges from Marshalsea, 45, 92; and Huffam, 78, model for Micawber, 253

Dickens, Katey, 38 [19 and 20], 230 [4]; birth of, 49; growing up, 55; and her parents' separation, 56; marries, 58

Dickens, Mary ('Mamie'), *38* [**19** and **20**], 58, *230* [**4**]; birth of, 49; growing up, 55; and her parents' separation, 56

Dickens, Walter Landor, *230* [**4**]

Dickens, William, 42

Dickens Fellowship, founded, 259

Disraeli, Benjamin, 1st Earl of Beaconsfield, and Reform Bill, 146; CD and, 146

Dostoevsky, Fyodor Mikjailovich, 30

Doyle, Richard, 226; a subtle draughtsman, 210; his illustrations, 218, 219

Dust-heaps, 163

Dyson, A. E., 259

Eliot, George (*pseud. of* Mary Ann Evans), 257–8, 259

Eliot, T. S., 254

Ellis and Blackmore, 92

Engel, Monroe, *Maturity of Charles Dickens*, 259, 261

Executions, public, *93*, *153*; CD and, 92, 132; CD's protest against, 153–4, *140* [**20**]

Fabian Socialists, 166

Factory Acts, Mines Act, 157, 158; of 1833, 158; evasion of, 158–9; Ten Hours Act, 160

Field, Kate, *Pen Photographs of the Dickens Readings*, 189, 192

Fielding, Henry, 244–5

Fielding, K. J., 261

Fields, W. C., 168, *174* [**19**]

Fildes, Sir Luke, Furniss's portrait of, *197* [**5**]; mistake in his illustration, 216; *Edwin Drood*, 196, *224*, 225

Fleet Prison, Pickwick in, 91; and later editions of *Pickwick Papers*, 150

Fleming, Ian, 244

Ford, G. H., and rise in sales of *Pickwick*, 243; on CD's appeal, 259

Forster, E. M., and CD's 'flat and round characters', 23–4, 29–30

Forster, John, 9, *38* [**21**], 185; Lytton and, 22; CD and, 49, 55, 99, 124, 245, 248, 250; CD reads *The Chimes* at home of, 184–5; and CD's public readings, 185–6, 187; objects to Cruikshank's drawings, 212; Leech and, 218; on *A Child's History of England*, 221; on CD's huge public, 238; on moral intent in CD's novels, 248–9; and Lewes, 251–2; a loyal friend, 252; on CD's 'city of the mind', 254; and ending of *Great Expectations*, 256; on CD, 257

Freedman, Barnett, *204* [**25**], 226

Frith, William Powell, his portrait of CD, *36:* CD's opinion of, 223

Furniss, Harry, his portrait of Fildes, *197* [**5**]

Galsworthy, John, *Justice*, 150–1

Genet, Jean, 244

Gissing, George Robert, 252

Gladstone, William Ewart, 149

Graves, Robert, *The Real David Copperfield*, 246, 247; on CD, 259

Guinness, Alec, 168, *174* [**20**]

Hansom, Joseph Aloysius, 96

Harding, Lyn, *172* [**13**]

Harvey, Sir John Martin, 168, *174* [**17**]

Hibbert, Christopher, 261

Hogarth, George, commissions a series from CD, 46; becomes father-in-law of CD, 48; reviews *Sketches by Boz*, 238

Hogarth, Catherine, *see* Dickens, Catherine

Hogarth, Georgina, *39* [**23**]; and CD, 32; manages Dickens household, 55; her loyalty, 56; and death of CD, 61

Hogarth, Mary, 32, *35* [**12**]; lives with Dickenses, 49; death, 49

Holloway, John, 253

Holloway Prison, the 'silent system', *151*

Homes of Charles Dickens:
    Bayham Street, Camden Town, 32, *34* [**9** and **10**]; Dickenses go to live in, 44; CD joins his parents in, 74; Dickenses leave, 88; house demolished, 88
    1, Devonshire Terrace, Regent's Park, 76; Dickenses move to, 49; CD sublets, 51; Martha Joachim's York Buildings near to, 121
    48, Doughty Street, *47*, 49
    Gad's Hill Place, *40* [**30**]; CD's dream realised, 32, 43, 55–6; CD at, 57, 58, 60, 61; CD dies at, 63; public readings to pay for, 187; and London, 258
    4, Gower Street North, 88
    5, Hyde Park Place, *61*, 61
    26, Johnson Street, 92
    Lant Street Southwark, 88, 89
    Little College Street, Camden Town, 44–5, 89
    Tavistock House, Tavistock Square, 53, 57

Horsemonger Lane Gaol, Southwark, 91, 92

House, Humphry, on CD and politics, 147; on CD and the Poor Law, 154; on dust-contracting, 163; and Dickens studies, 242

House of Commons, CD a reporter in Press Gallery, 100, 145; CD refuses to stand for seat in, 142; CD slumbers in, 147

Huffam, Christopher, 78

Huxley, Aldous, 255

James, Henry, 258, 259

Jerdan, William, 243

Jerrold, Douglas, *185: Black-eyed Susan*, 183; *Rent Day*, 183; at reading of *The Chimes*, 184; CD raises fund for his widow, 186

Joachim, Martha, 119, 125; report of her death, 116; Miss Havisham drawn from, 118; significance to CD of her death in York Buildings, 121; and the bride in *The Lazy Tour* ghost story, 128, 129

Johnson, Edgar, his biography of CD, 9–10, 260, 261; on CD's childhood, 32; and quarrel between CD and Phiz, 222; and CD as a Christian, 254

Jonson, Ben, 23, 24

Jowett, Benjamin, 149

Joyce, James, 20, 29

Jung, Carl Gustave, 30

Keene, Charles Samuel, 210, 224

Kent, W. C. M., 189

King's Bench Prison, 91

Kingsley, Charles, 162

Kitton, Frederick, 219

Landseer, Sir Edwin Henry, 219

Laughton, Charles, 168, *176* [26]

Layard, Sir Austin Henry, 149

Leavis, F. R., 144, 261

Leech, John, *197* [2]; drawing for *The Battle of Life*, *199* [10]; illustrates *Mr Sponge's Sporting Tour*, 206; eager to illustrate CD's work, 209; a subtle draughtsman, 210; illustrates *Christmas Books*, 218

Lemon, Mark, *Mr Nightingale's Diary* with CD, 182

Lever, Charles James, 24; Phiz illustrates his works, 222

Lewes, George Henry, 251

Lindsay, Jack, 261; on CD, 8; on Dickens criticism, 242

London, 64, *65–72* [1-6]; Dexter on Dickens's London, 11–12; in early nineteenth century, 74–5; suburbs, 74–6; CD on view from railway train, 75; CD walks about, 76, 78; changing areas of fashionable London, 76–7; CD on himself as a child in, 78–81; CD on, 82; slums, 82–7; cholera epidemic in, 87; immigrants, 96; sanitation and drainage in, 161–5; London 'particulars', 165

Berners Street, its significance to CD, 129, 130; Ellen Ternan's home, 129–30

Bevis, Marks, 78

Buckingham Palace, 163

Camden Town (*see also* Homes of Charles Dickens), CD on, 74–5

City of London, 78

Covent Garden Market, CD on, 90–1

Field Lane, lodging house in, *85*

Finchley Road, CD on neighbourhood of, 75

Fleet Ditch, *162*

Golden Square, 84, 87

Grosvenor Square, CD on houses in Mews Street, 77

Gray's Inn Lane, 78, *79*, *80*, 94

Hungerford Stairs, blacking warehouse at, 44, 88; CD avoids, 88–9; the 'Swan', 89

Jacob's Island, *139* [17]; CD on, 87; filthy conditions in, 161–2

Lant Street (*see also* Homes of Charles Dickens), CD on, 87–8

Lea, river, 163

Limehouse, 78, 81

Oxford Street, nineteenth-century development around, 76; CD's description of houses in, 77; cess-pools close to, 163

Park Lane, CD on streets leading off, 77

Parliament Street, Red Lion, 89, *90*

St Giles, 82–3, *83:* the 'Rookery', 83–4; sewage floods tenements, 163

St Paul's Cathedral, 92; CD on sight of dome, 78

Seven Dials, 82–3; CD on, 84

Smithfield Market, 84; CD on, 91–2

Somers Town, *67* [4], 75, 78

Spitalfields, a soup kitchen in, *139* [16]

Thames, river, CD fascinated by, 81; mudlarks on, 81–2; steamers on, 89; polluted, 161–2, 163; used as water-supply, 163; under discipline, 164–5; the Embankments, 165

Thames Street, 84

Tom-All-Alone's, 87

Walworth, CD on, 75

Westminster Abbey, CD's burial in Abbey, 20, 32; fever in, 163

Wild Court, Great Wild Street, *86*

York Buildings, Marylebone, *122:* Martha Joachim dies in, 116; near CD's home, 121; significance of name to CD, 121–3

York Buildings, Strand, 121–2

Longfellow, Henry Wadsworth, on death of CD, 63

Lovett, William, 145

Lytton, Edward George Lytton Bulwer, 1st Baron, 54, *102* [4]; chairman at CD's farewell banquet, 19; and *Great Expectations*, 22, 256; *Not So Bad As We Seem*, 182; *The Lady of Lyons*, 183; CD and, 184, 252; Phiz illustrates for, 222

Macaulay, Thomas Babington, 1st Baron Macaulay, *102* [4]

MacDonald, Geoffrey, *102* [4]

Maclise, Daniel, *185*, 221; at reading of *The Chimes*, 184; does some illustrations for CD, 218, 219; his picture of CD's children, *230* [4]

Macready, William Charles, *38* [22]; CD enthralled by, 94; a Little Nell enthusiast, 251

Manning, Frederick George *and* Maria, *140* [**18** and **19**]; execution of, 92, 132, 153

Manning, J., 262

Marcus, Steven, on social satire in *Oliver Twist* and *Pickwick*, 251 and Dickens criticism, 261

Marshalsea Prison, 10, 32, 122; John Dickens in, 44, 88; used symbolically in *Little Dorrit*, 53; CD on, 91; John Dickens leaves, 92: demolition begins, 150

Masson, David, 252

Matthews, Charles, CD enthralled by, 94, 115–16, 179; his sketch 'No. 26 and No. 27', 115; CD applies for audition to, 179

Mayhew, Henry, his outspoken descriptions of slums, 87; and prostitution, 95; illustration from *London Labour and the London Poor*, 97

Melbourne, William Lamb, 2nd Viscount, 149

Mill, James, 144

Millais, Sir John Everett, his drawing of CD, *40* [**42**]; John Leech, *197* [**2**]; CD denounces 'Christ in the House of His Parents', 223; a precocious talent, 224; introduces Fildes to CD, 225

Millbank, 132; the fetter room, *136* [**8**]

Miller, J. Hillis, 259, 261

Mills, John, 168, *174* [**20**]

Ministry of Health, 164

Mitford, Mary Russell, 243

Monod, Sylvère, 261

Moody, Ron, *172* [**15**]

More, Paul Elmer, 261

Mudlarks (*see also* Scavengers), *81*, 81–2

Myddleton, Sir Thomas, 163

Newgate, in CD's works, 91–2, 132; the condemned cell, *136* [**9**]; effect of 'Boz's' visit to, 150, 153; reconstructed on lines of Pentonville, 150; public execution outside, *153*

Nicholson, Renton, *Dombey and Daughter*, 262

Nightingale, Florence, 148

Nisbet, Ada, *Dickens and Ellen Ternan*, 260

O'Casey, Sean, 160

O'Connor, Feargus, 145

Old Bailey, 132; temporary galleries, *137* [**10**]; visitors' and prisoners' compartments, *137* [**11**]

Onwhyn, Thomas, 'The Fat Boy', *203* [**21**]

Orwell, George (*pseud.* of Eric Arthur Blair), defends CD, 253; his criticism of CD, 257

Owen, Robert, 143

Palmer, Samuel, illustrates *Pictures from Italy*, 196, 219, *220*, 221, *221*

Parliament, CD refuses to stand for, 142; CD despises, 143, 145

Pearson, Hesketh, 222, 261

Peel, Sir Robert, 146–7

Penal reform, urgently needed, 150; capital punishment, 153–4

Pentonville, a 'model' gaol, 150; suicide at, *167*

Phiz, *see* Browne, Hablôt Knight

Pickwick, Moses, *176* [**25**]

Poe, Edgar Allan, a Little Nell enthusiast, 251; on necessity for exaggeration in creative writing, 252

Poor Law of 1834, CD contemptuous of, 154; purpose of, 154–5; Fabians achieve reform of, 166

Pope-Hennessy, Dame Una, 261

Portsea, 43

Prisons (*see also individual entries*). CD and the 'attraction of repulsion', 92; CD's horror of, 132; effect of childhood experience on CD, 149–50; effect of isolation on prisoners, 150; imprisonment for debt, 151–2; debtors' prison, *252*

Prostitutes, at 'penny gaffs', 94; CD avoids outspoken portrayal of, 95, 244–5; in CD's works, 244, 245

Public Health Act, 164

Publications:

All the Year Round, CD founds, 57; *Great Expectations* appears in, 57; CD writes on children in, 91; *The Woman in White* to appear in, 110; CD editor of, 222; CD communicates his ideas through, 238

Atlas, 243

Bentley's Miscellany, 48

Court Journal, 238

Daily Express, 260

Daily News, CD editor of, 51, 157; fascimile of CD's letter to, *140* [**20**]; circulation of, 159; CD denounces window tax, 165

Evening Chronicle, 46

Fortnightly Review, 251

Fraser's Literary Chronicle, 243

Household Narrative of Current Events, 'Narrative of Law and Crime', 116; facsimile of page from, *117;* deals with transportation of convicts, 119; reports a dress catching fire, 120; and *Great Expectations*, 131

Household Words, CD founds, 53, 57, 157, 222; the model for Miss Havisham described in, 113; *The Lazy Tour of Two Idle Apprentices*, 123, 126; the ghost story in *The Lazy Tour*, 124, 125–6, 127, 128, 129; CD on the Lancashire strike, 144; CD and electoral reform, 146; appointment system scourged in, 149; 'Ground in the Mill', 158–9; circulation of, 159, 238; purpose of, 159; article on dustheaps in, 163; *A Child's History of England* in,

Household Words–continued
221; CD communicates his ideas through, 238; *A Child's Dream of a Star*, *241*, 255–6; CD wants to re-name, 248

Literary Gazette, 243

Mirror of Parliament, CD on staff of, 46, 145; CD contributing to, 100

Moniteur des Arts, 63;

Monthly Magazine, CD's sketch for, 46, 100

Spectator, 243

Morning Chronicle, CD on staff of, 46; *Sketches by Boz* reviewed in, 238

Punch, 222

Satirist, 239–40

Times, The, and CD's funeral, 20; CD writes to, 153; 'The Cabman's Horse' printed in, 243; its title for CD, 263

True Sun, The, 100, 145

Quiller-Couch, Sir Arthur Thomas ('Q'), on CD, 14, 17; and Tolstoy and CD, 27

Rackham, Arthur, 226; *A ChristmasqCarol*, *227*

Railways, CD on chaos caused by building of 95–6; growth of, 96

Reform Bills, provisions of first, 145; CD and, 145–6; of 1867, 146

Reynolds, Frank, 226

Reynolds, G. B., 248

Rochester, CD as a child in, 43; CD's description of, 61

Ross, William, 252

Ruskin, John, 144

Sabbatarians, CD attacks, 160–1

Sanitation, 132, *139* [**16**]; non-existent in Jacob's Island, 87; CD campaigns for improvement in, 161; New River, 162–3; river pollution and water supply, 163; and the rich, 163; dust-contractors, 163; *Bleak House* and, 163–4; work of Metropolitan Board of Works, 164

Santayana, George, defends CD's exaggerations, 252; on caricature, 253; on humour, 253; on CD's insensibility, 257

Scavengers (*see also* Mudlarks), a bone-grubber, *98;* scavengers' circular, *99*

Scott, C. P., 159

Seymour, Robert, 11, 209, 243

Shaftsbury, Anthony Ashley Cooper, 1st Earl of, his work for social reform, 143; and child labour, 157

Shaw, George Bernard, sees CD as a revolutionary, 23; and CD, 166; on *Little Dorrit*, 166; on CD, 166

Slack, Robert C., 260

Smoke, Nuisance Act, 165

Smollett, Tobias, 244–5

Spilka, Mark, *Dickens and Kafka*, 252, 261

Spy, *see* Ward, Leslie

Stanfield, Clarkson, *185;* a friend of CD, 218–19, 331; CD's opinion of, 223

Stephen, Sir James Fitzjames, 251

Stephen, Sir Leslie, 29, 259

Stone, Frank, does some illustrations for CD, 218, 219; friend of CD, 221

Stone, Frank, 223

Stone, Marcus, 225; CD and, 83; 'The Boffin Progress', *215*, 216; succeeds Phiz, 223–4; poor quality of his work, 224

Storey, Gladys, 260

Surtees, Robert Smith, 209

Symons, Julian, 261

Taine, Hippolyte Adolphe, his estimate of CD, 245–6; and Dickens criticism, 251

Tenniel, Sir John, 218, 219

Ternan, Ellen, *39* [**26**]; CD and, 10, 16, 32, 56, 57, 124, 260; ashamed of the liaison, 21; and Estella, 22; in a train crash, 58; and the ghost story in *The Lazy Tour*, 127, 129; living in Berners Street, 129–30

Thackeray, William Makepeace, *102* [**4**], 188; and CD, 9, 259; *Vanity Fair*, 151, 246; eager to illustrate CD's work, 209

Thames, river *see* London

Theatre, the, CD goes to, 78, 93–4; 'private' theatres, 94

Thorndike, Dame Sybil, 168, *174* [**18**]

Tillotson, Kathleen, 242

Tolpuddle labourers, 143

Tolstoy, Count Leo Nikolaievitch, 26, 27

Topham, F. W., 221

Trade unionism, CD's attitude to, 143–4

Transportation, *see* Convicts

Tree, Sir Herbert Beerbohm, 168, *172* [**13**]

Trevelyan, Sir Charles Edward, 149

Trevelyan, G. M., 155

Trilling, Lionel, 12

Trollope, Anthony, *102* [**4**]; *The Three Clerks*, 148; and CD, 259

Vagrants, 96, 132

Villa Bagnarello, *50*

Ward, Sir Leslie (Spy), his sketch of CD, *15;* CD's opinion of, 223

Warner, Rex, 254

Waugh, Arthur, on CD's interest in his illustrations, 213; on Cattermole, 218; on CD's early success, 250

Webb, Beatrice, 23, 166, 255

Webb, Sidney, 23, 166

Weller, Mary, 32

Wellington House Academy, CD attends, 45, 92, 100

Whitman, Walt, 147

Williams, Bransby, 168, *169* [**1-8**]

Wilson, Angus, 11

Wilson, Edmund, 22, 25, 248

Woolf, Virginia, 259

Wordsworth, William, 149

Wright, Thomas, 260, 261

Yates, Frederick, plays in 'No. 26 and No. 27', 115; as Mr Pickwick, *239*

Yeats, William Butler, 30

Young, G. M., 165

Zola, Emile, 246

Works of Charles Dickens:

American Notes, 50, 59, 228

Barnaby Rudge, 10, *231* [**6**]; completed in 1841, 49; Newgate in, 91; mistake in illustration in, 215; to appear in *Master Humphrey's Clock*, 216; Phiz's illustrations for, 217; Cattermole's illustrations for, 217-18; 'The Maypole Inn', 217; Forster on, 249

Battle of Life, The, Doyle illustrates, 218; Leech's drawing for, *199* [**10**]

Bleak House, 31; changing critical opinion of, 16; symbolism in, 53; attacks insanitary conditions, 164; and London fogs, 165; descriptive passages from, 192-3; 'Tom-All-Alone's', 209; Phiz and, 211, 221; quality of illustrations, 219; CD announces his intent in preface to, 245; Henry James and, 259; property-situation in, 263; Chadband, Mr, 53, *177*, 208-9; Lady Dedlock, 87, 192, 194; Miss Flite, 118, 208-9; Mrs Jelleby, 53; Jo, 87, 96, 255; Mrs Pardiggle, 53; Esther Summerson, 255, 263; Mr Tulkinghorn, 192, 193, 194

Child's History of England, A, 221

Chimes, The, a satire, 51; CD reads aloud, 184-5; illustrations for, 219; Sir Joseph Bowley, 51; Alderman Cute, 51, 87; Alderman Filer, 51, 166; Trotty Veck, 219, 255

Christmas Books, purpose of, 249; their appeal, 249

Christmas Carol, A, *270* [**10** and **13**], a parable, 50; unsatisfactory earnings, 51; CD's first public reading from, 186; Leech illustrates, 218; huge sales, 219; page from Japanese edition; *240:* Forster on, 249; Bob Cratchit, 44; Ebenezer Scrooge, 50, 219; Tiny Tim, 219

Cricket on the Hearth, scenes from dramatisation of, *175* [**21, 22** and **23**]; CD's second public

reading from, 186; Doyle illustrates, 218; Landseer's illustration for, 219; Tilly Slowboy, 219

David Copperfield, 23, 31, 51, *270* [**12**]; plans for early chapters, *52:* subjective narrative in, 30; and CD's childhood, 53; Phiz's illustrations for, 210, 219, 221; mistake in illustration of, 215; still a best-seller, 240; Marathi translation of, *241:* Forster on, 249; tears in, 256; David Copperfield, 24, *41*, 44, 45, 55, 74, 210; Mr Dick, 257; Martha Endell, 95, 245; Mrs Gummidge, 209; Uriah Heep, 26, *169* [**5**], 256; Mrs Micawber, 25-6, 88; Wilkins Micawber, 23, 25-6, 91, *174* [**19**], 252-3, 254, 256; Miss Jane Murdstone, 208-9; Peggotty, 192; Daniel Peggotty, *169* [**6**]; Sophy, 256; Dora Spenlow, *41*, 55, 209, 255; Mr Francis Spenlow, 210; James Steerforth, 245; Mrs Annie Strong, 256; Dr Strong, 257; Miss Betsey Trotwood, 118, 256; Agnes Wickfield, 245, 255

Dombey and Son, 10, 196; 'Carker's dead!', 18; a turning point, 23; first masterpiece of CD's maturity, 51; Staggs's Gardens, 75; the father contemplates the new-born child, 194; Phiz's 'dark plates' for, *202* [**17**], 211; Phiz's work for, *211*, 211-12, 221; CD exacting over illustrations for, 213-14; CD's purpose, 250; Leavis values, 261; Harriet Carker, 75; James Carker, 211; Captain Cuttle, 215; Edith Dombey, 255; Florence Dombey, *176* [**27**], *268* [**7**]; Paul Dombey, junior, *176* [**27**], 194, *268* [**7**]; Dombey, Paul Dombey, senior, 51, 76-7, *170* [**9**], 194; Hon. Mrs Skewton, 257; Mrs Polly Toodle, 75; Mr Toots, 24, 25

Edwin Drood, Mystery of, 196, *224*, *225*; CD breaks down when writing, 9, 32; CD working on, 61; mistake in illustration, 216; Fildes illustrates, 225; John Jasper, 95; Mrs Sapsea, 23

Great Expectations, 11, 110-31; changing critical opinion of, 16; Lytton persuades CD to alter ending, 22; significance of Pip's sufferings, 57-8; illustration from, *114:* Stone to illustrate, 224; first version of the ending, 256; Estella, 22, 57, 129, 130; Miss Havisham, 110, 113, 116, 118, 128, 129, 130; Mr Jaggers, 208-9; Abel Magwitch, 120, 130; Philip Pirrip ('Pip'), 24, 57-8, 75, 91, 120-1, 129, 130; Mr Wemmick, junior, 75, 91; Mr Wemmick, senior (the Aged Parent), 75

Hard Times, *270* [**10**]; attacks mechanized industry, 53; and trade unionism, 143; stimulates middle class social conscience, 144; and indictment of drudgery, 159; its social purpose, 160; Leavis and, 261; Stephen Blackpool, 159-60; Josiah Bounderby, 143,